THE
TEN COMMANDMENTS

I
Do not worship any other gods besides Me.

II
Do not make idols of any kind.

III
Do not misuse the name of the LORD your God.

IV
*Remember to observe the Sabbath
day by keeping it holy.*

V
Honor your father and mother.

VI
Do not murder.

VII
Do not commit adultery.

VIII
Do not steal.

IX
Do not testify falsely against your neighbor.

X
Do not covet.

EXODUS 20:3–17, NLT

WRITTEN BY THE HAND of GOD

Experience God's Love *and* Blessing
Through *the* Liberating Power *of* His

TEN
COMMANDMENTS

BILL
BRIGHT

NewLife
PUBLICATIONS

Written by the Hand of God: Experience God's Love and Blessing Through the Liberating Power of His Ten Commandments

Published by
NewLife Publications
A ministry of Campus Crusade for Christ
P.O. Box 620877
Orlando, FL 32862-0877

Edited by Joette Whims
Production by Genesis Group
Cover by Koechel-Peterson Design

Printed in the United States of America

ISBN 1-56399-165-9 (h.c.)

Unless otherwise indicated, Scripture quotations are from the *New Living Translation*, © 1996 by Tyndale House Publishers, Inc., Wheaton, Illinois.

Scripture quotations designated NASB are from *The New American Standard Bible*, © 1960, 1962, 1963, 1968, 1971, 1972, 1973, 1975, 1977 by the Lockman Foundation, La Habra, California.

Scripture quotations designated NIV are from the *New International Version*, © 1973, 1978, 1984 by the International Bible Society. Published by Zondervan Bible Publishers, Grand Rapids, Michigan.

Scripture quotations designated NKJ are from the *New King James* version, © 1979, 1980, 1982 by Thomas Nelson Inc., Publishers, Nashville, Tennessee.

Scripture quotations designated TLB are from *The Living Bible*, © 1971 by Tyndale House Publishers, Inc., Wheaton, Illinois.

For more information, write: Campus Crusade for Christ International, 100 Lake Hart Drive, Orlando, FL 32832, USA

For my beloved wife, Vonette,
and in loving memory of my dear parents,
Forrest Dale and Mary Lee Bright

CONTENTS

Acknowledgments 8
Foreword *by Tim LaHaye* 9
Preface 11

**Part One: The Joy and Blessings of the
Ten Commandments**

1 Finding True Happiness 15
2 Why We Need the Ten Commandments 23
3 The Blessing of Obedience 39
4 God's Law Leads to Grace in Christ 55
5 Cheap Grace and Legalism 69

Part Two: The Goal of Loving God

6 You Shall Have No Other Gods Before Me 87
7 Do Not Worship Idols 103
8 Do Not Take God's Name in Vain 117
9 Keep the Sabbath Holy.....................131

Part Three: The Goal of Loving Others

10 Honor Your Parents 149
11 Do Not Murder 167
12 Do Not Commit Adultery 185
13 Do Not Steal 203
14 Do Not Bear False Witness 221
15 Do Not Covet 235

Part Four: Living by the Ten Commandments

16 The Principle of Sowing and Reaping 253
17 Choose Life! 269
Appendix A: The Four Spiritual Laws 275
Appendix B: The Spirit-Filled Life 280
End Notes 284

ACKNOWLEDGMENTS

God has used many people through the years to enhance my understanding of the truths that I have tried to communicate in this book. I am grateful for each of them.

I especially want to thank John Barber, whose help with research and writing was invaluable to the creation of this book. I appreciate so much Helmut Teichert for his oversight of this project, and I also want to thank the other team members for their significant contributions: Joette Whims, editor; John Nill, publisher; Tammy Campbell, editorial assistant; and Michelle Treiber, cover coordinator and print broker. My gratitude also goes to Lynn Copeland of Genesis Group for the design and page layout.

There is one person more than any other who deserves special recognition: my beloved bride of over fifty years, Vonette. Together, we have experienced many years of God's abundant love and blessing.

FOREWORD

When I started reading the manuscript for this book, I expected it to be a good read; after all, my friend of over forty-five years, Bill Bright, was the author and he already has several good books in print. Besides, the subject is one I am highly interested in and on which I had even thought of writing myself. But frankly, I was not prepared to find this such an incredibly interesting and helpful book dealing with one of the most important issues of our day—how modern Christians relate to the Ten Commandments.

I had forgotten what a great storyteller Bill is. This book is filled with some of the most interesting stories you have ever read, and each one illustrates an important point. I also admire his courage in dealing carefully with some almost forgotten issues in today's church. Our Lord said, "If you love Me, keep My commandments," yet few Christians even know them all or could recite them. In fact, I don't think many Christians even know where to look in the Bible to find them.

Yet our very happiness is dependent on keeping His commands. Our Lord said, "Blessed [or happy] are they who hear the word of God and keep it." The psalmist has said, "Blessed are those who walk in the law of the Lord." By contrast, miserable are those who do not. As a pastor counselor for many years, I have observed that everyone who came to me for help was miserable. My wife used to kid me and say, "It's your personality. You naturally draw miserable people to you." Actually, happy people never go to their pastor or a counselor and say, "I'm so happy I just can't stand it so I came to you for help." No, it is miserable people who seek out counseling.

Then I began to notice a pattern in the stories these unhappy people told. They had violated one or more of the laws or principles of God. In short, they had earned a right to be miserable by violating His laws. It didn't matter that they didn't obey them because they didn't know them; they were still miserable.

That is when I developed the understanding that God meant His commands, precepts, and admonitions for our good. After that I looked on my role as a counselor as that of a listener to discern what commands of God the individuals were violating. Then I would graciously confront them with the Word of God so they could seek His help in changing their behavior. The end result is happiness.

Everyone wants to be happy. It's natural. But few people realize that happiness does not just happen; it is the result of obeying the commands, precepts, and principles of God. That is what they are for. Jesus said it best: "If you know these things [the principles of God], happy are you *if* you do them!" This book will help you realize how very important God's commandments are and how practical they are in our modern era, and will offer many suggestions on how to obey them.

Bill Bright is one of the most productive soul winners and encouragers of other Christians to serve their Lord in this century. He has walked with God and kept His commandments for more than fifty years. No wonder he is one of the happiest and fulfilled men in our generation! He is seeking in this well-written book to share his happiness.

This book is about happiness—how to achieve it. Read it prayerfully; implement its teachings into your own life; and I guarantee the end result will be happiness. Actually, *I* can't guarantee anything. Your guarantee of happiness is based on the Word of God, including the words of Jesus in Revelation 22:13,14: "'I am the Alpha and the Omega, the Beginning and the End, the First and the Last.' Blessed are those who do His commandments..."

TIM LAHAYE
Author, Minister

PREFACE

One of the greatest promises of our dear Lord to all who love, trust, and obey Him is an abundant and fulfilling life. Jesus said, "The thief comes only to steal, and kill, and destroy; I came that they might have life, and might have it abundantly" (John 10:10, NASB). I can state categorically that in fifty-five years of following Christ, His promise of abundant living has been true in my life. Certainly I have faced difficult times. We all do. But through it all, Christ has always enabled me to experience overflowing peace, joy, happiness, and blessing even in the worst of circumstances.

Nonetheless, this remarkable life in Christ has not happened automatically. I have had a part to play—obedience. The fact is that absolutely no one can know the abundant life Christ offers without living in obedience to God's commands. This is why the Ten Commandments play such a critical role in my life. There is no escaping this irrefutable truth: When a person lives in obedience to God and His law, he experiences the most satisfying and rewarding life imaginable.

It is to this end that I want to encourage you to discover, or rediscover, the Ten Commandments and the immeasurable blessing God has in store for you when you commit yourself to keeping them in your heart and following them daily. Along with this book and the Ten Commandments, I also encourage you to read the Book of Deuteronomy, which was written to ancient Israel. Here you will find many commands and promises that you can apply to your personal life, church, community, and country. The Holy Spirit is waiting to help you!

WRITTEN
BY THE
HAND of GOD

PART ONE

The Joy and Blessings of the Ten Commandments

ONE

FINDING TRUE HAPPINESS

I t all started with a lapse of integrity, but it ended in tragedy. Lisa and her husband lived a seemingly wonderful life. They were active in their church and had a young son. People in their church respected them because they tried to live by the rules in God's Word. Although Lisa thought life was going pretty well, she couldn't erase the feeling that her life was not complete and happy.

Then Lisa and her husband made a questionable financial decision that began to change their lives. It seemed insignificant at the time, just a small bending of the rules. They justified their action and went on with their daily life—with money in their pockets that wasn't rightfully theirs.

As a result of breaking this financial rule, Lisa and her husband began relaxing other moral rules over the next two years. Looking back, Lisa says, "I didn't understand that in the long term, every action has a reaction—physical laws as well as moral ones. When you disobey one of God's commandments, it knocks everything out of line. Once we crossed over a moral line, we kept getting farther and farther away and the line became dimmer and dimmer. Once we decided not to keep a commitment in one area, our lack of commitment spread to other areas."

Finally, Lisa discovered that her husband had begun an affair with an old girlfriend. Their fourteen-year marriage crumbled into divorce.

Lisa felt hurt and angry. Hadn't she lived a "good" life? Why did this happen to her? To make her situation worse, many of her friends abandoned her. Even her pastor was insensitive to her situation and said, "Now we'll see what kind of Christian you are."

Lisa reacted by turning her back on God. She quit going to church and began hanging out in bars, attracting a new circle of friends. She went back to school, found a better job—and had a lot of "fun." For ten years, she lived a life so rebellious to God that no one would have recognized that she ever called herself a Christian. In all this time, she knew that one day God would hold her accountable, but she was not about to change! She was fed up with His rules and religion.

Then one Sunday morning—on a Mother's Day—she woke up early and felt a strange urge to go to church. She did not understand this urge because she certainly had not been thinking about God. She called a Christian friend who was living an equally wild life, and they attended church together.

It was a horrible experience. Lisa felt nervous, conspicuous, and awkward. After church, she and her friend headed straight for brunch and Bloody Marys.

Then, for some unexplainable reason, Lisa dug out her Bible and kept going to church. God began to do a work inside her. Although the change was not instantaneous, Lisa's life and attitudes made a 180-degree turn. What she discovered was that before her divorce, attempting to follow God's laws merely as a set of rules, without a heart of love, did not automatically make her happy. But when she wholeheartedly responded to God's love for her, His commandments took on a completely different significance. They were not only easier to obey, but they became a joy to her life. She discovered that obedience to God out of love, not merely obligation, brings true happiness.

On the other hand, Lisa also discovered that purposely disobeying God's laws prevented her from experiencing a joyful life too. In her quest for happiness during her rebellious years, Lisa says, "What I experienced in the world can't even come close to what God has to offer. I had 'good times' in my old life, but it can't hold a candle to God's love. My worldly lifestyle caused me and my family great harm and distress, but obeying God protects me and fills me with joy. My relationship with God is so precious that I wouldn't throw it away for anything."

Lisa regrets the things she did during those ten wild years. She says, "As a professing believer, I took God to places I had no business going. He loved me so much, and I chose to throw His love back in His face."

Lisa did not find happiness in rebellion or in merely following God's rules. True happiness comes from something much more—*a love relationship with our great God and Savior that leads to obedience.*

Happiness or Joy?

Many people have asked me, "How does a person find true happiness?" Most of us have puzzled over this question at some time in our lives, but many searchers never find the answer. After fifty years of ministry and an incredible life of adventure with our Savior and God, I can affirm the answer with certainty and great enthusiasm—obeying God and His Laws. Nothing in this world can match the joy and satisfaction of obeying and serving God in the way that pleases Him most. This inner joy is much deeper than emotional happiness.

But joy comes from more than just following a list of rules. True happiness is not measured in rules; it is found in love for God. Love for God results in obedience, which fulfills the rules. Therefore, successfully obeying God's Laws begins with one simple principle. Jesus said, "'You must love the Lord your God with all your heart, all your soul, and all your mind.' This is the first and greatest commandment" (Matthew 22:37,38). This verse explains true happiness in a nutshell. I have found no other way to experience the kind of joy that remains through hard times and good times, on mountaintop highs and valley lows, in days of plenty and days of need. All other commandments God has given us are wrapped up in this Great Commandment. Through our obedience, God will give us the power to serve Him by obeying His other commandments with a joyful and expectant heart. As Lisa discovered, loving God first makes following His rules jubilant and exciting.

I love God's Laws. Every year they become more precious to me —in fact, more precious than the air I breathe. Recently, I was diagnosed with pulmonary fibrosis, a disease for which there is no known cure unless God supernaturally intervenes. The process of the disease makes my breathing more labored as time passes. For nearly eighty years, breathing was automatic for me. I did not pay much attention to this natural part of my body function. But now, every breath I take is precious. Today, I know in a deeper way what a blessing air is and how wonderful it feels to take in a deep breath that invigorates internal organs, muscles, and brain.

Yet the passion I have for the air I breathe is miniscule compared to the passion I feel for God and His commandments. I feel as ardent about God's commands as the psalmist must have experienced thousands of years ago. He poured out his love for God's Law in the 119th Psalm, the longest chapter in the Bible. He writes, "I open my mouth, panting expectantly, longing for your commands" (v. 131).

My most fervent desire is to serve God with my whole heart, which fuels my desire to follow the rules He has given us. They are as vital to me as oxygen. Every morning and evening, I take time to pray through the Ten Commandments and ask God to enable me to apply them to my life. Because I know of God's unconditional love for me, I grasp the truth that His Laws are for my well-being and that they are the keys to my true and lasting happiness.

I remember former President Ronald Reagan, a devout believer in Christ from his youth, said on numerous occasions that if only the American people would "obey the Ten Commandments and the Golden Rule, the problems we face as individuals and as a nation would be solved."[1] The Ten Commandments bring joy and happiness to every part of life. They communicate the essence of how we must relate to God and to our fellow man.

But perhaps you are thinking, *This is too hard to do. I could never obtain the perfection that the Ten Commandments demand.*

The Ten Commandments, simple and profound as they are, are impossible for any of us to keep. We are imperfect humans who hopelessly fail to live up to God's standards in our own self effort.

So we try to ignore them. But that too is a recipe for disaster. For example, some people avoid going to the doctor so they will not hear bad news about their health. They feel if they ignore the symptoms, their illness will go away. At times, we treat the Ten Commandments in a similar way. Because we feel that knowing what God expects of us threatens our way of life, we turn our backs on God's rules.

There is a better way. It is using the Ten Commandments in the way God intended—as a gauge of our love for Him.

A Gauge for Life

At thirty-six seconds past 4:00 a.m. on March 28, 1979, a deadly chain reaction erupted. At Metropolitan Edison's Three Mile Island nuclear power plant near Harrisburg, Pennsylvania, the normal flow of cooling water to the reactor core was accidentally stopped. Consequently, a valve flew open that allowed water to drain out of the reactor core. A small amount of radioactive gas was released into the morning air, threatening the communities nearby. One of the most dangerous kinds of explosions known to man was now on its way—the meltdown of a nuclear reactor!

Two long hours passed before plant personnel discovered that there was a malfunction. Even then, the operators did not understand where the problem was located. They began to frantically work to uncover what was wrong.

Shortly after 7:00 a.m., seven alarms went off, screaming that radiation levels were rising in the plant. As radiation in the plant's control room reached dangerous levels, the power plant was put on General Emergency.

By 11:00 a.m., all nonessential employees were ordered out of the plant. A core meltdown—the most serious kind of accident in nuclear energy—was almost certain unless something was done. What was wrong? Why couldn't the problem be corrected?

Finally, at 4:00 p.m., twelve hours after the accident had begun, plant personnel correctly diagnosed the problem and forced cooling water into the core. The meltdown had been averted. A later study showed that the reactor had come within *one hour* of a meltdown!

Why didn't the personnel recognize the danger in the first place or correctly diagnose the problem once they realized the reactor was malfunctioning? Part of the problem was that employees didn't read the gauges accurately. One indicator was hidden behind a hanging caution tag and a worker may have obscured another. Therefore, the operators failed to notice that the pipes leading to the auxiliary water pumps were closed causing the reactor to heat up. Because of these problems, the reactor almost exploded, releasing lethal doses of radiation into the air.

Still, the aftermath of the accident was enormous. It took the reactor three years to cool enough so that scientists could lower remote-control cameras into it. The cleanup took ten years to complete.[2]

Gauges are terribly important to the operation of any plant. The thick metal sides of the boilers prevent anyone from seeing how much water and steam are building up inside. That is why the boilers have gauges. If the gauges malfunction and the safety valves do not work as they should, workers may be killed or maimed.

I am sure you have seen pictures of old-time boilers. On the outside of the boiler is a tiny glass tube that serves as the gauge. The water level in the tube mirrors the water level in the boiler. When the tube is half full, the boiler is half full; if empty, so is the boiler.

This is similar to how the Ten Commandments function in our lives. How do you know you love God? You believe you love Him, but you want to *know*. Look at the gauge. Your obedience to God's holy commandments is the true measure of your love for God.

The Ten Commandments can also protect us from a slavish lifestyle of regulations. As I study and reflect on the Ten Commandments, I gauge my spiritual life as God sees it. On one hand, I can tell whether I am observing rules and regulations not mandated by God, which can add unbearable pressure to my life and lead me into bondage to manmade rules. On the other hand, by looking at my spiritual gauge, I can also see if I am failing to follow God's Spirit so that my spiritual life has no supernatural drive and direction. These ten brief statements plus the Golden Rule help keep my life in the center of God's will.

Only as we rely on God's power can we truly attain the standard that God sets for our behavior. When we observe the Ten Commandments in the power of God's Spirit, they liberate us to do what is essential to please God. They tie us into the love of God by helping us to get in step with what He has planned for our lives and for how He wants to protect us from wrongdoing and its consequences. His Commandments unlock the blessings God has in store for us.

These ten rules have been a vital part of any "success" I have experienced in life. The Ten Commandments have helped me build a wonderful relationship with my great Creator God and Savior, as well as with my beautiful partner for life, Vonette. Obeying these laws has enabled me to be a godly father to our two sons. God's Laws have guided me as I have directed a fruitful international ministry for five decades. I can recommend no other way of living and serving God.

I highly encourage you to memorize the Ten Commandments listed at the beginning of this book. Meditate on them and ask the Holy Spirit to help you obey them. They are keys that unlock God's love and blessing.

As we consider each of the Ten Commandments, I am sure you will see how simple yet complex each one is. Together, we can discover how God's Laws will liberate us and give us purpose and passion for loving God with all our heart, soul, and mind. And that truly is what brings us happiness and peace in this life!

T W O

WHY WE NEED THE TEN COMMANDMENTS

C an you think of a situation where your love for your children led you to create boundaries for their well-being? As a father, I faced many situations where I wanted to protect our sons from danger, and I did my best to do just that.

When our sons, Brad and Zac, were growing up, they liked to play with snakes and lizards. We had plenty of both at Arrowhead Springs, California, where we lived. Because our sons had no experience with harmful creatures, I had to give them some direction. I explained that although it was all right to play with lizards, they should stay away from snakes because a rattlesnake could kill them. On more than one occasion, Brad and Zac remembered my advice and avoided a possible deadly snakebite.

Vonette and I also cautioned our children about other health and safety issues. We warned them not to touch a hot stove or they would be burned. We also told them not to eat too many sweets but to always eat plenty of vegetables. Why did we give them these rules? Did we want to make our children's lives miserable? No, every barrier we established for our children was for their good, because we loved them.

In the Bible we find that God, our heavenly Father, has given us His Law—the Ten Commandments. Just like earthly fathers who give their children rules to safeguard them, God gave us His Ten Commandments for our protection and liberation. Although many people view the Ten Commandments as a "wet blanket" on their behavior, God's Law is for our guidance, encouragement, and safety.

I do not know any reasonable person who is upset with traffic laws or the law of gravity. Without laws designed to guide our conduct, life would be impossible. Likewise, God has given to us His perfect law so we can experience what Jesus called the "abundant life." If I violate any one of the Ten Commandments, I am the one who suffers because they are absolute spiritual laws of the universe. It would be foolish indeed for me to willingly break any one of God's Ten Commandments, because they exist for my good and His glory.

God's Supreme Gift to Israel

God's purpose for giving the Ten Commandments is not to assure the absence of evil but to ensure the presence of purity. Examining a photographic negative shows why God gave the Ten Commandments. The photosensitive material creates a negative image for light to pass through so the developer can create the bright, natural photograph. Just so, the Ten Commandments block out behaviors that ruin the picture-perfect plan God has envisioned for our lives.

Although God intended the Ten Commandments to provide rules for living, they are much more than a simple set of do's and don'ts. These Laws were meant as a supreme gift from God to be cherished and protected.

I can remember the excitement that filled our home on Christmas morning when Brad and Zac were young boys. They could not wait to open their presents. But with all the commotion and excitement that comes with Christmas, children can damage their gifts if they are not careful. So Vonette and I would gently remind the boys to be careful not to break their gifts. After all, Christmas presents hold a special place in the life of a child.

In the same way, God wants us to be careful not to break His commandments because He gave them to us as a special gift. The Ten Commandments deserve the highest place of honor and distinction in our lives. This is demonstrated by the special place that they occupied when God first gave them to the Jewish people. Before the nation of Israel could hear God's Law at Mount Sinai, they first had to prepare themselves through ceremonial cleansing. From this we learn that nothing unclean can dwell in the presence of a holy God. Furthermore, Mount Sinai, where God appeared to Moses, was to be off-limits. No one was permitted to approach the holy mount where God was. This reminds us that God's Law was no ordinary gift.

God did not bother dictating His commandments to Moses for him to record. God was His own secretary! The very finger of God wrote the commandments on tablets made of stone. This fact distinguishes the Ten Commandments from all other books of the Bible, which were given to men by inspiration of the Holy Spirit. Although the entire Bible is God's inspired Word, the Ten Commandments stand as God's *personal*, inscribed Word to man.

Another remarkable fact about the Ten Commandments is that God spoke them to Moses in an audible voice. Imagine the scene. The mighty voice of God declaring His will for man atop a smoke-filled mountain with peals of thunder and lightning filling the sky. I marvel at the very thought of it.

After Moses brought the tablets down from the mountain, they were placed inside the Ark of the Covenant. The Ark was a rectangular chest made of special shittim wood covered with gold. Later, Aaron's rod was placed in it, along with a golden pot containing manna. On top of the Ark was the mercy seat. It was made of pure gold and was held in place by a golden ridge or crown. Beaten out of the same piece of pure gold as the mercy seat were two cherubim with their wings overshadowing the Ark. The Ark of the Covenant was undoubtedly a very beautiful and expensive piece of furniture. And it was built to house the Ten Commandments.

Later, Solomon's Temple was built as a home for the Ark. It has been estimated that to construct Solomon's Temple and the Ark of the Covenant today would cost an estimated $2 billion! The inner sanctuary and altar of Solomon's temple were overlaid with gold. Even the floor was covered with gold. The doors were olive and pine-wood, also carved and covered in gold. There were 30 gold basins, 1,000 silver basins, 30 golden bowls, and 40 silver bowls. The altar of gold was placed in the Holy of Holies, the innermost part of the temple. King Solomon also had a bronze altar made. The doors in the gates between the courtyards were covered with bronze. This describes just *part* of the fabulous beauty of Solomon's Temple that housed the Ark of the Covenant and the Ten Commandments. What value God ascribes to His Law!

The awesome display of God's mighty power at Mount Sinai and the beauty of the temple remind us that the Ten Commandments are ten ways God says, "I love you." According to the well-known and highly respected theologian A. W. Pink, God gave the Law out of utmost love for His people. Pink comments, "Whatever of awful grandeur and solemn majesty attended the promulgation of the Law, nevertheless, it had its foundation *in love*, proceeding from God in the character of their gracious Redeemer."[1]

Many years after Moses received the Ten Commandments, the nation of Israel suffered great calamity as a result of repeatedly breaking them. Yet, through the prophet Jeremiah, God reminded Israel of His great love, saying, "I have loved you, My people, with an everlasting love" (Jeremiah 31:3). God's comfort revealed that His commandments had been given to help His people avoid disaster. Although ultimately Israel suffered the consequences of disobedience to God's laws, the Ten Commandments were based in God's love for His people.

Why, then, do we need the Ten Commandments today? Like Old Testament Israel, it is because we so desperately need God's love. From having no other gods before Him to not desiring things that are not ours to possess, the Ten Commandments serve as God's divine gauge to help us discover peace and blessing for our lives—and for our nation.

The Foundation for National Laws

I firmly believe that one reason the United States of America leads the world in so many areas today is that our secular laws were established on the foundation of God's Law. This basis can be traced back before the days of the Reformation.

The great theologian and reformer Martin Luther (1483–1546) saw in the Ten Commandments their ability to restrain evil. He taught, "The first use of the law is to bridle the wicked. This civil restraint is very necessary, and appointed of God, as well for public peace, as for the preservation of all things, but especially lest the cause of the Gospel should be hindered by the tumult and sedition of wicked, outrageous, and proud men."[2]

John Calvin (1509–1564) elaborated on the importance of the Law. Calvin emphasized the Law as a good and perfect gift from God. He believed that God dealt with people through covenant relationships. The central idea of covenant theology is that God's covenant with man contains God's stipulations and promises together with man's commitment to obey. For Calvin, the Ten Commandments formed the heart of the Old Testament understanding of covenant. Yet today, most people do not know about the profound influence of Calvin's views upon Western thought. Together with Calvin's view that man is sinful and that all rulers derive their authority to govern from God, Calvinists applied his views to the establishment of civil government in Europe and America.

The Puritans also had great respect for the laws of God. They believed that biblical law contained the essential principles of civil government. They saw that God's law revealed the character of God, who, being the ultimate Lawgiver, blesses all people who obey His commandments. In the Mayflower Compact of 1620 they declared that what they did was "for the glory of God and the advancement of the Christian faith." Soon, the General Court of Massachusetts of 1636 based its system of civil laws upon the revealed Word of God.

The influence of the Ten Commandments upon early America also came through the famous English jurist Sir William Blackstone (1723–1780). His *Commentaries on the Laws of England* played an important role in shaping law in the colonies and for years to come.

Blackstone believed that human laws were like scientific laws. They were God's creations, waiting to be discovered, just as Isaac Newton had discovered the law of gravity a century earlier.

Not surprisingly, Blackstone's influence upon law continues today. In Alabama, Judge Roy Moore was sued by the ACLU for hanging a plaque of the Ten Commandments in his courtroom. Dr. D. James Kennedy writes, "Judge Moore has written an eighty-seven-page affidavit on his defense, using Blackstone as his chief legal source. This unpublished treatise...documents very well how the laws of America are based on the laws of England, which in turn were based on the laws of God—in particular, the Ten Commandments."[3]

Biblical Law continued to provide the major source of authority for the Founding Fathers in their work of establishing a new nation. One study found that of 15,000 writings by the Founding Fathers included in newspaper articles, books, monographs, and other documents, 94 percent of all quotes either directly or indirectly cited the Bible.[4] The most cited thinker was Charles Montesquieu of France (1689–1755), whose best-known work was *The Spirit of Laws*. He believed that all law has its source in God and that laws made by humans should conform to the eternal laws of God.[5]

Many scholars agree that the "unalienable rights" of people as cited in the Declaration of Independence probably came from Blackstone's description of the rights of Englishmen under the British Constitution. The "Laws of Nature and of Nature's God" refer to natural law and to the written, moral law of God of which the Ten Commandments are central.

In his book *What if the Bible Had Never Been Written?*, D. James Kennedy points to several parallels between the Ten Commandments and Western law. The fourth commandment is the basis for the continuing observance of the Sabbath as a day of rest. The fifth commandment marks the nuclear family as the most important institution in Western civilization. The seventh commandment recognizes marriage as the bedrock of the family. The eighth commandment supplies the basis for private ownership. The ninth commandment forbids perjury. Because it is linked to all the commandments, the tenth commandment is the basis for a great amount of law.

Undermining the Integrity of the Ten Commandments

Unfortunately, the Ten Commandments have lost their place as an authority in the life of our nation. During the 19th century, the attack on the nature and authority of God's Law came from a very unlikely place—from anti-biblical forces within the Church. "Higher criticism," a new way of interpreting the Bible, was adopted by some seminaries. Higher criticism suggested that the stories found in the Bible are not historical, but are mere fables believers told and later wrote down as Scripture to lend credence to their faith.

The effect of higher criticism in the nation's leading seminaries was to undermine the faith of countless people entering the ministry. Once these newly trained clergymen took to the pulpits, their lack of fidelity to God and to the Scriptures spread throughout the churches.

While higher criticism was gaining prominence in theology, Charles Darwin's theory of evolution was becoming influential in science. Darwin rejected the idea of a created order and man's need for eternal standards. Instead, he suggested that man, having evolved from lower forms of life, is basically good. Although intended for science, Darwin's theories were later adapted for use in sociology, education, and politics. The result in America was a departure from a belief in biblical authority and law. No other time in history marked a clearer divide between orthodox Christian belief and a secularized view of life than the 19th century.

The Campaign to Abolish the Ten Commandments

The dawning of the 20th century was marked by a continuing struggle between liberalism and Christianity over the issue of biblical law. One of the most articulate defenders of the Christian faith during this period was J. Gresham Machen, who left his teaching post at Princeton to found the Westminster Theological Seminary. In his book *Christianity and Liberalism*, he wrote, "It is no wonder, then, that liberalism is totally different from Christianity, for the foundation is different. Christianity is founded upon the Bible. It bases upon the Bible both its thinking and its life. Liberalism on the other hand is founded upon the shifting emotions of sinful men."[6]

Machen's observation is no less true today. Choosing to live your life according to the firm foundation of the law of God rather than varying emotions is what distinguishes a life of joy and peace from a life marked by hopelessness and defeat.

Today, we are at the beginning of the 21st century. We continue to feel the dread effects of *Roe v. Wade*, the 1973 landmark decision legalizing abortion; *Engel v. Vitale* (1962), in which the Supreme Court removed prayer from public schools; and *Abingdon School District v. Schempp* (1963), in which the Court struck down Pennsylvania's in-school Bible-reading as a violation of the First Amendment.

Educators wouldn't think of omitting algebra from calculus, gravity from physics, or photosynthesis from biology, but merely faced with some peer pressure they omit these ten essential laws from life. To teach a curriculum without the Ten Commandments is to beat an empty drum, and such instructors stand intellectually naked before a world that knows better.

It is in this context that the abiding value of the Ten Commandments summons us to rediscover the blessings of obedience. Proverbs 29:18 says, "When people do not accept divine guidance, they run wild. But whoever obeys the law is happy." Unless God's Law is our constant guide, all we can expect is moral chaos. Happiness comes when we obey God's commandments, trusting that He alone knows what is best for our lives. Dr. Michael Horton, professor at Westminster Theological Seminary in Escondido, California, writes, "The Bible, particularly the Ten Commandments, calls us to discover our obligations to God and to our neighbors and society. It calls the people of God to their posts in society...as called-out men and women who have a heavy sense of moral duty—not to save their souls, for that is by grace apart from works, but to bring glory and honor to that gracious King."[7]

Reestablishing the Ten Commandments as the basis of our culture is the answer to our social problems.

Are the Ten Commandments Still Valid Today?

To this point, we have seen examples from history of the value of the

Ten Commandments. What we have not addressed is whether the Ten Commandments are still valid today.

Just because something has value does not mean it is binding upon our lives. People often ask, "If I'm under grace, do the Ten Commandments still apply to me?" While addressing the National Family Planning and Reproductive Association in Washington, D.C., media mogul Ted Turner said the Ten Commandments are "a little out of date." He added, "If you're only going to have 10 rules, I don't know if prohibiting adultery should be one of them."[8]

Sadly, many people agree with Ted Turner. The Ten Commandments no longer occupy the place of honor and respect they so rightly deserve. This is a terrible tragedy. The Ten Commandments are timeless. They are absolutely as important today as when Moses delivered them millenniums ago. We violate them at our own peril.

Yet today in America, a relativistic mindset toward biblically based morality is sweeping every area of society. A Barna Research Group survey asked, "Is there absolute truth?" Amazingly, 66 percent of American adults responded that they believe that "there is no such thing as absolute truth; different people can define truth in conflicting ways and still be correct." The figure rises to 72 percent for those between the ages of 18 and 25.[9]

The Ten Commandments stand as a towering refutation to those who believe there is no truth. The commandments contain the essence of God's unchangeable and absolute truth. When we follow the Ten Commandments, we benefit because they do more than steer us in the right direction, they also keep us from taking the wrong path. They set the boundaries that protect us from the quicksand we surely will encounter in life.

Without righteous law, we would live without direction. In this regard, the Ten Commandments serve three vital functions for our society.

*First, if obeyed, the Ten Commandments
serve as a basis of trust within society.*

When you are driving your car and approach an intersection with a green light, you proceed through the light without a second thought. Why? Because you trust other drivers to know what a red light means.

But in some parts of the world, drivers routinely run red lights. In those places, making it through an intersection becomes an obstacle course. What if there were no laws against murder or robbery? Your trust that no one would harm you would be greatly diminished.

The basic tenets of the Ten Commandments allow our society to function. Although our country is beginning to have serious problems in several areas that the Ten Commandments address, we still have a social agreement on other areas which allows our businesses, neighborhoods, and government to function.

Second, the Ten Commandments restrain evil in the world.
Without laws that are fair and just, society turns into anarchy. Just think what would happen if we didn't incarcerate murderers or child molesters. What if we allowed people to take whatever they pleased no matter who owned the objects? That's the function that the Ten Commandments serve for society—as a guideline for identifying and punishing evil.

The Ten Commandments are the signposts of civilization. Where they have not been posted, humanity has been systematically molested, denigrated, and slaughtered. We ignore them to our grandchildren's peril. We mock them to our own condemnation. We publish and obey them to our eternal reward.

Third, the Ten Commandments elevate the quality of life for society.
The matchless benefits of obeying the Ten Commandments enrich our health, our families, our finances, and our social lives. For example, stress can kill, but if you know you are okay in the eyes of God, where's the pressure? Money is important, but if you know you are earning all you can honestly and spending only because of legitimate needs, you have enough and are content. Families can be patched together with mixed motives, or they can be eternally sustained by marital fidelity—which immediately protects against wrenching problems of disease, divorce, and discouragement. Social acceptance may help esteem, but when we know our hearts are right with the living God, we find ourselves seeking to give away our joy in Him rather than aching for someone's approval.

The Ten Commandments and the Believer

In addition, the New Testament teaches that although we receive Christ by grace, the Ten Commandments still play an important role in the life of the believer. Paul, for example, encouraged young Timothy to live by the Old Testament Scriptures that include the Ten Commandments. "All Scripture is inspired by God and is useful to teach us what is true and to make us realize what is wrong in our lives. It straightens us out and teaches us to do what is right. It is God's way of preparing us in every way, fully equipped for every good thing God wants us to do" (2 Timothy 3:16,17).

The viewpoint that the Law does not apply to the believer today is a dangerous error known as "antinomianism." But Jesus said, "Don't misunderstand why I have come. I did not come to abolish the law of Moses or the writings of the prophets. No, I came to fulfill them. I assure you, until heaven and earth disappear, even the smallest detail of God's law will remain until its purpose is achieved" (Matthew 5:17,18).

New Testament references to the Ten Commandments prove the continuing importance of the Ten Commandments for our lives.

- First commandment—You shall have no other gods before Me: "You must love the Lord your God with all your heart, all your soul, and all your mind" (Matthew 22:37).

- Second commandment—Do not worship idols: "For we walk by faith, not by sight" (2 Corinthians 5:7, NASB).

- Third commandment—Do not take God's name in vain: "What union can there be between God's temple and idols? For we are the temple of the living God" (2 Corinthians 6:16).

- Fourth commandment—Keep the Sabbath holy: "On the first day of the week, we gathered to observe the Lord's Supper" (Acts 20:7).

- Fifth commandment—Honor your parents: "You children must always obey your parents, for this is what pleases the Lord" (Colossians 3:20).

- Sixth commandment—Do not murder: "You have heard that the law of Moses says, 'Do not murder. If you commit murder, you are subject to judgment.' But I say, if you are angry with someone, you are subject to judgment! If you call someone an idiot, you are in danger of being brought before the high council. And if you curse someone, you are in danger of the fires of hell" (Matthew 5:21,22).

- Seventh commandment—Do not commit adultery: "You have heard that the law of Moses says, 'Do not commit adultery.' But I say, anyone who even looks at a woman with lust in his eye has already committed adultery with her in his heart" (Matthew 5:27,28).

- Eighth commandment—Do not steal: "The commandments against adultery and murder and stealing and coveting—and any other commandment—are all summed up in this one commandment: 'Love your neighbor as yourself'" (Romans 13:9).

- Ninth commandment—Do not bear false witness: "So put away all falsehood and 'tell your neighbor the truth' because we belong to each other" (Ephesians 4:25).

- Tenth commandment—Do not covet: "I would never have known that coveting is wrong if the law had not said, 'Do not covet'" (Romans 7:7).

Even if I didn't know the Bible, I would still study the Ten Commandments for these reasons:

1. They are facts of history.

2. They are unique: Written by God Himself in a public manner, delivered to a mere mortal who broke them, etched a second time by the finger of God, and despite thousands of years, they remain intact and unrevised.

3. The greatest person of history, Jesus of Nazareth, embraced, quoted, and intensified them.

4. Jewish history cannot be explained without them.

5. The courts of Western civilization have posted and published them.

6. The Magna Carta cannot be understood without them.

It would be inconsistent, even unthinkable, for the God of an orderly creation to have overlooked setting in motion laws governing interpersonal relationships.

Truly, the Ten Commandments are vital to us today!

The Timeless Spirit of the Law

The Ten Commandments are sometimes called the Decalogue. They have God as their Author, holiness as their theme, and the exposure of ungodly hearts as their purpose.

Consider the powerful reality of ten statements carved in stone, 5,000 years old, and still cutting hearts to the quick. They go where no glib tongue nor guileful technology can travel to show us all how desperately wicked we are.

Some believe that Jesus gave new laws in His Sermon on the Mount. But this is not true. Rather, Jesus applied the *true* meaning of the Ten Commandments to His time. In Matthew 5, which records His sermon, Christ makes reference to several Old Testament laws including sanctions against murder, adultery, and divorce. Jesus mentions these laws to refute the teachings of the Pharisees. They were a group of Jews who, in an effort to appear as though they were conforming to the Law, twisted its meaning. In time, their "commentaries" on the Law gained a higher place among the Jewish scholars than did the Law itself. For example, in these commentaries, the Pharisees limited adultery to the "act" and not to the private wrestling of the heart.

Jesus reminded the Pharisees that the intent of the seventh commandment exceeded mere outward conformity but spoke to the lust of the heart. He made the scope of the Law contain the very sins of the heart the Pharisees thought they had escaped through legal hairsplitting. Jesus affirmed that the Ten Commandments are as vital to New Testament believers today as they were to Old Testament saints.

History has shown that every person and culture that fails to ascribe a place of honor to the law of God eventually falters and fails. But as Proverbs 29:18 says, "Whoever obeys the law is happy."

Over the next three chapters, I will discuss some important issues regarding the Law. We will look at, among other things, how the subjects of law and grace are related in the Bible and how *together* they can facilitate your walk with Christ. We will examine how you can experience a *balanced* walk with Christ by avoiding the extremes of cheap grace and legalism that often are associated with the Ten Commandments. And we will see how the Law can help you discover the grace and power of God.

May God bless you as we consider these truths together!

LIFE APPLICATION

Set Your Heart's Gauge

Commit the following verses to memory. Then, when you are tempted to break one of the Ten Commandments, recall these commands from God.

- 2 Timothy 3:16,17—"All Scripture is inspired by God and is useful to teach us what is true and to make us realize what is wrong in our lives. It straightens us out and teaches us to do what is right. It is God's way of preparing us in every way, fully equipped for every good thing God wants us to do."

- Proverbs 29:18—"When people do not accept divine guidance, they run wild. But whoever obeys the law is happy."

Gauge Your Spiritual Growth

Ask yourself the following questions. If one or more areas pose problems for you, ask God how you can deal with them through the power of the Holy Spirit.

- In reflecting on your moral standards, how do they stack up against the Ten Commandments?

- How are the Ten Commandments practiced in your home? What needs to be changed?

- Do you cherish the Ten Commandments? Why or why not?

- How are others harmed when citizens in your community break the Ten Commandments?

- How does your community benefit when citizens keep the Ten Commandments?

- How has keeping the Ten Commandments made you happier?

- How has breaking the Ten Commandments made you miserable?

Walk in the Power of the Holy Spirit

To emphasize the importance of each of the Ten Commandments, write each one out and make a statement about how it applies to your daily situations. (They are found in Exodus 20:1–17.) Ask God to help you make His Laws the center of your life and family through the power of His Spirit. You may want to post the Commandments and your applications in your home for everyone to read. Explain to each person how the Commandments serve as a gauge of their spiritual growth rather than as rigid rules.

THREE

THE BLESSING OF OBEDIENCE

America is a place of overworked and overburdened people who struggle each day with a world of concerns. We work to provide for our families, pay a never-ending mound of bills, raise children, and do a list of other things that challenge us to keep it all together. Add to this our church, which looks for our time and energy, and our children, who anticipate that we will have all the answers to life. Soon the pressures seem insurmountable. But perhaps our greatest sense of spiritual pressure comes from the burden we often feel when we are not dealing effectively with sin.

When I decided to write a book about keeping the Ten Commandments, I well knew about the many pressures people face. I felt many people would respond to this teaching by saying, "I am already overwhelmed and feel like I am not living the way I should, and now you want to lay the Ten Commandments on me?" Please relax. I want to use this chapter to address your concerns and to show you from the Bible how the Ten Commandments can aid you in finding peace in the midst of your stressed existence. How does this work?

Let us look at several misconceptions people have about the Ten Commandments and the solutions to the problems these misconceptions produce.

The Ten Commandments and Self-Effort

The Bible is extremely clear that no one can earn God's blessing through a life of toil and good works. Just read through the Ten Commandments, and without a moment's hesitation, you will concede you have failed to live up to God's perfect standards. Either you did not give God first place in your life, you did not honor your father and mother, you violated the Sabbath, you lied, you looked at another person with lust in your heart, or you desired something that belonged to someone else. Whatever our wrongdoing, our lives are proof to the testimony of the Scriptures that "all have sinned; all fall short of God's glorious standard" (Romans 3:23).

When I think about my failure to live according to God's perfect law, I am driven to the truth of the cross of Jesus Christ and His incredible work of salvation on my behalf. I am reminded of my own sinfulness and what a worm I am in the sight of a holy and just God.

The gospel of our Lord is not only a message of love and forgiveness; it is also an indictment of our sinfulness. The cross of Jesus Christ is God's opinion of us. It says that our sins are an affront to Him. Without the mercy of God poured out at Calvary, we would be the ones suffering the full penalty for our sins—a penalty brought about by our failure to comply with God's holy standards. It is our spiritual poverty in light of these facts that must drive us to a greater sense of our need for God's divine grace.

When the prophet Isaiah caught a vision of God in all His perfection, splendor, and majesty, he exclaimed, "Woe is me, for I am ruined! Because I am a man of unclean lips" (Isaiah 6:5, NASB). Once Isaiah gained a sense of his true condition before the God of the universe—a mere sinner justly deserving God's displeasure—he was ready to be cleansed of his sin and filled with God's power. Only then could he take on the work of being God's mouthpiece to the nation of Israel.

Isaiah's experience before God teaches me a very important lesson.

It says that accomplishing great things for God requires a new kind of doing. Before God can use me as an instrument of His grace, I first must be "undone." In other words, I must be reminded of my sinfulness, cast myself upon the grace and mercy of God, and draw from the power of His Holy Spirit to accomplish all He has called me to do. If being undone does not precede my doing, I am prone to serve God in the power of my own fleshly strength. It is then that exhaustion and eventual burnout and failure loom on the horizon.

Rest in God

Dear beloved, the reason people feel so overburdened by the many cares of life is not because they need more rest. It is because they need more rest *in* God. The Ten Commandments facilitate this rest because they point us away from our strength, which has proven incapable of meeting the righteous requirements of the Law, to serving Christ in the power of the Lawgiver.

Because the Law reveals our inability to be what God has called us to be, we can admit our failure, be filled with His Holy Spirit, and live His commandments with joy and confidence. Then all our service will be accomplished for God out of a heart of love and joyful gratitude for what Christ has done for us and not from our own human resolve, which produces frustration and defeat.

The late Dr. Jack Miller, founder of World Harvest Missions, used to say to missionaries, "How can you bring the gospel to the nations if you have not been mastered by the gospel yourself?"

Let me ask you, have you been "mastered by the gospel"? Before you take on the challenges of each day, do you look to the cross and see Jesus in your place, taking upon Himself the consequences of *your* disobedience to God's Law? Do you fall at His feet and permit Him to empower you by His grace and His Holy Spirit?

The first step in being "undone" is to receive Jesus Christ as your Savior and Lord. This decision brings you into the family of God and provides for you eternal life and joy. No one can begin to obey the Ten Commandments without first making this decision. If you have never received Christ as your Savior, turn to Appendix A, "The Four Spiritual Laws." What you learn by reading through these pages and applying them to your life will help you begin an adventure with God—the greatest adventure the human spirit can ever know.

The Gift of Grace

D. L. Moody was a great evangelist whose ministry dominated the last four decades of the 19th century. Hundreds of thousands of people were touched by his preaching. But for the first several years of Moody's ministry, he complained of ineffectiveness. Then when Moody was in a state of despair, a fellow minister told him, "The world has yet to see what God will do with a man fully consecrated to Him."

Moody resolved, "By the grace of God, I will be that man!"[1]

Dear friends, true effectiveness for Christ is achieved in this life when you totally surrender to God and to His matchless grace. Grace is for sinners. Grace has been defined by the acrostic GRACE: God's Riches At Christ's Expense. If you are not sensing His grace lifting and enabling you to defeat your spiritual enemies and to conquer all the challenges of the day, is it not because you forget to tell Him at the start of each day that you are a sinner in need of His grace? With the Holy Spirit's help, you will find the strength you need to live a life of fruitful abundance, even in the midst of the strongest opposition.

Sailors in the northern oceans frequently observe icebergs traveling in one direction in spite of strong winds blowing in the opposite direction. The icebergs are moving against the winds, but how? The explanation is that the icebergs, with eight-tenths of their bulk under the water surface, are caught in the grip of strong currents that move them in a certain direction no matter which way the winds rage.

In the Christian life, no matter how strongly the winds of challenge blow in opposition, the believer who has a depth of living in the currents of God's empowering grace will always move forward.

The Ten Commandments Cure Performance Mentality

Although God's grace and power are readily available, one of the great problems I have witnessed among believers is what I call a "performance mentality." The world we live in is based on a merit system. We are encouraged to believe that love and affirmation come to us as a result of what we do, not who we are. We are made to think the world rewards only the deserving. We are thus driven to perform for acceptance—searching inappropriately for the approval of others and desperately wanting to be loved.

The rock star Madonna remarked, "My drive in life is from this horrible fear of being mediocre that's always been pushing me, pushing me. Because even though I've become somebody, I still have to prove that I'm *somebody*. My struggle has never ended, and it probably never will."[2]

Tennis great Chris Evert, recalling the final years of her career, said, "I was depressed and afraid because so much of my life had been defined by my being a tennis champion. I was completely lost. Winning made me feel like I was somebody. It made me feel pretty. It was like being hooked on a drug. I needed the wins, the applause, in order to have an identity."[3]

The Approval of God
In his letter to the church at Corinth, Paul addressed the emphasis on externals and the need to perform for recognition. He writes, "'The person who wishes to boast should boast only of what the Lord has done.' When people boast about themselves, it doesn't count for much. But when the Lord commends someone, that's different!" (2 Corinthians 10:17,18).

When I see my reflection in the holy Law of God, I see a picture of a man in need of grace. Grace is "unmerited favor" because no man can earn God's acceptance through meticulous adherence to the Law. God has accepted and approved me by virtue of Christ's work and righteousness and not on account of my observance of the Law. This is what causes me to "boast in the Lord," which in turn, provides me strength for the day.

I firmly believe that seeking for approval from God and others through performance rather than divine grace is rooted in a spiritual insecurity that does not understand the depths of God's complete acceptance of His children in Christ. Indeed, we must rest in the absolute approval and unmerited favor of God as it is provided in Christ.

Bruce Larson shares the following anecdote in his book *Wind and*

Fire:

> A few years ago I almost drowned in a storm at sea in the Gulf of Mexico when I found myself swimming far from shore, having tried to reach my drifting boat. I got into that predicament through my own stupidity, something not unusual at all. I can remember saying, "Well, this is it." The waves were seven or eight feet high, and the sky was dark with gale force winds and lightning. I was drifting out to sea when the Word of the Lord came to me and saved my life.
>
> What I thought He said was, "I'm here, Larson, and you're not coming home as soon as you think. Can you tread water?" Somehow that had never occurred to me. Had I continued my frantic effort to swim back to shore, I would have exhausted my strength and gone down.[4]

Many believers have found that working to win the approval of God and man has only exhausted their strength. What we need is divine grace. It will be ours the moment we stop our frantic struggle and rest in God's gracious and saving mercy.

St. Augustine remarked, "You have made us for Yourself, and the heart of man is restless until it finds its rest in Thee."[5] Performance mentality only makes us weary of the struggle. Resting in Christ gives us increased strength and joy to more than finish whatever God has in store for us. Performance mentality results in failure; resting in Christ results in adventurous living.

The Ten Commandments are positive influences in our lives. Let us look at several ways they help us build a productive and joyful life.

The Ten Commandments Enable God's Power to "Show Through"

One Sunday on their way home from church, a little girl turned to her mother and said, "Mommy, the preacher's sermon this morning confused me."

The mother said, "Oh? Why is that?"

The little girl replied, "Well, he said that God is bigger than we are. Is that true?"

The mother replied, "Yes, that's true, honey."

"And he also said that God lives in us. Is that true, Mommy?"

Again the mother replied, "Yes."

"Well," said the little girl, "if God is bigger than us and He lives in us, wouldn't He show through?"[6]

Wanting God to "show through" in our lives should be the desire of every believer. But like the little girl, many believers assume that just because God is bigger, He will show through all the time. This is not the case. Living a life of consecrated service before almighty God requires commitment.

As I previously stated, because the average believer is already committed to so many things, he finds it difficult to spend time with God in regular prayer and Bible study. Add to this the need to obey the Ten Commandments, and it is no small wonder people begin to "feel the crunch." What is the answer? *It is found in continuing to apply the gospel to our lives.*

Since I became a believer in 1945, I have seen any number of people going to spiritual counselors and attending discipleship seminars seeking a "plan" that allows them to integrate principles of spiritual growth into their hectic schedules. As I observed these people, what struck me was their assumption that the gospel is only good for salvation, while some other plan is required to grow as a believer. They believe Jesus provides eternal salvation from hell but do not realize He also provides daily salvation from the power of sin.

God's Power and Spiritual Growth

For many years Campus Crusade for Christ has helped to train millions of pastors and laymen in biblical principles for spiritual growth, so please do not misunderstand me. There is nothing wrong with being trained in principles of spiritual growth so you can live an abundant and effective life for Christ. In fact, training is essential. The problem is in seeking training that minimizes the continuing role of the gospel in the process of spiritual growth.

It is my firm belief that growing as a believer requires a fundamental understanding and commitment to the gospel as the foundation of all spiritual growth in the Christian faith. Let me explain what I mean and how the Ten Commandments can assist you.

In writing to the church at Rome, Paul says, "I am not ashamed of this Good News about Christ. It is the power of God at work, saving everyone who believes—Jews first and also Gentiles" (Romans 1:16).

When we read or hear this marvelous passage of Scripture, we are inclined to think about the power of the gospel which breaks the chains of sin and which, together with the Spirit of God, ushers in newness of life to the heart of the penitent sinner. But when we are looking for a means to grow in the grace of the Lord, our tendency is to say, "The gospel enabled me to find eternal life in Christ, but now I need something else to grow as a believer."

Paul's use of the word "salvation" carries a double meaning. It can refer to the gift of salvation, which is ours the moment we trust in Christ and receive Him into our hearts by faith. Or it can refer to the believer's future blessing in heaven when salvation will be experienced not just in part, but in all its glorious fullness.

Taking the latter meaning of the word into consideration, the gospel of Jesus Christ remains the power of God in our lives to produce spiritual growth until the day that we see Jesus face to face in heaven.

But practically speaking, how does the gospel function as a source of power in your life to help you through your daily struggles?

God's Power and Our Trust in Him

Everything in the Christian life requires *power*. Salvation results when we place our full trust upon the finished work of Christ—in His death, burial, and resurrection—for the forgiveness of our sins. God responds to our faith by forgiving our sins and granting us the free gift of eternal life in Christ Jesus. The power to perform this spiritual transaction belongs to the gospel, working in conjunction with the Holy Spirit.

Just think what an incredible accomplishment God works in our lives through a simple act of trust on our part. We were dead in sins and trespasses, spiritually separated from God, and on our way to a fiery hell without hope. But in a split second, God transferred us into His heavenly kingdom, made us His children, afforded us His Holy Spirit, and gave us eternal life, rich and free. This is amazing power!

I am sharing these truths with you to make a point. The principles that operated together to produce your salvation are the same principles that give you power for your daily living. Say, for example, you are facing a busy day with many problems that surfaced at the last second. You are tired, frustrated, and looking for an answer. What do you do?

What did you do when you received Christ? You admitted your sinfulness to God and by faith trusted in the finished work of Christ for the forgiveness of your sins. In turn, God was faithful, through the power of the Holy Spirit, to rescue you from your helpless estate as a sinner, to make you His child, and to give you a new life.

Now let us return to your dilemma. How do you overcome in the midst of it? Go to God in a moment of prayer and tell Him you are a sinner in need of His *continuing* grace and forgiveness. Remember the finished work of Jesus Christ for the forgiveness of your sins. As someone has explained, "Preach the gospel to yourself!" What will happen? The same power of God that brought you from spiritual death to eternal life will now come streaming into your life in a fresh way to provide the way of victory over your pressing circumstances. God will place at your disposal *all* the spiritual resources you will need to overcome the particular challenging situation you are facing.

Please think of it this way. If the power of the gospel can get you to heaven, it can get you through a day. You need not look any further.

God's Power and Walking with Christ
By itself the Law is *powerless* to provide eternal life. Paul writes, "The law of Moses could not save us, because of our sinful nature. But God put into effect a different plan to save us. He sent His own Son in a human body like ours, except that ours are sinful. God destroyed sin's control over us by giving His Son as a sacrifice for our sins. He did this so that the requirement of the law would be fully accomplished for us who no longer follow our sinful nature but instead follow the Spirit" (Romans 8:3,4).

The Law cannot function as an instrument to overcome life's challenges and to provide the abundant life. The great 19th century preacher Charles Spurgeon remarked of the Law's purpose, "The Law is meant to lead the sinner to faith in Christ, by showing the impossibility of any other way. It is the black dog to fetch the sheep to the shepherd, the burning heat which drives the traveler to the shadow of the great rock in a weary land."[7] Although Spurgeon is speaking about the role of Law in justification, the principle that the Law also leads to Christ in our living of the Christian faith is no less true.

Notice that the text above says we should walk "according to the Spirit," not according to the Law. So then, one role the Law plays in our daily walk with Christ is to reveal our sin and to drive us to the source of hope and strength that is found in the gospel of Jesus Christ. Apart from the deadening effect of the Law, no one would feel the need to cast himself at the mercy of Christ.

Walking in the power of the Holy Spirit is the only way a Christian can consistently obey the Ten Commandments and live above his circumstances. Appendix B, "The Spirit-Filled Life," explains how you can walk in the Spirit on a daily basis. If you are unfamiliar with this concept, I encourage you to apply the principles before you read any further.

The Ten Commandments Help Train Us in Righteousness

Every prizefighter needs a trainer to help condition him for the fight. Paul writes, "All athletes practice strict self-control. They do it to win a prize that will fade away, but we do it for an eternal prize...I am not like a boxer who misses his punches. I discipline my body like an athlete, training it to do what it should. Otherwise, I fear that after preaching to others I myself might be disqualified" (1 Corinthians 9:25–27).

Although Paul does not specifically mention the Ten Commandments, the standard for Paul's self-control and discipline was the Law. Without its continuing role in his life, Paul would have been an out-of-shape boxer, beating the air with no way of knowing if his behavior was hitting the mark. From this perspective, the Ten Commandments should not be perceived as a burden, but rather as a coach who is committed to helping you defeat every challenger life throws into the ring.

There is a story about the creation account called *The Fable of the Birds*, which also makes this point, but from a different perspective. All the newly created animals were walking around discovering what it was like to be alive. All except the birds. They were doing nothing but complaining because God had given them a heavy burden that He gave no other animal—those awkward appendages on their shoulders. God must be punishing them somehow. Why did they have to carry these things around, making it hard to walk? "Why?" they asked. "Why us?"

Finally, two or three of the more adventurous birds began to move their appendages. They began to flutter them, and soon they discovered that the very thing they had regarded as a burden actually made it possible for them to fly. No other animals could fly. The "heavy burden" turned out to be a beautiful gift.

Many of us act like those foolish birds. We regard God's call to obedience as an awkward appendage to our lives—weighing us down. Thou shalt not! Thou shalt! Heavy burden it is until we discover that God's Law is really the wind of the Spirit, enabling us to fly as no other creature can fly![8]

The Ten Commandments Help Us to Abide in Christ

The usual practice in viticulture, the care of vines, is for the branches to be pruned back each year to cleanse them. A vine produces certain growths called "sucker shoots," which start to grow where a branch joins the stem. If allowed to grow, they dissipate the life of the vine through sustaining so many branches that the vine produces little or no fruit but produces mainly leaves instead.

Every vinedresser knows how important it is to prune away these little sucker shoots to ensure plentiful fruit. Since the shoots grow right where the branch joins the stem, creating a tight cluster where dirt, leaves, and other debris collect, the pruning is basically a cleansing process.

Jesus used the analogy of the vinedresser to explain the process God uses to make us more like Christ in attitude and behavior. He said, "I am the true vine, and My Father is the gardener. He cuts off every branch that doesn't produce fruit, and He prunes the branches that do bear fruit so they will produce even more" (John 15:1,2).

The Father's work in our lives is to find a branch that is beginning to bear fruit, beginning to produce the likeness of Christ, then to cut it back. He trims off the troublesome shoots so that we may bear more fruit.

What is the goal of this pruning? God wants to bring us to a place where we are abiding in Christ. Jesus said, "Remain in Me, and I will remain in you. For a branch cannot produce fruit if it is severed from the vine, and you cannot be fruitful apart from Me" (John 15:4).

Jesus Commands Us to Abide in Him

How can we know with certainty that we are abiding in Christ? By following the Ten Commandments in the power of the Holy Spirit. Jesus said, "When you obey Me, you remain in My love, just as I obey My Father and remain in His love" (John 15:10). What an incredible level of importance Jesus ascribed to the Ten Commandments—to remain obedient to them is synonymous with abiding in His love.

Our Savior also reaffirmed this in John 14:21–23: "'Those who obey My commandments are the ones who love Me. And because they love Me, My Father will love them, and I will love them. And I will reveal Myself to each one of them.' Judas (not Judas Iscariot, but the other disciple with that name) said to Him, 'Lord, why are You going to reveal Yourself only to us and not to the world at large?' Jesus replied, 'All those who love Me will do what I say. My Father will love them, and we will come to them and live with them.'"

Abiding in Christ Leads to Joy

Certainly the Bible is full of other commandments beside those God delivered to Moses at Mount Sinai. But all the other laws found in Scripture directly relate to the Ten Commandments in some way. What does Jesus promise us if we abide in His commandments and consequently in His love? Joy overflowing! He said, "I have told you this so that you will be filled with My joy. Yes, your joy will overflow!" (John 15:11).

Nonetheless, throughout the centuries men have pursued joy

through every other avenue imaginable. The consequences of looking for joy in these other places are truly tragic.

- *No joy in unbelief*—Voltaire was an infidel of the most pronounced type. He wrote: "I wish I had never been born."

- *No joy in pleasure*—Lord Byron lived a life of pleasure, wealth, and nobility. He wrote: "The worm, the canker, and grief are mine alone."

- *No joy in money*—Jay Gould, a millionaire, had plenty of money. When dying, he said: "I suppose I am the most miserable man on earth."

- *No joy in position and fame*—Lord Beaconsfield enjoyed more than his share of both. He wrote: "Youth is a mistake; manhood a struggle; old age a regret."

- *No joy in military glory*—Alexander the Great conquered the known world in his day. Having done so, he wept in his tent before he said, "There are no more worlds to conquer."

Others seek joy in alcohol and drugs. Substance abuse is well known among the wealthy, famous, and powerful as they seek in vain for the joy and peace that only Jesus can give.

Where then is real joy found? The answer is simple. In abiding in Christ, in His love, and in His commandments!

A life lived with the Ten Commandments as its guide is anything but a life of encumbered living. If anything, God's Law offers a solution to the weary and overstressed who worry that the Ten Commandments represent an even bigger pile from which we must dig ourselves. When we abide in Christ, we do not "sweat the small stuff." We have an eternal perspective and live to please Someone who loves us unconditionally. We experience the blessing of obedience—and a great part of this blessing is joy that springs up within us and cannot be extinguished by circumstances or people. We do not live like those around us, but live with a sense of purpose and a communion with God that sustains us through trying times. He is our Source of joy, just as He is the source of the commandments that lead to joy.

In fact, rather than robbing our lives of happiness and fulfillment, the Ten Commandments point the way to a fuller and more exciting adventure than we could otherwise experience. In our next chapter, we will look at how the Law leads to grace.

LIFE APPLICATION

Set Your Heart's Gauge

Commit the following verses to memory. Then, when you are tempted to turn your spiritual focus away from God to other things, recall these commands from God.

- Romans 8:3,4—"God destroyed sin's control over us by giving His Son as a sacrifice for our sins. He did this so that the requirement of the law would be fully accomplished for us who no longer follow our sinful nature but instead follow the Spirit."

- John 15:10—"When you obey Me, you remain in My love, just as I obey my Father and remain in His love."

Gauge Your Spiritual Growth

Ask yourself the following questions. If one or more areas pose problems for you, ask God how you can deal with them through the power of the Holy Spirit.

- At this point in your life, do the Ten Commandments add pressure to your life? If so, why?

- Which of the Commandments are most difficult for you to follow?

- How does meditating on the Ten Commandments bring you closer to God?

- Which good works are you doing out of self-effort and which are you doing in the power of the Spirit?

- What evidence from your life can you find that you are basing your self-worth on a performance mentality rather than on the Lord?

- Can you name an incident this week where God has helped you to obey His Law?

- Are you trying to overcome life's challenges through the Law or through the power of the Holy Spirit?

- What areas of your life is God pruning? Are you abiding in Christ through the pruning process or responding negatively?

Walk in the Power of the Holy Spirit

Joy is a mark of those who are abiding in Christ. Joy is a command of God rather than an emotion. When you encounter times of difficulty—whether minor or major—practice living in joy. Thank God for the problem and rejoice that He has allowed it to come into your life. Keep reaffirming this attitude through prayer until your emotions follow suit.

Remember, Scripture commands us to "give thanks for everything to God the Father in the name of our Lord Jesus Christ" (Ephesians 5:20) and promises "that God causes everything to work together for the good of those who love God and are called according to His purpose for them" (Romans 8:28).

F O U R

GOD'S LAW LEADS TO GRACE IN CHRIST

R ecently, I was seated next to a woman in an airplane. I asked if she was interested in reading through a small booklet, *The Four Spiritual Laws*, with me. After reading it, she explained that she was already a believer.

Because I pray every morning, in fact throughout the day, that God will lead me to the people whose hearts He has prepared for me to talk to about Him, I knew that God had something to say to her. So I took the blue booklet, *Have You Made the Wonderful Discovery of the Spirit-Filled Life?* and gave it to her to read. This booklet presents many Scripture passages showing how to live a victorious Christian life in the power of the Holy Spirit. Out of the corner of my eye I saw that the woman read the booklet several times. Then I noticed tears streaming down her cheeks.

She turned to me and said, " Thank you so much that you gave me this booklet. There is no way that you could know how appropriate it was. I am a Christian, but I am having an affair with a man. And the man with whom I am having the affair is waiting for me at the airport to take me to his home so we can live together. Now I know where I will turn to get the strength to withstand this temptation. I will turn down my friend and return to my husband."

What motivated this woman to return to her husband? It was the transforming power of God's Word, His Law, in her heart. The more she saw herself in the mirror of God's Word, the more she was driven to her knees in need of God's grace to overcome her desire to leave her husband for another man. I never had to quote the seventh commandment to her, "Do not commit adultery." The Spirit of God made it clear to her.

How does this happen? God writes His Law upon our hearts the more we experience the grace and mercy of our loving God.

The Ten Commandments Guide Us to God's Grace

The story of that woman is an example of how the marvelous grace of God relates to the Ten Commandments. Let us examine three ways the Ten Commandments guide us to God's grace.

First, the Ten Commandments helped bring the promises
of the Old Testament to fulfillment in the New Testament.
Paul says that the Ten Commandments act as a "guardian." What does Paul mean by guardian? He says, "Think of it this way. If a father dies and leaves great wealth for his young children, those children are not much better off than slaves until they grow up, even though they actually own everything their father had. They have to obey their guardians until they reach whatever age their father set ... But when the right time came, God sent His Son, born of a woman, subject to the law. God sent Him to buy freedom for us who were slaves to the law, so that He could adopt us as His very own children" (Galatians 4:1–5).

Paul's point is that God never intended the Law to act as a basis for salvation. Rather, God instituted the Law as a way to harness or to control history. From the beginning of time, God had a specific date in mind when He planned to send Jesus into the world. Paul refers to this as the "fulness of the time" (Galatians 4:4, NASB).

By Noah's day, however, man's sin covered the earth. Sin was so strong and extensive that it threatened to jeopardize the earth along with God's redemptive timetable. So God sent a flood and wiped man from the face of the earth but saved righteous Noah and his family.

By the time of Abraham, sin once again had increased to where it threatened to shortcut God's plan of sending Jesus Christ into the world. But God had already promised never to destroy the earth again by a flood. So this time God gave His Law as a way to bridle man's sin. This way the promise of salvation given to Abraham was placed in guardianship until the time when people could receive the fulfillment of the promise in Christ Jesus. (See Galatians 3:19.)

Paul says it was not God's intention to replace faith with works using the Ten Commandments. Instead, the Law was given to make sure that the gift of the gospel promised to us in Abraham would someday be ours in Christ Jesus. The Ten Commandments served as history's caretaker, or guardian, ensuring that all the blessings that rightfully belong to God's children would arrive on time.

A story is told of how God intervened to guard the life of Ira D. Sankey, the long-time musical associate of Dwight L. Moody. One Christmas Eve, Sankey was traveling by steamboat up the Delaware River. Asked to sing, Sankey sang the *Shepherd Song*. After the song ended, a man with a rough, weatherbeaten face came up to Sankey and asked, "Did you ever serve in the Union Army?"

Sankey replied, "Yes, I did, in the spring of 1860."

The man asked, "Can you remember if you were doing picket duty on a bright moonlight night in 1862?"

Sankey was surprised and said, "Yes, I did."

The stranger said, "So did I. But I was serving in the Confederate army. When I saw you standing at your post I said to myself, 'That fellow will never get away from here alive.' I raised my musket and took aim. I was standing in the shadow completely concealed while the full light of the moon was falling upon you. At that instant, just as a moment ago, you raised your eyes to heaven and began to sing. Music has always had a wonderful power over me, and I took my finger off the trigger. 'Let him sing his song to the end,' I said to myself. 'I can shoot him afterwards. He's my victim and my bullet cannot miss him.' But the song you sang then was the song you sang just now.

"I heard the words perfectly: 'We are Thine, do Thou befriend us; Be the guardian of our way.' Those words stirred up many memories in my heart. I began to think of my childhood and my God-fearing mother. She had many, many times sung that song to me. But she died all too soon, otherwise much in my life would no doubt have been different. When you had finished your song, it was impossible for me to take aim at you again. I thought, 'The Lord who is able to save that man from certain death must surely be great and mighty,' and my arm of its own accord dropped limp at my side."[1]

Just as this simple song worked to guard the life of a great man of faith, God used the Ten Commandments to safeguard His plan of bringing Jesus Christ into the world. Think about it. God wanted His best for you and me. He knew the exact minute and second that the birth of the Jesus would take place. Paul says, "When the right time came, God sent His Son, born of a woman, subject to the law" (Galatians 4:4). The Ten Commandments were God's way of bringing order into the world to ensure that nothing would interfere with Jesus' arrival.

Second, the Ten Commandments help us
continue to live the Christian life.

Someone once calculated that in America we have thirty-five million laws trying to enforce Ten Commandments. This fact reminds us how impossible it is for anyone to gain God's acceptance by the works of the Law. Indeed, the apostle James reminds us that if we break even one of God's laws, we have in effect broken all of them. He writes, "The person who keeps all of the laws except one is as guilty as the person who has broken all of God's laws" (James 2:10).

Once an elderly lady went to the post office to mail a Bible as a gift to a friend. The clerk inspected the package, shook it, then asked, "Is there anything breakable in here?"

The woman thought for a moment, then replied, "Only the Ten Commandments."

Since the time of Moses, the Ten Commandments have shown

people their sin and hopelessness and their need for the grace of God in Christ Jesus. Again, God never meant the Ten Commandments to act as a means of earning salvation. Rather, God's Law provides a way for people to see their total inadequacy to live by God's standards.

Pride, selfishness, and concern over the things of this world are just a few of the wrong attitudes that keep us from the perfect obedience demanded by the Ten Commandments. Paul writes, "No one can ever be made right in God's sight by doing what His law commands. For the more we know God's law, the clearer it becomes that we aren't obeying it" (Romans 3:20). Our failure shows us our need for grace.

It is amazing how powerful God's timeless principles are when it comes to revealing our sin and shortcomings. One old story tells of a smalltown newspaper editor in west Texas who had some space to fill so he had the Ten Commandments set in type and ran them in the paper without comment. Seven men left town the next day and another wrote, "Cancel my subscription. You're getting too personal."

TV host Merv Griffin was interviewing Charlton Heston on his television program. Heston is, of course, the actor who played the part of Moses in *The Ten Commandments* and also starred in *Ben Hur*. Griffin asked Heston if any of the characters he had portrayed in his religious movies had changed his spiritual outlook. Heston did not answer the question directly. He thought a moment, then simply said, "Well, Merv, you can't walk barefoot down Mount Sinai and be the same person you were when you went up."[2]

This is the real significance of the Ten Commandments. Because they reveal God's perfect holiness, we see ourselves as God sees us— in need of His grace and forgiveness. We will never be the same.

Third, the Ten Commandments help us experience grace.
Who is God's grace for? It is for sinners. Romans 3:23 says, " All have sinned; all fall short of God's glorious standard." It also says that anyone who sins breaks the Law of God: "Those who sin are opposed to the law of God, for all sin opposes the law of God" (1 John 3:4). The cost of sin is death. And death means eternal separation from God.

God knew we could not keep His Law so He did something wonderful. God became a man—the person we know as Jesus Christ. In the form of a man, God lived the perfect requirements of the Law in our place. Romans 3:24 says, "Yet now God in His gracious kindness declares us not guilty. He has done this through Christ Jesus, who has freed us by taking away our sins." By receiving Christ as Savior and Lord, we can know that all our sins are forgiven and that some-day we will be with Christ in heaven.

Paul writes emphatically about the advantages we gain through God's grace: "For He has rescued us out of the darkness and gloom of Satan's kingdom and brought us into the Kingdom of His dear Son, who bought our freedom with His blood and forgave us all our sins" (Colossians 1:13,14, TLB). Why would we want anything less?

But today the relationship between the Ten Commandments and God's grace has often been presented in a misleading way. Like two heavyweight fighters sparring off against one another in the ring, law and grace have been presented as two old warriors battling for our hearts and minds. But the fact is law and grace are absolutely, beauti-fully intertwined. To seek to live in accordance to the Ten Command-ments always results in blessings. Even non-Christians who choose to live in accordance with God's moral laws benefit from the positive results that follow, whereas even Christians who choose to violate those laws will suffer the consequences.

This is one reason I begin and end every day on my knees reading the Bible and meditating briefly on the Ten Commandments. Fre-quently I ask God if I am breaking any of His holy commands, and if so, to reveal what I can do to amend my ways. Why? My daily walk with Christ depends on it. The Ten Commandments are irrevocable, and we should know and obey each of them for our own well-being and for our pathway to grace.

The Ten Commandments in the Life of the Believer

Can you recite the Ten Commandments? This question is not meant to embarrass you, but to make a point. How can we live out God's commandments if we do not know them? And let's be honest. When most Americans hear of the Ten Commandments, they do not think of God's unbendable moral code given to protect and provide an abundant life for them. They think of an angry God who is out to ruin their fun. But actually the opposite is true. The Ten Commandments were given by God for our blessing. There are three outstanding reasons why the Ten Commandments still hold an important place in the life of a believer and lead to grace.

First, the Law reflects the nature of God.
The Bible never speaks of God as a mere abstract concept. Rather, it describes Him as a God who is very involved in His creation. The Ten Commandments lie at the very heart of God's involvement with us. They reveal His will and His ways and His heart of grace, which are beneficial to us personally and to society at large. With the influence of the Ten Commandments working in our world, crime, adultery, and murder (to name just a few of society's ills) would be curbed. The fact is that every crime that takes place in America violates at least one of the Ten Commandments. Imagine all the pain and heartache that could be prevented if people used these commandments as their guide for living.

A *Wall Street Journal* editorial some time ago asked, "Why, if there are more than 50 million evangelical, born-again Christians in the United States, is there an epidemic of crime, abortion, drug addiction, alcoholism, and divorce?" Are Christians not supposed to be the salt of the earth and the light of the world? Obviously, the answer is that true believers must do more than profess faith in Christ—we must demonstrate our faith by our godly lives. There is no clearer way to accomplish this than by obeying the Ten Commandments. As we demonstrate the nature of God to others through our observance of the Ten Commandments, we will, by our authentic living, lead even more unbelievers to the throne of grace.

Second, the Law promotes respect for God.
Proverbs 1:7 says, "Fear of the Lord is the beginning of knowledge." A healthy, reverential fear of the God who created all heaven and earth, the eternal One who gave us life and who can take it, is the very bedrock of human wisdom. Today, most Christians have lost that reverential fear of God and as a result have lost their basis for under-

standing. We clearly live at a time when believers, due to superficial knowledge of the holiness and majesty of our great God and Savior, treat Him in a far-too-casual manner.

Once, a small child ran to her parents for protection during an especially noisy nighttime thunderstorm. They assured her that it was perfectly safe for her to return to her bed, saying, "God is always there with you."

The little girl replied, "I know God is with me, but I want a God with a face!"

It is our nature to reduce God to our size. In the Old Testament, the pagan nations worshiped rocks, statues, bugs, the sun, the moon, and a list of things that made people feel more comfortable with their gods. Little has changed. Albert Schweitzer's observation that modern man has created a god in man's own image becomes truer with each passing day. We are not secure with the God of the Bible who "just is," a God who has no form or tangible manifestation. The god of modern man has become a product of his own imagination and behavior.

A recent Gallup survey on religion in America reported some unexpected results. It seems that on the surface, Americans are just as religious as we were in 1947. At that time, 95 percent believed in God, 90 percent prayed, 73 percent believed in the afterlife, 41 percent attended religious services regularly. Compare this with more recent statistics: 96 percent believe in God, 90 percent pray, 71 percent believe in the afterlife, 41 percent attend religious services.

Except for slight variations, we are about as religious as we were fifty years ago. The difference is that society is slipping ever closer to the brink of moral disaster. I find the results of this survey troubling. It suggests that our collective faith appears to be somewhat shallow. We have maintained a form of belief while abandoning the substance. Our faith is not translating into moral reform in our personal lives or in our culture. I believe this ethical gap is caused by a "knowledge gap" with respect to God's character and laws. Even the small percentage who have retained intellectual understanding of God's Laws are increasingly losing a working knowledge of them. And when we lose our knowledge of God's laws, we also lose our attitude of respect toward Him.

Third, the Law reveals our growth in God.

The Ten Commandments serve as a yardstick for our spiritual walk. God measures all things. Here are some interesting facts from the prophet Isaiah:

- The oceans of the world contain more than 340 quintillion gallons of water, yet God holds them "in the hollow of His hand" (40:12, NASB).

- The earth weighs 6 sextillion metric tons, yet God says it is but "dust on the scales" (40:15, NASB).

- The known universe stretches more than 30 billion light-years (200 sextillion miles), but God measures it by the width of His hand (40:12, NASB).

- Astronomers claim there are at least 100 billion galaxies and each galaxy is made up of about 100 billion stars. To such mind-boggling math, Isaiah reminds us that God calls each star "by name" (40:26, NASB).[3]

But how do we measure our lives before our God? By the Ten Commandments! Jesus said, "Those who obey My commandments are the ones who love Me. And because they love Me, My Father will love them, and I will love them. And I will reveal Myself to each one of them" (John 14:21). According to Jesus, obedience to His commandments is a yardstick of the true spiritual condition of our lives. Although obedience to the Law does not produce the Spirit-filled life, we know we are living in the power of the Spirit to the degree we obey God's commandments and experience the power, joy, excitement, and adventure of the Christian life.

Today, we are a nation of people who claim to believe in God, and yet most of us know the Ten Commandments only secondhand. This has had a devastating effect. We are tempted to think of the Ten Commandments as little more than a set of quaint rules, completely outdated for our modern world. But as the well-known TV personality Ted Koppell once remarked in a speech at Duke University, "[The Ten Commandments] are not the Ten Suggestions."

During World War II, an American plane flew a mission in Africa.

Under the cloak of nighttime, the pilots flew toward their destination of Benghazi in North Africa. A strong tail wind pushed the plane much faster than expected. When the instruments revealed they had reached their destination, the crewmembers kept flying. They felt the instruments must be wrong so they pressed on looking for a beacon light that was already miles behind. Eventually, the plane ran out of fuel and the entire crew died when they crashed in the desert.[4]

Emotions can be a dangerous guide. But we can always know that our lives are on course by following the Ten Commandments. They are an accurate gauge for living according to God's standards.

When God gave the world the Law, He gave us His transcendent standard. It goes beyond what we can see, hear, feel, or smell. It is a standard untouched by human hands. God's Laws do not bend or shift depending on the era in which we live, the circumstances in which we find ourselves, or the environment in which we were raised. The Ten Commandments were given to the ancient Hebrews as a beacon to the world, a standard for everyone to know what God expects in relation to Him and others. For the believer, the Ten Commandments serve the larger purpose of showing us where we are in our spiritual growth. Our spiritual journey is so much more enjoyable when we know we are doing the things that are pleasing to our God.

Obeying Through Empowering Grace

The fact that a believer is no longer *under* the Law does not mean he is *without* the Law. God still requires us to obey His commandments. We do this not in our own strength, but in the power of the Holy Spirit. To illustrate, let me share a story. One of my very dear friends, a leader of many Christian causes in his city, always appeared to be radiant and joyful in every situation where I observed him.

One day as I was flying through the community and had a few moments at the airport, I called him and asked, "How are you doing?"

He said, "I'm miserable. I wish the Lord would take me home."

I was shocked. I had never heard such words from him.

He went on to say, "You think I'm a victorious Christian. I'm not. I'm a miserable sinner. I've been unfaithful. Ever since I became a Christian I've put on an act. I've tried to convince people that I was a very wonderful Christian, but I am constantly failing the Lord. I've tried everything I know to please God but nothing works for me."

I felt impressed to read to him Romans 7 where Paul says, "The good that I wish, I do not do; but I practice the very evil that I do not wish... Wretched man that I am! Who will set me free from the body of this death?" (vv. 19,24, NASB).

"That is the story of my life," he said through his tears.

I explained to my friend that there is no possible way he could live a victorious life, no matter how many masks he may wear or how many resolutions he may make. The only One who could live the Christian life is the Lord Jesus Himself through the enabling of the Holy Spirit. Then after reviewing the highlights of Romans 7, I went into the great and glorious passage of Romans 8:1: "There is therefore now no condemnation for those who are in Christ Jesus" (NASB).

No one is capable of obeying God's Law in his or her own strength. But through the power of the Holy Spirit in us, we can lead productive, obedient lives. If we follow after the Holy Spirit and no longer obey the old, evil nature within us, we find the key to our liberation from a life of spiritual defeat. I cannot live the Christian life unless the Holy Spirit enables me, no matter how long I pray, fast, beg, and plead. I am not capable of pleasing God in my own strength and neither are you.

John Newton, the author of the hymn *Amazing Grace*, had great difficulty with his memory. In the latter days of his life, a friend asked if he still had a poor memory. Newton replied, "Yes, I do, but I remember two things: I am a great sinner and I have a great Savior; and I don't suppose an old slave trader needs to remember much more than that." Newton never forgot his need for grace and the enabling of God's Spirit.

The source of the Christian's strength lies in God's grace and the Holy Spirit's empowerment, not in exertions of willpower or self-effort.

Yet sometimes we devalue the grace we have in Christ. And at times our reliance on the Ten Commandments can contribute to our failings as believers. In the next chapter, we will look more closely at the relationship between the Law and grace.

LIFE APPLICATION

Set Your Heart's Gauge

Commit the following verses to memory. Then, when you are tempted to turn your spiritual focus away from God to other things, recall these commands from God.

- Galatians 4:4,5—"When the right time came, God sent His Son, born of a woman, subject to the law. God sent Him to buy freedom for us who were slaves to the law, so that He could adopt us as His very own children."

- Romans 3:24—"Yet now God in His gracious kindness declares us not guilty. He has done this through Christ Jesus, who has freed us by taking away our sins."

Gauge Your Spiritual Growth

Ask yourself the following questions. If one or more areas pose problems for you, ask God how you can deal with them through the power of the Holy Spirit.

- How have the Ten Commandments safeguarded your life in specific ways?

- Do you ever feel that you have to keep the Ten Commandments to gain God's acceptance? What is wrong with this feeling?

- How are you integrating the Ten Commandments into your daily walk with God?

- Can you recite the Ten Commandments?

- How would you say the Ten Commandments have helped you have a holy fear of God?

- How have you experienced more grace in your Christian life through obeying God?

- Do you regard the Ten Commandments as suggestions or commandments from God in your daily walk with Him?

- What reaction do you have when you break one of the Ten Commandments? What does that say about your walk with God?

- What is your source of strength?

Walk in the Power of the Holy Spirit

Develop a reverential fear for God. In your daily times with Him, meditate on Scripture verses that pertain to His might, power, wisdom, and infinite character. Begin with passages such as Psalm 30 and 93, Isaiah 6 and 40:12–26, and Revelation 1:9–18. Use them to praise God for His greatness and the glory of His Son, Jesus Christ.

FIVE

CHEAP GRACE AND LEGALISM

The Parthenon in Athens, Greece, is considered one of the world's architectural wonders. Begun in 447 B.C., it has grand Doric columns and is built with beautiful marble. Its architectural lines are a reminder of the importance of balance. Seen as a whole, its symmetry is striking.

Yet taken part by part, the Parthenon is a mass of inconsistencies. There is not a single straight line in the architecture. No two steps are the same size or placed the same distance apart. Even the floor is not exactly square or level. The horizontal lines are inclined slightly, and the columns are slightly larger in the center than at either the top or the base. Yet the remarkable fact is that the Parthenon is built in gorgeous proportion and balance.[1]

The example of the Parthenon illustrates a simple fact: We, too, are a mass of inconsistencies. Our lives are filled with extreme views that we struggle to reconcile, so we must constantly strive for proportion and balance.

But unlike the Parthenon, our lack of balance does not make a beautiful whole. Consequently, the world is full of people who live anything but balanced lives. Extreme sports, extreme eating habits, and extreme attitudes about life mark the present-day culture. Lopsided thinking and acting threaten to cause our world to collapse. What is so sadly lacking in today's world is balance. This is also true of many followers of Christ. We have a tendency to migrate toward the extremes. As believers, we must find the equilibrium that Jesus taught in God's Word.

In our study on the Ten Commandments, we must avoid two extremes: cheap grace and legalism. Both are unbiblical. Each leads to particular problems in our Christian life. Let us first look at cheap grace.

The Seductive Charm of Cheap Grace

"Cheap grace" is a term coined by the late German theologian Dietrich Bonhoeffer. His observations of the church still ring true in our day. "Cheap grace is the preaching of forgiveness without requiring repentance, baptism without church discipline, communion without confession, absolution without personal confession. Cheap grace is grace without discipleship, grace without the cross, grace without Jesus Christ, living and incarnate."[2] In essence, cheap grace is grace without complete surrender to the Lordship of Christ.

Clearly, the Bible teaches that salvation is free to all who would truly repent and trust in Christ. But it also teaches that those who receive salvation are responsible to live a life of good works—to "prove their repentance by their deeds" (Acts 26:20, NIV). Paul writes, "God saved you by His special favor when you believed. And you can't take credit for this; it is a gift from God. Salvation is not a reward for the good things we have done, so none of us can boast about it. For we are God's masterpiece. He has created us anew in Christ Jesus, so that we can do the good things He planned for us long ago" (Ephesians 2:8–10).

The reason we were created is to do good works that give glory to God. This does not mean we are to do good works to earn God's acceptance. Rather, it means that God has a wonderful plan for our lives. He created us to spend eternity with Him and to share our faith with others, to live obediently, and to do the many things that are part of building and establishing His number one priority—the kingdom of God.

Think about it. God created you with a specific task in mind. He saved you from your sin and selfishness to equip you for a marvelous life of service in His kingdom. The Ten Commandments facilitate this goal by providing guidance and direction for life. And what is especially exciting about God's plan for you is that according to Paul, God had this plan in mind even before He created the world. What possible sense would it make to receive God's wonderful grace and then live life according to your own plan? That is cheap grace. But costly grace is much different.

The Beauty of Costly Grace

You can always tell when spring has arrived. Signs advertising yard sales begin popping up all over. If you have ever had your own yard sale, you know people want to get "something for nothing." But did you know that the world is full of people looking for "yard sale religion"? They want religion for nothing. They seek forgiveness without repentance and the blessings of the church without the fruit of a changed life.

But we must never forget that unlike people who discard their junk at a yard sale, God gave the very best He had in Jesus Christ. Although grace is free, it was not cheap. It cost the very life of Jesus. He died the worst possible death on our behalf so that we might be free from the power of sin and have the gift of eternal life. Peter writes, "You know that God paid a ransom to save you from the empty life you inherited from your ancestors. And the ransom He paid was not mere gold or silver. He paid for you with the precious life-blood of Christ, the sinless, spotless Lamb of God" (1 Peter 1:18,19).

As a young agnostic, I was offended by any discussion of the cross and the blood of Christ. It seemed so distasteful, so superstitious and pagan. My "aesthetic" nature rebelled at the thought. Then one day God sovereignly opened my mind as I was studying the Scriptures. Suddenly, I found myself on my knees, overwhelmed with a deep sense of gratitude. Christ's death on the cross and the shedding of

His blood for my sins suddenly became the major focus of my life. My sins were forgiven, cleansed, and washed away for eternity because He died on the cross and shed His blood for me.

Although I may do things in this life that might grieve or quench the Spirit, God's forgiveness is always there. I am so privileged to have the absolute assurance of God's Word that all of my sins are forgiven and that one day I will spend eternity in the presence of the glorious, mighty, holy Creator God and Savior and worship Him for all eternity. When I take communion, I find myself again and again in tears of gratitude when I think of how unworthy I am of God's love.

Jesus did not die for only those whom He called His friends. The Bible says that Jesus died for us even when we were God's enemies: "God showed His great love for us by sending Christ to die for us while we were still sinners" (Romans 5:8).

Bonhoeffer remarks about costly grace, "It is costly because it costs a man his life, and it is grace because it freely gives a man the only true life. It is costly because it condemns sin, and grace because it justifies the sinner...Costly grace confronts us as a gracious call to follow Jesus, it comes as a word of forgiveness to the broken spirit and the contrite heart. Grace is costly because it compels a man to submit to the yoke of Christ and follow Him; it is grace because Jesus says: 'My yoke is easy and My burden light.'"[3] Costly grace calls us to follow Jesus Christ with our whole heart, mind, soul, and strength.

We must never treat God's gracious forgiveness as a free ticket to live as we want. The expense of a life—God's only begotten Son—was paid upon a cruel, Roman cross so that we could receive His forgiveness and experience a life of peace and happiness. Costly grace inspires us to live by the Ten Commandments. This obedience, in turn, benefits us in all areas of our lives. King David writes, "Happy are people of integrity, who follow the law of the Lord" (Psalm 119:1). So not only is grace costly because of the price Christ paid for us, it is also priceless for us in the way it enriches our lives.

Costly Grace and the Exchanged Life

A great truth that helps overcome an attitude of cheap grace is what some call the "exchanged life." Paul writes to the church at Galatia, "I myself no longer live, but Christ lives in me. So I live my life in this earthly body by trusting in the Son of God, who loved me and gave Himself for me. I am not one of those who treats the grace of God as meaningless. For if we could be saved by keeping the law, then there was no need for Christ to die" (Galatians 2:20,21).

Paul's new life was a testimony to the exchanged life. He did not treat the grace of God lightly. He allowed Christ to live His life in and through him. By grace, God offers to take away our sin in exchange for His righteousness. Paul writes, "God made Christ, who never sinned, to be the offering for our sin, so that we could be made right with God through Christ" (2 Corinthians 5:21). We exchange our depraved life of sin for Christ's life of righteousness.

But just as eternal life is a costly gift from God, so is a life of obedience. We can live by the Ten Commandments only as we allow Christ to manifest His life in ours. Jesus is the One who lives the Law of God through us. We simply become part of the process. We do this by dying to self daily and surrendering the throne of our lives to Christ as a way of life.

Let me offer a personal example. I begin each day on my knees worshiping God. I acknowledge His Lordship and remind myself that I am nothing more than a suit of clothes for Him to wear. I have exchanged my life of failures and defeat for His life of victory. So my life is an exchanged life. It is the abundant life. He is my life, and I do not have any rights. I have been bought with a price, the price of His sacrifice on the cross for me. This outlook makes a vast difference in my perspective.

First Corinthians 13 records, "[Love] will hardly even notice when others do it wrong" (v. 5, TLB). Many times people have criticized me, attacked me, and on occasions have tried to destroy my ministry in different ways. Many times I have received harsh letters from people to bring issue with things that I have said or done. What is my response? I write them a letter of love. But it is not Bill Bright writing. My nature is to be very defensive and to react negatively. But Christ living in me motivates me to respond in love. His costly grace, freely given to me when I was still His enemy, inspires me to love those who treat me badly.

Costly Grace and a Thankful Heart

It was late in the afternoon and cold. The hot breath of the weary miners fogged the windows of the bus. Half the fathers in the village worked in the coal mine outside the small Irish village and made their way home each day on the company bus to a waiting family and a hot meal. The roads were slick with ice. It was one of those times that you dare not put on the brakes or turn sharply for danger of skidding off the road. The driver carefully guided his precious cargo down the narrow incline that had a solid rock wall on the right and a sheer cliff on the left that dropped to the quarry below.

As the bus approached the village, through the dim light, the men could see the form of a small boy sitting in the street playing in the snow, his back turned to the fast-approaching bus. An eerie hush descended on the bus as the men realized the horror of the situation. In just a few split seconds, the driver would be forced to make a decision no man ever wants to make—to attempt to stop suddenly or to swerve, which would mean certain death for half the fathers and husbands in the small village, or to continue on, which meant certain death to the oblivious boy ahead. In those few seconds he must decide. The boy? Or the men?

With tears in his eyes, the bus driver made his decision to sacrifice the boy and spare the lives of the men on the bus. The men awaited the impact. When the bus finally stopped, the driver was the first one out of the bus. He ran back to pick up the lifeless body of his own son. How can anyone describe or even imagine the anguish that man experienced that day as he chose to sacrifice his own son to save the lives of those men?[4]

This moving story actually happened. Would you have made the same decision that father made? This story illustrates another powerful motivation in living according to costly grace—gratitude. Do you think those men whose lives were spared were not grateful to that father? Of course they were. Likewise, God gave His only Son so we might live. Let us be thankful that God did not spare His own Son in securing for us salvation that we so desperately needed. But instead, let us spurn cheap grace and live obediently to the One who interceded on our behalf.

In Luke 17, the Bible tells a story of ten lepers. As Jesus was on His way toward Jerusalem, ten lepers stood and cried out, "Jesus, Master, have mercy on us!" Miraculously Jesus healed all of them of their disease. But only one of them turned and said, "Praise God, I'm healed!" He ran and fell at Jesus' feet and thanked him. But what about the other nine? They failed to thank Jesus for their healing and walked away (vv. 11–18).

When we look at the Ten Commandments, we see ten ways to practice costly grace and say "thank you" to Jesus. Obeying His commandments is not difficult if our hearts are full of thankfulness. Christ healed our broken relationship with our heavenly Father. God's judgment and wrath have been turned away. Eternal life is ours. And Christ's promise? To live inside us through his Holy Spirit—helping, comforting, and strengthening us each day in all of life's challenges. How can we respond with anything less than a life of total surrender and obedient gratitude?

But someone might say, "I don't want to know more about Christ's commands. I'm already experiencing tremendous guilt because I am not able to live up to what I already know. I'm burdened enough!"

If this is your attitude, either you are not a believer or you have not surrendered your life to the Lordship of Christ and are not allowing the Holy Spirit to control your life. We need to carefully consider both possibilities because many people have gone through a ritual of becoming a believer and being baptized, but do not have assurance of salvation. Ask yourself, "If I were to die today, do I know for sure that I would go to heaven?" If you are not able to answer with a positive exclamation, then it is quite possible you need to review the steps of salvation. To do so, prayerfully read through the steps in Appendix A.

If you are sure you are a Christian and still feel a tremendous burden of guilt, ask yourself, "Am I really living in the power of the Holy Spirit?" If you live in the power of the Holy Spirit, Christ, who took upon Himself your guilt and shame, will carry your burden. You need to surrender your feeling of guilt to Him. See Appendix B to review how you can experience the Spirit-filled life.

The Dangerous Lure of Legalism

On the opposite end of the spectrum from cheap grace is another danger: legalism. This is the belief that we can earn God's acceptance by observing religious rituals or by adhering to a set of religious works.

In 1947, Dr. Henrietta Mears, Dr. Louis Evans Jr., Dr. Richard Halverson, and I started a group called the Fellowship of the Burning Heart. We likened ourselves to "kamikaze pilots" for Christ. We were totally sold out to God and agreed to do anything Christ asked of us, even to the point of death. We dedicated our lives to a strict code of spiritual discipline. We arose early to pray for at least an hour. We were committed to reading our Bibles daily, memorizing Scripture, witnessing, and living lives of total surrender before almighty God.

What became of the Fellowship of the Burning Heart? It burned out! Before long, we were all spiritually exhausted and fell miserably short of our goal. We realized we simply could not maintain the high standards we had created for ourselves. Although it was our sincere desire to glorify Christ through our commitment, our fellowship was legalistic. We had not abandoned godly living. Rather, in our zeal we had reduced the awesome experience of walking with Christ in the power of His resurrection to a mere set of rules and regulations devoid of the true power and grace of God. I came away from that experience with a fresh commitment to shun religious formulas and to simply surrender my life to Christ to live His life in and through me in the power of His Holy Spirit.

Legalism was also a problem in Jesus' day. The Pharisees had developed an elaborate system of laws intended to make life easier. Instead, their 613 laws—365 negative commands and 248 positive laws—only complicated life and drew people further away from God. For example, law 345 chastened people "not to remove the entire beard, like the idolaters." Many debates, however, revolved around how much of his beard a man could shave and remain in compliance with the law. Additionally, the sheer number of laws made it almost impossible to know if you were in compliance. The result was spiritual insecurity and confusion.

Legalism has also been a problem throughout church history. During the early 16th century, a monk by the name of Martin Luther was suffering from spiritual insecurity. He sought inner peace through a legalistic form of monastic living. In the hopes his religious works would earn his salvation, Luther would crawl up and down flights of stairs praying until his knees were bloody. Although he was a committed churchman, the rules and regulations that made up Luther's way of life provided little relief for his sin-sick soul.

On a mission to Rome in 1510, Luther was appalled by the corruption he found in the Church. The Pope's emissaries were raising funds to rebuild St. Peter's Cathedral by the sale of indulgences—taking money in exchange for the "forgiveness" of sins. Soon Luther began to learn about "justification by faith" rather than by works and realized that all his works were wood, hay, and stubble compared to the riches of God's grace freely offered in Christ. Luther gratefully placed his trust in Christ's death rather than in his good works for his salvation.

To protest the practice of indulgences and other Church problems, on October 31, 1517, Luther nailed his 95 theses on the church door at Wittenberg. The Reformation of the Church had begun.

Legalism Produces a Bad Crop

The writer of the Book of Hebrews was very concerned about legalism. Jewish believers were reverting to meticulous adherence to the ceremonial law as a way of gaining God's acceptance. The writer contrasts a life of faith with trusting in works. Hebrews 6:7,8 says, "When the ground soaks up the rain that falls on it and bears a good crop for the farmer, it has the blessing of God. But if a field bears thistles and thorns, it is useless. The farmer will condemn that field and burn it." Following are ten ways legalism produces "thorns and thistles" in our lives:

- Legalism kills love for God (Revelation 3:14–22).

- Legalism places human tradition above God's Word (Mark 7:5–9).

- Legalism hinders our vision of God (Matthew 23:13–15).

- Legalism overlooks the needs of others (Luke 10:25–37).

- Legalism is a source of selfish pride (Matthew 18:1–4).

- Legalism produces rivalry and deception (Luke 20:9–20).

- Legalism causes us to view others with contempt (Luke 18:9–14).

- Legalism denies our freedom of conscience (Mark 2:23–28).

- Legalism emphasizes externals (Mark 12:38–40).

- Legalism makes us Pharisees and hypocrites (Mark 10:1–12).

From the Pharisees, to Luther's day, to our own, history reveals a natural tendency toward "works righteousness." These come from a wrong view of God's Law. But the problem is not with the Law. Paul says, "But still, the law itself is holy and right and good" (Romans 7:12). What, then, is the source of legalism? It is within us. When we treat the Law legalistically, it quickly becomes our taskmaster. Human rules soon follow. But God never intended us to obey the Ten Commandments through slavish adherence. This produces death. His commandments become a source of life to us when, in the power of the Holy Spirit, we invite Christ to direct our steps.

The great preacher Charles Spurgeon made a statement I could make myself, "I have found, in my own spiritual life, that the more rules I lay down for myself, the more sins I commit. The habit of regular morning and evening prayer is one which is indispensable to a believer's life, but the prescribing of the length of prayer, and the constrained remembrance of so many persons and subjects, may gender unto bondage, and strangle prayer rather than assist it."[5]

No matter how much we may try to reform ourselves through legalistic behavior, we can never achieve the newness of life that God wants us to experience in Christ. The following story illustrates our inability to reform ourselves. A man with a very large nose marries a woman who also has a large nose. Before they have children, both husband and wife have plastic surgery performed to reduce the size of their noses. Shortly thereafter, the wife finds out that she is pregnant. Will the child have a large nose or a regular nose—one that reflects their heredity or the surgical change? Obviously, the child will reflect the genetic make-up of the parents and will likely be born with a large nose.

Likewise, changing ourselves on the outside through legalistic conduct does very little to produce change within. Only Christ can change a human heart, give us spiritual life, and enable us to lead fruitful lives in accordance with God's Law.

The Bible's Cure for Legalism

What is the answer to defeating legalism in our lives? Paul explains, "When we place our faith in Christ Jesus, it makes no difference to God whether we are circumcised or not circumcised. What is important is faith expressing itself in love" (Galatians 5:6).

Circumcision was a Jewish ritual that expressed a heart of obedience to God. It was an outward sign of an inward attitude. But what was important to God was not the outward physical sign but the inward heart of love and obedience toward Him.

Paul's simple yet profound point is that when we are walking by faith in the Son of God and loving people, we do not have a heart for sin. God's Law is written on our hearts as we love Him wholeheartedly and love others as ourselves.

The Christian life is not reams of rules that hang around our necks like a noose that tightens with every sin. It is a life of freedom. The Ten Commandments are designed to assist us in our exciting journey with Christ. If we try to produce the Spirit-filled life by obeying the Ten Commandments in our own effort, we are doomed to fail. But the Bible says to consistently walk by faith and to show love for God and others. Then God will produce obedience to the Ten Commandments in us the way a tree bears its precious fruit.

Jesus says, "I am the vine; you are the branches. Those who remain in Me, and I in them, will produce much fruit. For apart from Me you can do nothing" (John 15:5). Just as the sap brings nutrients up through the vine to the branches, which then produce fruit, we produce the fruit of Spirit-filled living by abiding in Christ through the power of the Holy Spirit.

A Personal Lesson

The biggest problem any of us have as believers or nonbelievers is self, or ego. The unbeliever thinks, "All I have to do is work hard, get some breaks, and the world will be my oyster." In college, many years ago, I became student body president, editor of the yearbook, and a member of Who's Who. I graduated as the outstanding student, and many other honors also came my way. Later I went to Hollywood where I went into business and enjoyed a considerable measure of success. But I knew nothing of God's plan for my life. In my ignorance, I believed I was the master of my own fate. Then through the influence of my mother's prayers and the First Presbyterian Church of Hollywood, I met the One who created the universe, the promised Messiah. Soon I discovered that the real key to success and happiness was found in total surrender to Him as Lord of my life. It became obvious to me that if He could create and run this universe, He could surely run my life better than I could.

Let me encourage you to stop seeking the acceptance of men or even God's acceptance based on how well you perform in life. Simply abide in our loving Savior, allow Him to abide in you, and you will soon find yourself living for the glory of God—the kind of life for which you long and pray.

Achieving a balance takes walking with Christ moment by moment. This has been my emphasis for more than fifty years. When my life is in spiritual balance, I am joyful and content.

Yet over the years, I have been accused of teaching both cheap grace and legalism. Critics charge I promote cheap grace or "easy believism" because I stress the love of God in evangelism. But at Campus Crusade for Christ, we have *always* emphasized faithful obedience to Christ in our staff training and in the discipleship training we have offered to millions of people around the world.

On the other hand, the charge of legalism has also been laid at my feet because of my commitment to prayer and fasting. In fact, the thought that I was being legalistic occurred to me one day as I was preparing for a forty-day fast. I thought, *But I already have God's full acceptance. What more of God's love and acceptance can I possibly gain through fasting?* Then the truth came to me. My fast was not a means to win God's approval, but a way to develop a closer, more intimate relationship with Christ. On October 19, 2001, I will turn eighty years of age and will have walked with Christ for more than fifty-five years. Yet, I am keenly aware of my fleshly propensity toward both cheap grace and legalism. This is why each day I surrender to Christ and rely on the power of His Holy Spirit to guide me in the path of the gospel so I might live a life that brings maximum glory and honor to Him.

You too can live a balanced life according to the Ten Commandments by living under costly grace. It is attitude that counts. As we go into the next sections of our study, commit yourself to repudiating the extremes of cheap grace and legalism. Instead, develop an attitude of praise and thankfulness with service to God and others.

In the next two sections, we will examine each of the Ten Commandments. Christ brilliantly summarized the Law into two distinct groups through His use of two Old Testament commands when He said, "'You must love the Lord your God with all your heart, all your soul, and all your mind.' This is the first and greatest commandment. A second is equally important: 'Love your neighbor as yourself'" (Matthew 22:37–39).

The first group of commandments (1–4) addresses our obligations *toward God*, while the second group (5–10) speaks of our obligations *toward each other*. The first command follows the *shema* (Deuteronomy 6:4–9), which was a confessional statement central to Israel's life and worship. The second command comes from the laws of social order (Leviticus 19:18), which were a part of Israel's civil law.

As we study the chapters ahead, remember that obeying the Ten Commandments is not to be a burden. Rather, it is a joyous experience with Christ when you follow these two simple principles: love God with your whole heart, soul, and mind, and love your neighbor as yourself.

LIFE APPLICATION

Set Your Heart's Gauge

Commit the following verses to memory. Then, when you are tempted to turn your spiritual focus away from God to other things, recall these commands from God.

- Ephesians 2:8–10—"God saved you by His special favor when you believed. And you can't take credit for this; it is a gift from God. Salvation is not a reward for the good things we have done, so none of us can boast about it. For we are God's masterpiece. He has created us anew in Christ Jesus, so that we can do the good things He planned for us long ago."

- Galatians 2:20,21—"I myself no longer live, but Christ lives in me. So I live my life in this earthly body by trusting in the Son of God, who loved me and gave Himself for me. I am not one of those who treats the grace of God as meaningless. For if we could be saved by keeping the law, there was no need for Christ to die."

Gauge Your Spiritual Growth

Ask yourself the following questions. If one or more areas pose problems for you, ask God how you can deal with them through the power of the Holy Spirit.

- What in your life is unbalanced regarding grace versus legalism?

- Can you say before God that you have surrendered every part of your life to Him?

- Are you living the "exchanged life"? What evidence do you have?

- Does your love for God reflect the gratitude you feel toward Christ's sacrifice for you?

- Do you feel guilty about failing to measure up to the Ten Commandments? What is the source of this guilt? What do you need to do about it?

- Are your good deeds done out of a legalistic attitude or from a walk of faith?

- What rules do you have for yourself that do not reflect God's Word? Are these rules keeping you in bondage?

- How are you balancing your freedom in grace and your responsibility to obey God's laws?

Walk in the Power of the Holy Spirit

Abiding in Christ means walking in His Spirit moment by moment. Reread the material in Appendix B. Practice a lifestyle of being filled with the Spirit. Do this for a week, then look back to see how God has worked in your life.

WRITTEN BY THE HAND of GOD

PART TWO

The Goal of Loving God

YOU SHALL HAVE NO OTHER GODS BEFORE ME

Many years ago in Brooklyn, New York, Thomas K. Beecher substituted as a speaker at the Plymouth Church for his famous brother, Henry Ward Beecher. Many curiosity seekers had come to hear the renowned Henry Beecher speak. When Thomas Beecher appeared in the pulpit instead, some people got up and started for the doors.

Sensing that these people were disappointed because he was substituting for his brother, Thomas raised his hand for silence. Then he announced, "All those who came here this morning to worship Henry Ward Beecher may withdraw from the church. All who came to worship God may remain."[1]

Thomas Beecher was implying that all humans have the tendency to replace rightful focus on God with a preoccupation on other things. How many times have you been in a worship service and found yourself thinking about finances, a recent argument with your spouse, or the problems at your job? Our daily schedules also testify to the fact that we do not make God primary in our lives. Although we may not recognize or admit it, we let other things take God's place.

When I was a young Christian, I was not as sensitive to how we can place other things—even the good things in our lives—before God. I was tempted to give Vonette, my children, or even my ministry more effort and time than I gave to God. I soon learned that we can become so excited about serving the Lord that our good works can rob us of the joy of intimacy we have in Christ. We can become so busy "doing" God's work that we neglect to spend time with Him.

God expects to be first in our lives. Therefore, anything that takes our focus and worship away from Him becomes a god to us.

God Expects our Worship

The first commandment spoke directly to the issue of whom ancient Israel was to worship. It says, "God instructed the people as follows: 'I am the LORD your God, who rescued you from slavery in Egypt. Do not worship any other gods besides me'" (Exodus 20:1–3). This law reflects the "great and foremost" commandment of the Old Testament: "You must love the LORD your God with all your heart, all your soul, and all your strength" (Deuteronomy 6:5). Jesus affirmed this commandment when He said, "You must love the Lord your God with all your heart, all your soul, and all your mind" (Matthew 22:37). Therefore, this commandment is also to be our great priority.

God gave this commandment to Moses at Mount Sinai not long after He had miraculously delivered His people out of Egypt. Without question, God was to be the number one priority in the Hebrews' hearts and minds.

Why did God preface His first commandment with mention of His mighty deliverance of His people from Pharaoh's ruthless control? He wanted to jog the Israelite's memory of the plagues of Egypt and the parting of the Red Sea. Through those and other miracles, God reminded the ancient Hebrews, and reminds us today, that He alone has the power to set people free from spiritual bondage to sin. Therefore, He alone has the legitimate right to our worship. He will obviously not tolerate any rival gods.

False Gods Steal Our Worship

The world is a place of "false gods" that beg for our allegiance. Without exception, every false god, from Confucius to New Age philosophy to materialism, says that people are basically good or that they can better themselves. All man needs is a spiritual stimulant, not a Savior.

The God of the Bible, however, presents Himself as perfectly holy and man as totally sinful in need of forgiving grace. The gospel of Jesus Christ presents an uncomplimentary picture of humanity. It says that all people are sinners who can do nothing to meet God's standards. The Bible emphatically states that human redemption is not found in religious rituals or relentless self-effort. Rather, mankind is hopelessly lost and in desperate need of God's loving mercy.

Think about it. Is the Bible's picture of mankind made up by mere humans like the views of other religions? Why would any person invent a religion that puts himself down? Would he purposely defame his own character as sinful and insist that salvation can be found only in One greater? Only God would draw this picture.

Let's consider a few of these false gods and the consequences for putting them first in our lives.

False Religions

God will not share His glory with false gods. False religions like Buddhism, Islam, and Hare Krishna promise lasting peace and fulfillment but cannot deliver on their promises. They offer intellectual salve, but no spiritual renewing of the mind. A temporary peace, but not a "peace that surpasses all understanding." A back-scratcher for your religious itch, but no soothing for the deep needs of your soul.

Fame and Fortune

Another type of false god is fame and fortune. J. C. Penney was a man who discovered nothing but disappointment after years of serving these gods of materialism. I came to know J. C. Penney in his later years. He was a great man of God who left behind a merchandising empire and a tremendous legacy that has inspired countless individuals to a life of faith and obedience to Christ.

It was not until the department store magnate was an older man that he committed his life fully to Jesus Christ. For many years, he was primarily interested in becoming a success and in making money. Looking back at his life, he confessed, "When I worked for six dollars a week at Joslin's Dry Goods Store back in Denver, it was my ambition, in the sense of wealth in money, to be worth one hundred thousand dollars. When I reached that goal, I felt a certain temporary satisfaction, but it soon wore off and my sights were set on becoming worth a million dollars."

Penney and his wife worked hard to expand the business. Then one day Mrs. Penney caught a cold and developed pneumonia, which claimed her life. At that point, Penney realized that having money was a poor substitute for inner peace. "When she died," he said, "my world crashed about me. To build a business, to become a success in the eyes of men, to accumulate money—what was the purpose of life? What had money meant for my wife? I felt mocked by life, even by God Himself."

Soon Penney was financially ruined and in deep distress. It was then that God could deal with his self-righteous nature and his love for money. After that, Penney received Christ and through the years that followed had a powerful influence for our Savior. He built one of the great Fortune 500 companies on the Golden Rule: "Do unto others as you would have them do unto you." He testified of God's working in his life. "I had to pass through fiery ordeals before reaching glimmerings of conviction that it is not enough for men to be upright and moral men. But as I was earnestly seeking God's aid, it was forthcoming, and a light illumined my being. I cannot otherwise describe it than to say that it changed me as a man."[2]

Setting up success as your god cannot change the needs of your heart. Instead, success becomes a demanding taskmaster that will not satisfy the deepest needs of your soul.

Self-Esteem and Pride

For most of my early life I was the "lord of my life, the master of my fate." I had no God, no Savior, no knowledge of God's Word, the Bible. I was a humanist, a materialist who worked day and night to build my own materialistic empire. In my ignorance, I was a happy pagan.

Like I did then, many people today make self a god. In fact, the practice of making self-esteem the ultimate priority in life has become a major national movement.

We can see evidences of this movement in our schools. Johnny cannot read or write, but learning is not as important as feeling good about himself. Research agrees, right? Not according to a recent issue of *Psychological Review*. Three researchers, Roy Baumeister of Case Western Reserve University and Laura Smart and Joseph Boden of the University of Virginia, thoroughly examined the literature and concluded that a much stronger link connects high self-esteem to violence. They write, "It is difficult to maintain belief in the low self-esteem view after seeing that the more violent groups are generally the ones with higher self-esteem."

The study's conclusion was: "Certain forms of high self-esteem seem to increase one's proneness to violence. The pursuit of high self-esteem for everyone may literally end up doing considerable harm ... Perhaps it would be better to try instilling modesty and humility."[3] This conclusion flies in the face of conventional wisdom.

William B. Swann, Jr., a psychology professor at the University of Texas at Austin, studied the workings of the self-esteem concept for fifteen years. Swann sees a backlash building against the message of self-esteem. One teacher, for example, told Swann that she had been advised by the school counselor not to ask a certain student any questions unless she was sure the boy knew the answer so that she would not damage his self-image. "So she stopped asking him questions," Swann says. "The kid gets ignored and less knowledgeable, and it actually makes the problem worse."[4]

From an increase in violence to a marked drop in education standards, the world's message of self-esteem has proven its ability to produce a generation that is suffering both morally and intellectually. Now allow me to be clear. I am not opposed to cultivating a healthy self-esteem. God wants us to have a proper self-image. There is nothing wrong with feeling good about a job well done or rejoicing in the successes of our children. But it is wrong to allow a godless pride to take root in our hearts and supplant God's place in our lives.

Jesus admonished us to love our neighbors as ourselves. A healthy self-esteem is based on the knowledge that we are made in the image of God, who loves us unconditionally.

In essence, a prideful view of self is making one's self a god. Ever since Lucifer attempted to usurp the throne of God and Adam and Eve wanted to be as wise as God, all people have been infected with pride. It is the source of all rebellion against God and His holy Word. It is no wonder, then, that research proves the destructive influences of pride among a broad spectrum of people from many walks of life.

Nevertheless, most people are reluctant to admit to ungodly pride. But allow me to ask some questions. Do you remember the argument you had with your spouse—the one you *had* to win? Do you recall the dirty deed someone did to you that you could not forgive? Why is it that you feel good about yourself when it is your idea to do a task but you feel a tinge of resistance when your spouse asks you to do it? Because the root problem is pride. Our sinful nature wants to be in control. In fact, pride is the cause of most defense mechanisms and insecurities that rule our lives, which in turn, lead to destructive patterns of depression and despair.

Appearances

Someone might say, "But I am not living in depression and despair. I have a nice job, a family, and a wonderful home."

The Pharisees of Jesus' day had nice jobs, families, and wonderful homes. Yet Jesus likened their hearts to tombs of "dead men's bones." What they did in the name of God, they really did to make themselves look holy in the eyes of other people.

Today, many Americans are also preoccupied with the idea of maintaining "appearances." While our suburbs are showcases with perfectly manicured grass, many of our sons are strung out on drugs and too many of our daughters are pregnant at age fifteen. Couples suffer silently as their marriages crumble, while the television has become our escape to keep us from thinking about our failed expectations. Unfortunately, many believers value the approval of others above what God thinks of them. As a result, they miss out on God's best.

Do not waste your life chasing after earthly false gods that never satisfy. God's Word is filled with promises of tremendous blessings for the person who puts God first and rejects all manmade "gods." Come to the glorious realization of the first commandment: that *permanent* satisfaction is attainable only when you receive Christ by faith and give your *whole life* to the worship of God—Father, Son, and Holy Spirit —one God revealed in three Persons.

God Has a Right to Our Worship

Scripture gives us many reasons *why* we should put God first in our lives.

First and foremost, God created us. The psalmist declares, "You made all the delicate, inner parts of my body and knit me together in my mother's womb" (Psalm 139:13). And Paul writes, "We are God's masterpiece. He has created us anew in Christ Jesus, so that we can do the good things He planned for us long ago" (Ephesians 2:10). Taken together, these verses teach that God is our Creator who designed us for a specific task—to live for Him in total devotion.

On the other hand, not to live for Him can result in total disaster. How important is it to fulfill the design for which God created us? Imagine trying to cook your dinner in a washing machine rather than in an oven. You place your casserole in the wash tub, turn on the machine, and leave. What will you find when you return for your food? A big mess! Your washing machine was not created to prepare food.

By filling our hearts and minds with the gods of this world, we allow ourselves to be used for wrong reasons. We were created for "good works," not to be filled with trash. Small wonder, then, that our life becomes a mess when we fill it with unwholesome things. But when we live for the reason we were created—to worship God with our whole heart, mind, and soul—everything in life falls into its rightful place and fulfills its intended purpose.

For more than fifty years it has been my primary goal in life to love, trust, and obey my great creator God and Savior. Why? Because if He actually created 100 billion or more galaxies and loved me enough to leave His place of glory to die on the cross for my sins and give me eternal life, how could I possibly not want to live totally and completely for Him? Plus, He has given me the Holy Spirit to enable me to live for Him.

Second, God is our powerful Protector. The Bible says, "God is our refuge and strength, a very present help in trouble" (Psalm 46:1, NASB).

Looking back at historical events, we can see how God protected people in the past. When Napoleon's massive French army was preparing to attack Feldkirch, a little town on the Austrian border, the citizens didn't know what to do. When they spotted soldiers on the heights above the little town, a council of citizens was hastily summoned to decide whether the townspeople should try to defend themselves or display the white flag of surrender.

That fateful day happened to be Easter Sunday, so the townspeople gathered in the local church, as was their custom. The pastor rose and said, "Friends, we have been counting on our own strength, and apparently that has failed. As this is the day of our Lord's resurrection, let us just ring the bells, have our services as usual, and leave the matter in His hands. We know only our weaknesses, and the power of God to defend us."

The council accepted his plan, so they rang the church bells. The enemy, hearing the sudden peal, concluded that the Austrian army had arrived during the night to defend the town. Before the service ended, the enemy broke camp and left![5]

No matter what threatening circumstances are encountered by those of us who truly trust our Lord, our all-powerful God is always with us. He constantly shields us from harm, even when we are unaware of the danger. Who is more worthy of our worship and devotion?

Third, God is the sovereign Ruler of the universe. One reason God refuses to share His honor is because only He is able to accomplish everything that He has planned for us. In His plan, He led the nation of Israel out of Egypt and through the wilderness to the Promised Land. Without Israel's *complete attention* focused on God, they would likely have gotten lost, or worse, perished along the way.

God has a place of incomparable blessing in store for all of His children—heaven. What part of your life are you allowing God to control on your way there? Are you inviting Him to direct your religious activities, but not the rest of your life?

Many of us have been affected by cultural pressures and are experts at compartmentalizing our lives. We reserve God for a compartment on Sunday, but on Monday morning, we set God aside and put on our business face or our homemaker face.

Jesus said, "If anyone wishes to come after Me, he must deny himself, and take up his cross, and follow Me" (Mark 8:34, NASB). If you are struggling in an area of your life, try putting God first in that area. For example, if you struggle with singleness, put God first by accepting whatever His plan is for your life. If you struggle with finances, put God first by giving Him back the fruits of your labor through your tithes and offerings given joyfully because of who He is and all He has done for you. Then He will lead you through all your difficulties.

Worship God by Keeping Him First

Our worship must be for God and God alone. Today, people all over the world are turning from worshiping rival gods of wood and stone to worshiping the true God.

The people of Chalyaphum, Thailand, worshiped a large rock in the center of town. They brought their problems to the rock, and a "watcher" interpreted the rock's counsel. One man had served as the rock's watcher for fifteen years. Throughout this period, he never once left the rock! The rock site was his home.

None of the local believers dared to share their faith in Christ with the watcher. They felt that his loyalty to his "god" was so deep that he would not consider any other way of worship.

Then one day a Campus Crusade for Christ missionary who served locally with the Here's Life Training Center shared the good news of Christ with the man. To the amazement of everyone in town, the man eagerly invited Christ into his heart. When the missionary invited the man to attend a follow-up session for more teaching, he brought his entire family, who joined him in committing their lives to Christ.

You may be thinking, *I would never bow down to some carved piece of wood or seek advice from a stone.* And you probably never will. However, Satan is far craftier than that. The "gods of this world" do not need to be idols in the literal sense, but rather they can be anything or anyone whom we serve, follow, or honor above God. A god is anything or anyone who monopolizes our thinking and our affections.

G. Campbell Morgan, author and preacher at Westminster Chapel in London during the early 20th century, observed, "Every man needs a god. There is no man who has not, somewhere in his heart, in his life, in the essentials of his being, a shrine in which is a deity whom he worships...The question is whether the life and powers of man are devoted to the worship of the true God or to that of a false one."[6]

I am reminded of a dear, wonderful woman, a pillar in her church who was worth many millions. She didn't have to worry about what she would wear or where she would live or any other material need. But her wealth had become her god. She would fall into depression whenever the stock market dropped causing her to lose some of her fortune. Consequently, she became very insecure. She was depending on her bank account instead of on our Lord.

Please permit me to ask you a difficult question. What consumes your mind each day? Is it your work, your future, sex, or perhaps a loved one? The answer will help you determine what you have allowed to occupy God's rightful place of priority in your life.

One of my favorite, most meaningful promises from God's Word is recorded in Matthew 6:33, "Seek first His kingdom and His righteousness, and all these things will be given to you as well" (NIV).

Have you made seeking God and serving Him your highest priority? Consider how much effort, resources, and quality time you invest in personal interests, goals, or things versus what you commit to God. Whatever occupies your thoughts and your schedule is quite likely your "god."

Worship God by Giving Him the Glory

The first commandment includes God's right to receive *all the glory* in all things.

Toward the end of his life, composer Franz Joseph Haydn was present at the Vienna Music Hall, where his oratorio *The Creation* was being performed. Weakened by age, the great composer was confined to a wheelchair. As the majestic music built to a climax, the audience was caught up with tremendous emotion. When the passage "And there was light!" was reached, the chorus and orchestra burst forth in such power that the crowd could no longer restrain its enthusiasm. The vast assembly rose in spontaneous applause.

Haydn struggled to stand, and when he did, he motioned for silence. With his hand pointed toward heaven, he said, "No, no, not from me, but from thence comes all!" Haydn refused the glory but gave all the praise to the Creator and fell back into his chair exhausted.[7]

God says, "I am the Lord *your God.*" The word *God* in the original Hebrew is *Elohim*, which means the supreme object of worship. Thus, God does not identify Himself as a god of the wind, rain, or fire, but as the only transcendent Creator God—the supreme object of worship!

We tend to narrowly define worship as going to church on any given Sunday. But worship is much, much more than that. The word "worship" comes from the old English *worth-ship*, which means "to ascribe worth or value to something or someone." It is recognizing and submitting to the awesome majesty of God in every area of life moment by moment, seven days a week.

Worship not only involves singing and praising God, but also includes how we think and live. A. W. Tozer eloquently writes, "Worship is to feel in your heart and express in some appropriate manner a humbling but delightful sense of admiring awe and astonished wonder and overpowering love in the presence of that most ancient Mystery, that Majesty which philosophers call the First Cause, but which we call Our Father Which Art in Heaven."[8]

Worship helps us begin to appreciate who God is and expresses an attitude of gratefulness and awe toward our holy Lord and Savior.

Worship God through Sacrificial Living

Because God is infinite and almighty, the first commandment distinguishes our worship of Him from all other earthbound devotion. Worship of God differs not only in *degree* from all other worship we may ascribe to people or things, but also in *kind*. God is not only *more important* than your job, family, and future, He is also *in charge* of your life.

Worship, then, must include our willingness to sacrifice anything God requires. The Bible illustrates this principle through the life of

Abraham, who is known as the "father of the faithful." Abraham was willing to sacrifice his only son, Isaac, as an act of worship before God. At God's command, he took his son up the mountain, bound him, and placed him on the altar he had built. He raised the knife to kill his son. Before he could harm Isaac, God said, "Abraham!...Do not hurt the boy in any way, for now I know that you truly fear God. You have not withheld even your beloved son from Me" (Genesis 22:11,12). Abraham's trust in God was so strong that he knew God would raise Isaac from the dead if he sacrificed him to the Lord.

The story of Abraham reminds us that very often there is a price to pay in worshiping God. God sacrificed His only Son at Calvary for you; now He may call upon you to sacrifice a personal goal, a relationship, or a job that does not represent His best for you. We must be willing to lay everything on our "worship altar" to God.

Our sacrifice of worship includes giving our very lives, as many have done as martyrs before us. In the famed Twelfth Legion of Rome's imperial army were forty soldiers who professed their faith in Jesus Christ. One midwinter day in A.D. 320, their captain informed them that Emperor Licinius had sent out an edict commanding all soldiers to offer sacrifices to pagan gods.

These Christian warriors said, "You can have our armor and even our bodies, but our hearts' allegiance belongs to Jesus Christ."

Because of their stance, they were marched onto a frozen lake and stripped of their clothes. At any time they could have renounced Christ and been spared from death. Instead, they huddled close together and sang their song of victory, "Forty martyrs for Christ."

That freezing night, one by one, thirty-nine men fell to their icy deaths. Then the only man left alive stumbled to the shore and renounced Christ.

The officer in charge of guarding these men had secretly come to believe in Christ. The faith and sacrifice of the thirty-nine martyrs inspired him so much that he walked out onto the ice. Throwing off his clothes, he joined the other martyrs, confessed his faith in Christ, and took the place of the man who had broken ranks. At sunrise, the Roman soldiers found the forty martyrs of Sebaste, men who gave their all in the worship of Christ.[9]

Worship God with Wholehearted Love

In Mark 12, Jesus is asked by a scribe, "Of all the commandments, which is the most important?" (v. 28).

Jesus replied, "The most important commandment is this: 'Hear, O Israel! The Lord our God is the one and only Lord. And you must love the Lord your God with all your heart, all your soul, all your mind, and all your strength" (Mark 12:29,30). Jesus summarized the intent of the Law into a single concept—that we should love God with our *whole heart, soul, mind, and strength*. Here is a breakdown of what Jesus said:

- **Heart.** The devotion of my heart must be directed to God. The center of my being must be first aimed toward Him and His glory. He must be first in my ambitions and motives.

- **Soul.** My affections and emotions are to be ablaze with desire to worship and serve Him.

- **Mind.** My thought life must belong to Him so that my mind will be pure, disciplined, and ruled by His revealed will.

- **Strength.** All my energy, power, and strength must be surrendered to Him.

Another way to express Jesus' summary of the Law is *to surrender your whole life completely and irrevocably to God and never look back*.

An experience described by Dr. Christiaan Barnard, who performed the world's first heart transplant operation, illustrates this single focus. He was talking to one of his transplant patients, Dr. Philip Blaiberg. Suddenly, Barnard asked, "Would you like to see your old heart?"

Blaiberg said that he would.

Dr. Barnard went to a cupboard, took down a glass container, and handed it to Blaiberg. Inside the container was Blaiberg's old heart.

For a moment, Blaiberg stood there in stunned silence—the first man in history ever to hold his own heart in his hands. Finally, he spoke, "So this is my old heart that caused me so much trouble." He handed it back, turned away, and never looked back.[10]

Jesus taught that the real problem with man is that his spiritual heart is sick (Mark 7:1–23). But God has the remedy. He declared through the prophet Ezekiel, "I will take away their hearts of stone and give them tender hearts instead" (Ezekiel 11:19). The Bible also says, "Therefore if any man is in Christ, he is a new creature; the old things passed away; behold, new things have come" (2 Corinthians 5:17, NASB).

Just as Dr. Blaiberg was unwilling to look back at his old heart that caused him so much trouble, so the believer should never return to his false gods or his former manner of life. God deserves nothing less than *all* our worship, praise, and thanksgiving.

The Puritan writer George Swinnock remarked, "Worship comprehends all that respect which man oweth and giveth to his Maker ...It is the tribute which we pay to the King of kings, whereby we acknowledge his sovereignty over us, and our dependence on him ...All that inward reverence and respect, and all that outward obedience and service to God, which the word enjoineth, is included in this one word—worship."[11]

Shortly before his death, Moses said before all Israel, "See, I have set before you today life and prosperity, and death and adversity; in that I command you today to love the LORD your God, to walk in His ways and to keep His commandments and His statutes and His judgments, that you may live and multiply, and that the LORD your God may bless you in the land where you are entering to possess it" (Deuteronomy 30:15,16, NASB).

What a wonderful promise from our loving God! Today many millions have accepted the lie that true happiness comes only from pursuing self-centered goals. But in their hearts, they know otherwise.

Since 1945, I have experienced and observed the truth of God's promises, His faithfulness, and His unconditional love for all who trust and obey Him. I have also observed the heartache and tragedy of believers and nonbelievers alike who violate His laws and reject His love and forgiveness. Turn to God today with your whole being. Worship Him only. And God promises to generously lavish upon you and your family more abundant blessings than all your self-serving devotion can ever produce!

LIFE APPLICATION

Set Your Heart's Gauge

Commit the following verses to memory. Then, when you are tempted to turn your spiritual focus away from God to other things, recall these commands from God.

- Exodus 20:3—"Do not worship any other gods besides Me."

- Mark 12:29,30—"The most important commandment is this: '. . . The Lord our God is the one and only Lord. And you must love the Lord your God with all your heart, all your soul, all your mind, and all your strength.'"

Gauge Your Spiritual Growth

Ask yourself the following questions. If one or more areas pose problems for you, ask God how you can deal with them through the power of the Holy Spirit.

- What evidence can you find in your life that you are or are not putting God first?

- What consumes your thoughts each day? Is anything more important than God in your life?

- When you attend a worship service at your church, is your focus on God or on other things?

- Are you worshiping God wholeheartedly, or are you just going through the motions?

- What have you sacrificed for God this week? This year? What have you denied yourself for Christ's sake?

- When you think of true happiness, what comes to your mind? Is your first thought of God?

- Has a false god, such as religion, fame, materialism, career pursuits, self-centeredness, or pride, stolen your devotion to God?

Walk in the Power of the Holy Spirit

Putting God first in everything requires consistent and practical steps of faith. Begin by examining your heart before God. Is He your first priority? Are you worshiping only Him? Confess any areas in which you struggle, giving God complete control. Ask the Holy Spirit to help change your life so you are completely devoted to God. Meditate on Psalm 95:1–7 and 96:1–9. Worship God with these psalms and commit yourself to worship only God with your life's devotion.

SEVEN

DO NOT
WORSHIP IDOLS

In a tale from ancient India, four royal brothers each decided to master a special ability. They went their separate ways. After a certain amount of time had passed, the brothers met to reveal what they had learned.

"I have mastered a science," said the first, "by which I can take but a bone of some creature and create the flesh that goes with it."

"I," said the second, "know how to grow that creature's skin and hair if there is flesh on its bones."

The third said, "I am able to create its limbs if I have flesh, the skin, and the hair."

"And I," concluded the fourth, "know how to give life to that creature if its form is complete."

Then the brothers went into the jungle to find a bone so they could demonstrate their specialties. As fate would have it, the bone they found was a lion's.

The first brother added flesh to the bone; the second grew hide and hair; the third completed it with matching limbs; and the fourth gave the lion life.

Shaking its mane, the ferocious beast arose and jumped on its creators. It killed them all and vanished contentedly into the jungle.[1]

We too have the capacity to create what can devour us. Goals and dreams can consume us. Possessions and property can destroy us. People whom we have placed on a pedestal can fall and shatter our trust. As we saw in the previous chapter, the world is a showcase of gods calling for our heart's commitment. Each one has the ability to shipwreck our futures on the rocks of despair.

But God has a better plan. He calls us to shun the gods of life and to worship Him alone. And God's promise for our obedience? To lavish upon us love and blessings in abundance.

Worshiping God's Way

The second of the Ten Commandments speaks to the issue of worshiping idols. It says, "Do not make idols of any kind, whether in the shape of birds or animals or fish. You must never worship or bow down to them, for I, the LORD your God, am a jealous God who will not share your affection with any other god! I do not leave unpunished the sins of those who hate me, but I punish the children for the sins of their parents to the third and fourth generations. But I lavish My love on those who love Me and obey My commands, even for a thousand generations" (Exodus 20:4–6).

The first thing to notice about the second commandment is its relationship to the first commandment. At first glance, there does not appear to be a great distinction between the first two commandments. Both forbid false worship and both direct our hearts to God. However, there is an important difference. Whereas the first commandment tells us *Who* to worship, the second tells us *how* to worship the one true God. Why does God tell us how we are to worship Him?

Human nature is a peculiar thing. If left to our own devices, we are liable to do the right thing the wrong way. This is like the little girl who wanted to please her mother very much. Mother had a slight tear in her favorite dress and was planning to sew it after a brief nap.

But her daughter thought, *I know. I'll sew Mother's dress, and when*

she wakes, she'll have no more work to do, and she will be so pleased.
So the little girl sat on her own bed working hard while her mother
slept in the other bedroom. She was so pleased to finish her work
before her mother woke up.

When her mother awoke, she walked into her little girl's bedroom
only to find a sad face staring up at her. Mother asked, "What is it?
What's wrong?"

Her daughter replied, "I'm so sorry. I sewed your dress to the bed
sheet!"

Our worship of God is like this story. We do not please Him merely by having good intentions. Like the little girl who did not know
how to sew, if it is our desire to please our holy God, we must know
how to properly come before Him. We must worship God according
to the pattern of worship He has established in the Bible. Otherwise,
we presume upon our heavenly Father, which displeases Him and
creates heartache for us.

The Sin of Human Presumption

The Old Testament illustrates what happens when people come before God in human presumption. Aaron the priest had four sons who
also were priests—Nadab, Abihu, Eleazar, and Ithamar. At first, they
were faithful to perform their duties as God instructed them, and
God was pleased to accept their sacrifices on behalf of the people.

Then it happened. Nadab and Abihu put their own fire in their
censors, set incense on them, and offered profane fire before the
Lord. They knew what God wanted but chose to go against His law.

Then holy fire went out from the Lord and consumed Nadab and
Abihu. They died on the spot. Moses said to Aaron, "This is what the
LORD meant when He said, 'I will show Myself holy among those who
are near Me. I will be glorified before all the people'" (Leviticus 10:3).

What was the great sin of Nadab and Abihu? They presumed they
could worship God in any fashion and He would still be pleased. But
God had not commanded them to offer their own fire rather than
what God had mandated. God had already revealed through Moses
the acceptable manner for worship. Nadab and Abihu demonstrated
arrogance and presumption before God. Therefore, their sacrifice was

an abomination before the throne of heaven.

No one today will die instantly because they fail to worship God in an appropriate manner. We now live during a period of "God's deferred judgment." Nevertheless, the judgment of God is coming. Now is the time to examine our hearts to see if we truly know Christ personally and worship Him with all our heart, mind, soul, and strength. Religious presumption is no substitute for an exciting and life-transforming intimate relationship with Christ.

Genuineness in Worship

How then should we worship God? The second commandment does not address a prescribed order for corporate worship; rather it speaks to the *heart* of worship. The late pastor and author Ray C. Stedman captures the essence of the commandment when he observes:

> Worship is a heartfelt encounter of men and angels with the true God. It is an act of attention to the living God who rules, speaks and reveals, creates and redeems, orders, and blesses. The essence of worship is genuineness. It is to be with all your heart, your soul, and your mind. Worship may find expression in thought, in prayer, in praise, in song, in body position, and in activity such as dancing or uplifting of arms—but without genuineness all becomes false worship. Jesus instructed the woman at the well in this matter, saying: "But the hour is coming, and now is, when true worshippers will worship the Father in spirit and in truth, for the Father seeks such to worship him" (John 4:23, RSV).

Today America is marked by the sin of religious presumption. Many think God is impressed by formal religion but ignores the condition of their own heart. There is little of the "genuineness" in worship and in life as addressed by Stedman. Because many Americans have nice homes, fancy automobiles, and wonderful families, many think that God favors them.

But underneath the superficial picture of the happy American family is a gnawing awareness that all is not well. The things many dreamed about as children turn out to be little more than fleeting rainbows. These things satisfy for a while, but then as if dissolving into thin air, the thrill soon vanishes. Other people attend church and say prayers with their children before meals and at bedtime, hoping that their nominal faith will someday translate into joyful living. But sadly, for many that day never arrives.

There is an answer. Genuine worship of God does not come from religious activities, but is an *attitude*. It does not come through nominal religion, but through an *exciting* personal *relationship*. It begins the moment you turn from the false gods of religion, avoid presumption, and set aside your pride to receive Christ as your Lord and Savior. Tell Him about your loneliness and despair—how the substitute gods have failed to provide you with lasting peace. Perhaps for the first time in your life, talk to God from your heart, and He will listen. He is the God who shows lovingkindness to a thousand generations. He will bless you and your family if only you seek after Him with all your heart and soul.

No End to Idols

So far, we have considered the object of true worship—God—and have identified the substitute gods that may replace God's pre-eminence in our lives. We truly are a race that sets up false idols. When we consider the "how" of worship, we are thrust into a world of possible attitudes and actions that contend for our devotion. When Paul visited the ancient city of Athens, he discovered people worshiping so many idols that to make sure none had been overlooked, an altar was erected to the "unknown god"!

There are many ways we can practice idolatry without bowing before carved pieces of wood or stone. Permit me to point out several ways that we allow idolatry to pervade our attitudes.

We practice idolatry when we are motivated by greed.
Paul considered greed such a pervasive sin that he put it in a group of other pernicious sins. He writes, "Therefore consider the members of your earthly body as dead to immorality, impurity, passion, evil desire, and greed, which amounts to idolatry" (Colossians 3:5, NASB). The excessive striving for more money, power, and things is idolatry. We become idolaters when we allow tangible things to become our gods and we therefore worship objects rather than our great God and

Savior.

In the case of materialism, our worship turns into greed. The consuming message of greed is everywhere—TV game shows, frivolous lawsuits, and advertisements. Greed turns politics into blood sport. It can consume most of your waking thoughts and even spill into your dreams. In today's world, even dedicated Christians become financially overextended. As a result, many live in bondage to anxiety. Their preoccupation with financial worry robs them of their joy in Christ and hinders their witness to others.

Phil and Beverly are prime examples. This fine young Christian couple loved the Lord and invested their time, talent, and treasure in serving Him through their local church. Then one day, Phil saw a computer system he just had to have. The couple did not have the money to buy it outright, but the merchant was more than willing to extend credit. Phil took the system home that night.

When the bills started coming, the financial pressure wasn't too bad. But soon Beverly saw two beautiful dresses on sale, which she charged on her credit cards. Then the transmission in their car went out. Before long, the minimum monthly payments on their charges were eating into their giving, savings, and discretionary funds. They found themselves struggling from paycheck to paycheck and arguing over whose fault the debts were. The joy that had been so evident in their lives turned into weariness and frustration. Eventually, Phil had to quit some of his volunteer work at the church so he could moonlight to make extra income.

I am convinced that one of the most visible witnesses we can project to our neighbors is how we handle our checkbooks. Has your witness been hindered because you have been in bondage to debt?

We practice idolatry when we empower anything with godlike qualities. If we give power to anything other than God to save us, redeem us, or even lift us to a higher position in life, we make a graven image. The idol might be a doctor you hope will save you, a mate who will solve all your problems, or perhaps that house you believe will make you happy. Maybe your idol is a business or a political party. Anything we place our faith in besides God quickly becomes an idol.

Not a single idol can provide fulfillment in life the way that God can. Hideyoshi, a Japanese warlord who ruled over Japan in the late 1500s, commissioned a colossal statue of Buddha for a shrine in Kyoto. It took 50,000 workers five years to build the statue. The work had barely been completed when the earthquake of 1596 brought the roof of the shrine crashing down and wrecked the statue.

In a rage, Hideyoshi shot an arrow at the fallen colossus. "I put you here at great expense," he shouted, "and you can't even look after your own temple."[2]

Any idol we worship will eventually turn to dust in our hands. As Christians, God calls us to put away the idols that would claim our allegiance. When we do, we find that even greater treasures than we had dreamed possible are ours.

We practice idolatry when we live by sight rather than by faith.
Faith is believing in something we cannot see. But as humans, we have a tendency to desire the assurance of touch and sight so that we do not have to trust God in the spirit realm.

During the Middle Ages (A.D. 711–853), a religious debate called the Iconoclastic Controversy raged between the East and West over the place of images in worship. The controversy ended after many years of conflict, resulting in a ban on graven images in worship in the West. The conclusion reached was that anything which represented God to the point that it received the faith or worship belonging to God was wrong.

As beautiful as icons and relics may be, they are still lifeless objects. These objects we can see or touch cannot truly represent a God who is so awesome that He can be everywhere at once. They tend to redirect our focus from a Spirit God to the physical object itself.

Tragically, as fallen humans, we can let the tangible representations of our faith become idols to us. The people in the Middle Ages worshiped icons such as statues, imagining that these lifeless objects had special powers or significance. Like them, it is our human tendency to replace true worship with false. Can you imagine what would happen if we had pieces of Christ's cross or a section of the Ark of the Tabernacle today? People would worship these objects rather than God.

We must avoid the temptation of substituting what we can see for what we cannot see. A painting of Jesus created by a gifted artist can remind us of our glorious, magnificent Savior and what He endured for our sakes. But the painting should never become the central focus of our worship.

God wants us to take Him at His Word and not rely on some cheap imitation. To worship God through paintings, sculptures, or drawings only limits our understanding of the awesome magnitude of God and detracts from the revelation of God's divine attributes.

Do not misunderstand me. I am not suggesting that you should get rid of your cross lapel-pins, flannel graphs in Sunday school, inspirational videos, or paintings depicting Jesus. The second commandment does not prohibit the use of such items as long as these physical objects are viewed only as reminders of our great God and Savior and not as a way to produce a relationship with God or as a means to facilitate access before God.

Through His atoning sacrifice for our sins, Jesus has already provided complete access to the throne of grace for His children. No painting, sculpture, or icon can add to Christ's finished work.

This hymn by Walter Chalmers Smith says it well:

> Immortal, invisible God only wise,
> in light inaccessible, hid from our eyes.

God desires an intimate relationship with us, and wants us to cling to Him "by faith, not by sight."

We practice idolatry when we follow culture's dictates
rather than God's commandments.

What is culture? It is ways of thinking, living, and behaving that define a people and underlie their achievements. It is a nation's collective mind, its sense of right and wrong, the way it perceives reality, and its definition of self. Culture is the morals and habits parents strive to instill in their children. It is the obligations we acknowledge toward our neighbors, our community, and our government. It is the worker's dedication to craftsmanship and the owner's acceptance of the responsibilities of stewardship. It is the standards we set and enforce for ourselves and for others, our definitions of duty, honor, and character. It is our collective conscience.[3]

Culture becomes a personal idol when we supplant God's Word with what society believes. Today, the American conscience is showing a greater, not lesser, tendency to place collective thinking above godly principles. Perhaps no one has spoken more powerfully to the point on this subject than Pastor Joe Wright of the Central Christian Church of Wichita, Kansas, when he opened the Kansas State Legislature in January 1996 with this prophetic prayer:

> Heavenly Father, we come before you today to ask Your forgiveness and seek Your direction and guidance. We know Your Word says, "Woe on those who call evil good," but that's exactly what we have done. We have lost our spiritual equilibrium and inverted our values.
>
> We confess that:
>
> We have ridiculed the absolute truth of Your Word and called it pluralism.
>
> We have worshiped other gods and called it multiculturalism.
>
> We have endorsed perversion and called it an alternative lifestyle.
>
> We have exploited the poor and called it the lottery.
>
> We have neglected the needy and called it self-preservation.
>
> We have rewarded laziness and called it welfare.
>
> We have killed our unborn children and called it choice.
>
> We have shot abortionists and called it justifiable.
>
> We have neglected to discipline our children and called it building self-esteem.
>
> We have abused power and called it political savvy.
>
> We have coveted our neighbor's possessions and called it ambition.
>
> We have polluted our air with profanity and pornography and called it freedom of expression.
>
> We have ridiculed the time-honored values of our forefathers and called it enlightenment.
>
> Search us, O God, and know our hearts today; cleanse us from every sin and set us free. Guide and bless these men and women who have been sent to govern this great state. Grant them the wisdom to rule, and may their decisions direct us to the center of Your will. I

ask it in the name of Your Son, the Living Savior, Jesus Christ. Amen.

As you can imagine, the anti-God forces in the media and politics rose up in indignation, protesting this recognition and honor to the true God.

The Growing Influence of Cultural Idols

Several years ago, government officials in Washington, D.C., called on citizens to join in a day of prayer to ask God to restore that city from the destructive influence of drugs, crime, and poverty. Unbelievably, a local ACLU official confronted them and later told the *Washington Post*, "It is always inappropriate for government officials to ask citizens to pray." Our Founding Fathers would have been shocked to hear that governing authorities, whom Paul calls "ministers of God," should not call upon people of faith to pray. But this is the effect of cultural idolatry. Idols leave no room for God.

Another monument to cultural idolatry is the escalating divorce rate. Sixty percent of American children born today will see their parents divorced by the time they are eighteen. Of those children who have suffered this pain, half of them will see a second divorce before they are eighteen.[4] What is the root problem with marriages today? The world's idols are supplanting Christ at the center of marriage.

Some time ago I talked with a beloved friend, a minister who had left the pulpit and had his life crumble around him. When he divorced his wife, all kinds of problems resulted. Because I knew him to be a man of the Word, a man of prayer, a man who had unusual gifts and abilities to discern the will of God, and a man who had led thousands of people to Christ, I asked him how it all happened.

He quoted that statement, "Sin will keep you from God's Word or God's Word will keep you from sin." Then he said, "I knew and believed that. But with all the circumstances and all the comings and goings of my life, I ceased to depend on the Lord and His Word more and more until finally there was little time for God at all. And that is when it happened."

Years ago, my dearly beloved pastor, Dr. Louis Evans, Sr., used to say, "Marriage is God's idea, and only with His help can we work it out with joy." In spite of divorce statistics, I believe we can be optimistic about marriage and family life when we know that our Lord is working in the heart of each member of the family.

But perhaps there is no clearer example of cultural idolatry in the Church than the growing acceptance of homosexuality. There was a day when the Church viewed homosexuals with Christlike compassion and sought to minister to them. But today the question being debated by several mainline denominations is, "Should we ordain them?" Thankfully, among major denominations, only the United Church of Christ accepts the ordination of practicing homosexuals. Are more coming?

A related issue is the current controversy over the church's sanctioning of gay marriages. Some members of the 8.5 million member United Methodist Church are reeling after a church trial in March 1999 found an Omaha, Nebraska, pastor, the Rev. Jimmy Creech, *not guilty* of breaking church law for performing a same-sex ceremony. A jury of thirteen clergy voted 8 to 5 that Creech had violated the "order and discipline" of the church. Nine votes were necessary for conviction.[5]

Taking Every Thought Captive

Paul is very clear on how to destroy both the personal and cultural idols that offend our heavenly Father. He writes, "We are destroying speculations and every lofty thing raised up against the knowledge of God, and we are taking every thought captive to the obedience of Christ" (2 Corinthians 10:5, NASB).

Are you struggling in your thought life? Do you know someone else who suffers in the same way? The *inner struggle* is where the real battle against *all* idolatry lies. What are you doing to resist Satan's attacks? What are you doing to break his stronghold in the lives of others? Here are some suggestions on how to take *every* thought captive to Christ.

Pray without ceasing.

We can pray every moment of the day. However, it is not the amount of time in prayer that matters to God so much as the quality and genuineness of one's prayer life. Additionally, I encourage you to keep your thoughts focused on the Lord and your heart singing with praises as you go about your daily tasks. Whenever you encounter an idol in your life, immediately turn away from it and reaffirm your obedience to God. Take a moment to worship Him as the supreme Creator God.

Also, pray against the cultural idols that pollute our land. Ask God to stem the immoral tide that has been unleashed. Be specific about the issues that affect your community and neighborhood. God will hear and respond.

Live your life according to the Word of God,
not according to fleeting emotions.
When Jesus was tempted by the devil, He quoted Scripture. How much more must we rely on God's Word to keep us from the idolatry that tempts us? Be faithful in your devotional life and Bible study. Memorize Scripture verses and apply what you learn to your everyday life. The Word of God must be our constant guide.

Share your faith with others.
When your heart is focused on the needs of others, the idols that tempt you will flee. To the degree you "take captive" the personal idols of others through the ministry of the Word of God, the more America's cultural idols are destroyed. These strongholds cannot stand up against the testimony of God's faithfulness. The more your friends and loved ones respond to God's love, the more they will also be able to recognize and put away the idols in their lives.

Practice these three simple steps, and God will lavish His love upon you and your family—even for a thousand generations of those who obey His commands!

Once we put God first in our lives and remove any idols that usurp His preeminence, we can tackle another issue related to God's holiness and honor. In the third commandment, we will learn why it is so vital to respect God's name.

LIFE APPLICATION

Set Your Heart's Gauge

Commit the following verses to memory. Then, when you are tempted to worship things instead of God, recall these commands from God.

- Exodus 20:4,5—"Do not make idols of any kind, whether in the shape of birds or animals or fish. You must never worship or bow down to them, for I, the LORD your God, am a jealous God who will not share your affection with any other god!"

- Colossians 3:5—"Therefore consider the members of your earthly body as dead to immorality, impurity, passion, evil desire, and greed, which amounts to idolatry" (NASB).

Gauge Your Spiritual Growth

Ask yourself the following questions. If one or more areas pose problems for you, ask God how you can deal with them through the power of the Holy Spirit.

- In considering all you own, do your possessions occupy too large a share of your time? Your interest? Your love?

- Is there someone in your life who has become an idol to you because you care for him or her more than you love God?

- Is your worship genuine or merely ritualistic?

- Is how you worship more important to you than Who you worship?

- Have objects that represent God become the focal point in your worship instead of God? The crucifix? The Bible? Paintings or sculptures?

- When examining your daily life, are you walking by faith or by sight? Do you worship God in spirit and truth, or do you require physical things as part of your worship?

- When examining your lifestyle, is culture influencing your beliefs about right and wrong or are you following God's Word in everything? Do you agree with social consensus or with God's Word on sins such as divorce, homosexuality, and pornography?

Walk in the Power of the Holy Spirit

Reread Ray Stedman's quote about genuine worship. How can you include more genuine worship in your devotional life? Meditate on Psalms 106 and 115. Ask the Holy Spirit to show you if plans, possessions, or people have become more important to you than your relationship with God. When you worship, are you worshiping objects or our Spirit God? Identify any problem areas and ask the Holy Spirit to help you make the appropriate changes in your thought life and behavior.

EIGHT

DO NOT TAKE GOD'S NAME IN VAIN

A fter the American Civil War, the managers of the infamous Louisiana Lottery approached former Confederate General Robert E. Lee and asked if he would let them use his name in their scheme. They promised that if he did, he would become rich. Lee, a devout follower of Christ, straightened up, buttoned his gray coat, and shouted, "Gentlemen, I lost my home in the war. I lost my fortune in the war. I lost everything except my name. My name is not for sale, and if you fellows don't get out of here, I'll break this crutch over your heads!"

Misusing someone's name is always wrong. Have you ever asked an important friend if you could "drop his name" when attempting to secure a business deal? The only way that person will allow you to use his name is if he knows you and is confident that you will represent his name properly.

The third commandment speaks to this issue. It says, "Do not misuse the name of the LORD your God. The LORD will not let you go unpunished if you misuse His name" (Exodus 20:7). The term "LORD" (printed in capital letters in the English Old Testament) is God's personal name and is generally translated *Yahweh*. There is no name higher than God's name. His name is supreme among an entire universe of names. It is to be treated with a level of dignity and respect that reflects who God is.

The Meaning of a Name

In Jewish thought, a name is far more than an arbitrary identification. It is more than a random blending of sounds. A name conveys the basic nature of the thing named. It represents the reputation of the one named and recalls the deeds the person has performed. In fact, the Bible refers to a person's reputation as his "good name." Proverbs 22:1 says, "A good name is to be more desired than great riches" (NASB).

The Hebrew concept of a name is similar in that a name reflects the great worth and value of a person or object. Throughout the Bible, God instructs parents to give a child a specific name that reflects who he is and foretells his mission in life. For example, Isaiah means "the salvation of the Lord." Ezekiel means "the strength of God." And Jesus means "savior" or "deliverer."

God also changes people's names as He enters their lives and assigns them a new direction or task. Part of God's covenant with Abram was to change his name to Abraham, which means a "father of many nations." Jesus changed Simon the fisherman's name to Peter, which means "rock." Saul of Tarsus was never the same after his encounter with the risen Lord on the road to Damascus. God gave him a new name, Paul, that mirrored his new heart for Christ. Paul means "small in stature, big in love."

To Muslims, the most important ritual is to face Mecca while kneeling and saying their prayers. To Buddhists, writing prayers and muttering mantras on little scrolls and placing them in prayer wheels is essential. For the New Age follower, seeking spiritual attunement at "harmonic convergences" is the key to unlocking the meaning of the universe. For the Christian, the most vital element of prayer is coming before God in reverence and respect for His holy name.

Proper respect for the name of the Lord is so important that Jesus instructed His followers to begin their prayers by showing utmost reverence for the name of God: "Our Father in heaven, hallowed be Your name" (Matthew 6:9, NIV). To "hallow" means to consecrate, revere, or set apart. God's name is to be treated differently from all the other names on earth. Leviticus 22:32 declares, "Do not treat My holy name as common and ordinary."

God's name is so important that in heaven the very mention of it evokes worship. The name of the Lord was so sacred to the Orthodox Jews that they refused to utter it aloud. In their Scriptures, they replaced the name of God with a code word so they would not be tempted to say the name lightly.

Many people, however, take God's name lightly. We do this not only as a culture, but also in churches that have been influenced by post-Christian society. The sacred name of God is used so casually that many people have no idea of the power behind it.

The reason we become so flippant about God's name is rooted in how we feel about Him. Jesus says in Matthew 12:34, "Whatever is in your heart determines what you say." If we respect, love, and fear the Lord in our hearts, we will not want to dishonor His mighty name with our lips.

Most of us think of profanity when we hear the third commandment. Profanity is a terrible affront to God's holiness. But we can also profane God's name in other ways. Let us look at profanity and the ways we can take God's name in vain.

The Offense of Profanity

If you are like me, you cringe when someone uses profanity—especially when God's name is abused. God is my loving Father and I am His son. His Spirit lives within me, making my body His temple. He is awesome, mighty, powerful, and holy. To even consider taking my precious Lord's name in vain is unimaginable to me.

But if we who love the Lord react in this manner, how much more is God offended?

Paul urges us not to engage in profanity or unclean speech. He writes, "Don't use foul or abusive language. Let everything you say be good and helpful, so that your words will be an encouragement to those who hear them" (Ephesians 4:29).

In the past, people considered profanity an affront to God. On July 4, 1775, General George Washington dealt with the profanity his troops were using. He issued General Orders from his headquarters in Cambridge:

> The General most earnestly requires and expects a due observance of those articles of war established for the government of the Army which forbid profane cursing, swearing, and drunkenness.[1]

General Washington's reverence for God's name was therefore transmitted throughout his entire army.

There are two reasons we should avoid all profanity, especially using the name of the Lord.

Profanity calls into question who God is and what He has done.
Moses confronted Pharaoh saying, "Let my people go."

Pharaoh responded, "Who is the LORD that I should obey His voice to let Israel go? I do not know the LORD, and besides, I will not let Israel go" (Exodus 5:2, NASB). By denying God, Pharaoh profaned both God's name and reputation.

We do the same thing when we speak God's name in a vile or cursing manner. Our God is holy, above all, without peer. He holds the stars in His hand and rules the universe. He is perfect in all His ways. Using His magnificent name in jest or as a curse is impugning His glory. As His children who have received eternal life because of His love for us, why would we ever want to cast a shadow on His name?

When we publicly profane God's name, we reduce Him in the world's eyes to a mere cultural icon. Such words have the effect of minimizing God's mighty power before others. Using God's name in a curse also denies what He has accomplished. People who use God's name in profanity deny what He has done for His people throughout history.

Profanity is a lie.

Paul encourages us to "let no unwholesome word proceed" from our mouths. He also says, "So put away all falsehood and 'tell your neighbor the truth' because we belong to each other" (Ephesians 4:25). God considers profane all words that question His goodness and holiness. Essentially, they are lies. Satan used God's name wrongly in the Garden of Eden. He questioned God's truthfulness and perfect intentions when he tempted Eve. Satan knew what he was saying was a falsehood. We must never use God's name in a curse, throw God's name around for our own purposes, or speak about God in untrue terms, or we too will be guilty of profane lying.

The ninth commandment instructs us not to lie about our neighbor. But the third commandment warns us not to lie about God!

Watch Those Substitute Words

At first glance, the third commandment seems rather straightforward. It is very easy to assume that because you do not curse using God's name that you are not breaking this commandment. But there are other ways we can break this commandment and offend our loving God. One way is through the use of *substitute* words.

Do you remember Gomer Pyle on the television show *Andy of Mayberry*? He used words like "golly" as a way to make a point or to show surprise. Partly as a result of the influence of this old TV show and many others, substitute words like "golly," "gee," and "gosh" are in constant use in today's culture. But did you know these words are derived from the word "God"?

The Law of Moses clearly says that we are not to use God's name in vain—not in any way, shape, or manner. But do substitute words for "God" also violate the third commandment's prohibition against taking the Lord's name in vain? For Christians, obeying the spirit of the Law is just as important as obeying the letter of the Law. Seek God on this question, and I am confident He will reveal His answer.

More Walk Than Talk

Although the third commandment addresses our speech, it has far more to do with our walk than our talk. Dr. Lawson G. Stone, Ph.D., professor of Old Testament at Asbury Theological Seminary, observes, "The key to the entire Commandment lies in the word 'take.' What a shock it was to learn in my first-year Hebrew class that the word does not refer to speech! The Hebrew word means to 'carry, or bear.' It can refer to speech in formal ways, such as when we 'bear' good or bad tidings. Usually, though, it simply means to 'carry.' We are not to 'carry' the name of the Lord our God ineffectually so that it appears false."[2]

For many years, I have taught about the danger of living as a carnal or worldly Christian. This is a believer whose life is not controlled by the Holy Spirit and who knows little about the abundant or fruitful life promised in the Scriptures. The presence of continuing sin in this person's life shows he does not understand his spiritual heritage in Christ. The word "vain" means "useless, void of any real value." The worldly Christian bears God's name as if it were meaningless, void of any real value or power. The answer for him is to discover the basic and revolutionary concept of how to be filled with the Holy Spirit. It is only then that one can live joyously and effectively for Christ.

Once an indigenous Christian went to a missionary for counsel. He was troubled by the spiritual conflict going on within his heart. He wanted to do what God wanted him to do, but he frequently disobeyed God. He found that he was prone to do the evil things he did before he became a follower of Christ.

The native described this conflict within himself as a dogfight. He said to the missionary, "It is as though I have a black dog and a white dog inside me fighting each other constantly." The black dog, he explained, represented evil and the white dog represented good.

The missionary asked him, "Which dog wins the fight within you?"

After several moments of silence, the native said, "The dog that wins is the one to which I say 'sic em.'"

Man has a free will; he is a free moral agent. We can choose to carry God's name in a respectful manner.

Even as Spirit-filled believers, we can decide whether we will obey the dictates of the flesh or the leading of the Spirit. Whether a believer lives a consistent, Spirit-filled life is determined by the frequency with which he says yes to the leading of the Spirit and no to the temptations of the flesh.

For the Christian, the old sin nature, if not properly dealt with, can become a major hindrance to living supernaturally. A believer who, for any variety of reasons, does not properly deal with his old sin nature is said to be living in a state of worldliness.

A carnal Christian is usually a miserable person—even more miserable than the nonbeliever. Disobedience in the life of the believer is the height of taking God's name in vain.

Some or all of the following traits may characterize the carnal Christian:

Ignorance of spiritual heritage	Jealousy
Unbelief	Guilt
Disobedience	Worry
Impure thoughts	Discouragement
Poor prayer life	Critical spirit
No desire for Bible study	Frustration
Legalistic attitude	Aimlessness
Loss of love for God and for others	

How are you carrying the Lord's name? Do you have unconfessed sin in your life? Are you living in a manner that is well below God's best for you? Are you bringing glory or shame to God's name?

The Vanity of Life

Did you know that we also take God's name in vain when we waste our lives on meaningless, time-consuming things that are of no consequence?

How would you like to spend two years making phone calls to people who are not home? Does this sound absurd? According to one time-management study, that is how much time the average person spends in a lifetime trying to return calls to people who never seem to be in. Not only that, we spend six months waiting for the traffic light to turn green and another eight months reading junk mail.

These unusual statistics should cause us to reevaluate how we spend our lives. To bear God's name in a fitting manner means managing our time well. The Scriptures say, "Make the most of every opportunity for doing good in these evil days. Don't act thoughtlessly, but try to understand what the Lord wants you to do" (Ephesians 5:16,17). Look at your life. How many things rob you of the time that you could be using for the Lord? You will see how vital it is that you do not busy yourself "in vain."

Then there is the vanity of hard work. King Solomon said, "So now I hate life because everything done here under the sun is so irrational. Everything is meaningless, like chasing the wind. I am disgusted that I must leave the fruits of my hard work to others. And who can tell whether my successors will be wise or foolish? And yet they will control everything I have gained by my skill and hard work. How meaningless!" (Ecclesiastes 2:17–19).

Once there was a young lady who purchased her very first car. She was excited over its metallic red paint that seemed to sparkle in the sun and its beautiful interior, with its fresh leather smell. Each day, the young lady felt as though life had taken on new meaning.

One day as she was telling her friends all about how much her new car meant, one young man asked, "Why did you buy the car?"

She answered, "So I can drive to work."

The man said, "And why do you go to work?"

She said, "In order to pay for my car."

Suddenly, the young lady saw the man's logic. She thought, *Is this what life is all about? A vicious treadmill?*[3]

The psalmist says, "We are merely moving shadows, and all our busy rushing ends in nothing. We heap up wealth for someone else to spend" (Psalm 39:6). Working hard to have nice things is no guarantee your life will not be lived in vain. Only Christ can provide true meaning to your life's labor.

Entrusted with His Mighty Name

It is sobering to think that God has entrusted His name and reputation to fallible creatures like us. We are finite; He is infinite. We are imperfect; He is absolute perfection. The psalmist asks, "What are mortals that you should think of us, mere humans that you should care for us?" (Psalm 8:4).

Nevertheless, God says, "I shall be your God, and you shall be My people." And Hebrews 11:16 declares that God is pleased to be called our God. So then, we must not disappoint God and the trust He has placed in us, His children. In every way our lives must reflect the integrity of the name which is above all others—the name of the Lord.

In the Sermon on the Mount, Jesus foretold a day when many would come to Him and say, "Lord, Lord, did we not prophesy in Your name, and in Your name cast out demons, and in Your name perform many miracles?" But Jesus will say to them, "I never knew you; depart from Me, you who practice lawlessness" (Matthew 7:22,23, NASB).

Today the world is filled with people whose mouths profess the name of Christ, but whose lives say otherwise. Our Lord is not interested in an easy profession, but in the pattern of our lives. Certainly, we will sin. We all experience momentary lapses into disobedience. But the real test is how quickly we bounce back in the power of the Holy Spirit.

We bear a mighty name. We cannot permit God's name to appear powerless, empty, or false before a watching world.

Dishonoring God's Name Is Costly

The third commandment includes an incentive that should not go unnoticed. God promises that if we disobey this law, He will *lovingly chasten* us to bring us back to our senses. God says, "The Lord will not let you go unpunished if you misuse His name" (Exodus 20:7).

These are not the words of a mean, vindictive judge who gets pleasure in punishing people. Rather, God knows that we will suffer in life unless our hearts and minds place Him first in our thoughts and speech. So He disciplines us for our good. The Lord's discipline is *always* redemptive.

Dr. Billy Graham, commenting on God's discipline, said, "The Bible says, 'whom the Lord loveth He chasteneth.' If life were all easy, wouldn't we become flabby? When a ship's carpenter needed timber to make a mast for a sailing vessel, he did not cut it in the valley, but up on the mountainside where the trees had been buffeted by the winds. These trees, he knew, were the strongest of all. Hardship is not our choice; but if we face it bravely, it can toughen the fiber of our souls.

"God does not discipline us to subdue us, but to condition us for a life of usefulness and blessedness. In His wisdom, He knows that an uncontrolled life is an unhappy life, so He puts reins on our wayward souls that they may be directed into paths of righteousness."[4]

I fell in love with my sons, Zac and Brad, as newborns when I held them in my arms; I love them more today now that they are grown men. But I used to spank them when they were disobedient. Often I would shed more tears than they did. But then I would say, "Why did I spank you?" Usually, one would respond, "Because you love us."

You would never discipline your neighbor's children. Why? Because they are not yours. God "spanks" us because He loves us. His discipline proves that we are His children. Thank God for His discipline when you need it because it shows you belong to Him and that He will *never* forsake you!

Appreciate the Value of His Name

How can we resist taking God's name in vain? Remember that taking God's name in vain reflects a *cavalier attitude* about God. As I stated earlier, the word "vain" means "useless, void of any real value." But is God without any real value? That is unthinkable. Then ask yourself if taking His name in vain in such a casual fashion reflects the true nature and work of almighty God in your life.

Once Vonette was flying to an important speaking engagement. The man seated next to her repeatedly used the Lord's name in vain. Finally Vonette could not take it any longer. She exclaimed, "Sir, your words are highly offensive because you are talking about the most important person I know!"

The man sat silently stunned. Then in a low voice he apologized and confessed that using God's name in this way was a problem for him. He was so sorry.

To avoid using God's name in vain, we must consider it holy and precious. During the sinking of the *Titanic*, a frightened woman was fortunate to find a place in a lifeboat that was about to be lowered into the raging North Atlantic. Before the crew cast off, she suddenly thought of something she needed, so she asked permission to return to her stateroom. She was granted three minutes or the boat would leave without her.

She ran across the deck that was already slanted at a dangerous angle. She raced through the gambling room with money rolled to one side, ankle deep. She came to her stateroom and quickly pushed aside her diamond rings and expensive bracelets and necklaces as she reached to the shelf above her bed. She grabbed three small oranges. Then she quickly found her way back to the lifeboat and got in.

Thirty minutes earlier, the woman would never have chosen a crate of oranges over the smallest diamond. But death had boarded the *Titanic*. One blast of its awful breath had transformed all values. Instantaneously, priceless things had become worthless; worthless things had become priceless. In that moment she preferred three small oranges to a crate of diamonds.[5]

Do not wait until your life is sinking in sorrow and distress to evaluate what is most precious to you. Appreciate the immense value of what God has done for you. Then God's name will take on a whole new meaning as you cherish and esteem it. Respect God's name. Revere it. Treasure it in your heart and in your speech, and God will bless you as you do.

We have seen in this chapter the immense importance God attaches to His name. Honor it, cherish it, and revere it. His name speaks volumes about His character—the awesome, majestic, and loving God whom we serve and worship. In His grace He permits us to bear His name before a watching world. Carry His name high; lovingly correct those who treat it disrespectfully. God will honor your faithfulness.

So far in the first three commandments, we have learned about the Person we must put first in our lives and how we must worship and respect Him. The next commandment ties up the first three by giving us guidelines on when to worship and revere God.

LIFE APPLICATION

Set Your Heart's Gauge

Commit the following verses to memory. Then, when you are tempted to use God's name in a way that does not honor Him, recall these commands from God.

- Exodus 20:7—"Do not misuse the name of the LORD your God. The LORD will not let you go unpunished if you misuse His name."

- Leviticus 22:32—"Do not treat My holy name as common and ordinary."

Gauge Your Spiritual Growth

Ask yourself the following questions. If one or more areas pose problems for you, ask God how you can deal with them through the power of the Holy Spirit.

- How are you using God's name when you pray? Is it sacred and special or has it become ordinary and even meaningless?

- Do you struggle with profanity? How does using God's name in vain hurt your testimony to others and your relationship with God?

- Are you aware when you use substitute words for God's name, such as "gosh" and "golly"?

- How are you "bearing" Christ's name in your daily life? Is your life a good testimony for Christ? Are you living in the power of the Holy Spirit?

- Are you investing your life in meaningless goals or things? Or are you dedicated to honoring God with your life and fulfilling Christ's purposes?

- What do you do when others misuse God's name in your presence? Do you indicate your disapproval or are you more concerned with their acceptance of you?

- How much do you treasure God's name? What is the evidence that you do?

Walk in the Power of the Holy Spirit

Ask the Holy Spirit to help you respect God's holy and precious name. Practice respecting and revering God's name. Whenever you pray, speak about God, or use His name in any way, demonstrate a reverential attitude in your heart. Speak about God as the most precious Person in your life. Explain to people who use His name in vain how important He is to you and how their actions make you feel. Use the opportunity as a way to share your faith in Christ with others.

NINE

KEEP THE SABBATH HOLY

Wandering deep into the dark forest, Tom and Betty looked for the perfect tree. "A large oak would work best," said Tom.

"I'll see if I can find one," replied Betty.

The year was 1941, shortly after the start of World War II. The newlywed couple had been married for two weeks and planned to settle down in the same town they both grew up in. Then Tom was called to serve his country. Now matters were out of their control. Tom and Betty would have to wait to move to their hometown.

"Here's an oak!" exclaimed Betty. It was an old oak. But the playful squirrels that ran quickly up its massive limbs offset its many years.

Tom and Betty looked at each other as if to agree that this was indeed the right tree. Tom drew his knife and began to carve their initials in the tree's trunk. "It will be here forever, my love," said Tom.

"Someday soon, you'll be back," Betty sobbed. "But until then this tree will stand as a reminder of what we have."

Like Tom and Betty's initials carved on that tree, God carved the

Sabbath day observance into our week. It stands as a reminder of God's incredible love for His creation. Understanding our fleshly limitations, He gave us a day to rest in Him from all our hectic labors. The Sabbath also reminds us of God's great love in Christ, in whom we can find rest for our weary souls.

A Day to Rest for the Glory of God

The fourth commandment says, "Remember to observe the Sabbath day by keeping it holy. Six days a week are set apart for your daily duties and regular work, but the seventh day is a day of rest dedicated to the LORD your God. On that day no one in your household may do any kind of work. This includes you, your sons and daughters, your male and female servants, your livestock, and any foreigners living among you. For in six days the LORD made the heavens, the earth, the sea, and everything in them; then He rested on the seventh day. That is why the LORD blessed the Sabbath day and set it apart as holy" (Exodus 20:8–11).

Keeping one day in seven holy to the Lord is required by the fourth commandment. Although it was created for our benefit, the type of rest required on the Sabbath day is a special rest *to the Lord*. It is a rest that is to be observed on the Lord's terms and for *His glory*.

In the New Testament, the "Lord's Day," Sunday, replaced the Jewish Sabbath for followers of Christ because the Lord Jesus rose from the dead on Sunday (John 20:1). The Day of Pentecost also occurred on Sunday (Acts 2:1). As a result, the first Christians came together on Sunday, the first day of the week, to worship and celebrate communion (Acts 20:7). Barnabas, one of the leading church fathers, supported this view: "We keep the eighth day [Sunday] with joyfulness, the day also on which Jesus rose again from the dead."[1] Thus believers look forward on the first day of the week, symbolizing that we look forward to Christ's magnificent return.

Dr. J. Vernon McGee explained what this change meant to him. One day a man came to him and said, "I'll give you $100 if you will show me where the Sabbath day has been changed."

McGee answered, "I don't think it has been changed. Saturday is Saturday; it is the seventh day of the week, and it is the Sabbath day

...The seventh day is still Saturday, and it is still the Sabbath day."

Then the man who had challenged McGee got a gleam in his eye and said, "Then why don't you keep the Sabbath day if it hasn't been changed?"

McGee answered, "The *day* hasn't changed, but I have been changed. I've been given a new nature now, I am joined to Christ; I am a part of the new creation. We celebrate the first day because that is the day He rose from the dead."

This change from Saturday to Sunday is what Paul means when he writes in Colossians 2:14 that the ordinances have been nailed to the cross. All commandments are part of Christ's kingdom and we celebrate and observe them from that perspective. That is why I worship God on Sunday rather than on Saturday as the Old Testament believers did.

A Cultural Tug-of-War

Once there was a day when Sunday observance and rest was a mainstay of American culture. That has changed. Today, retail stores and professional sports operate seven days a week. In fact, it is difficult to find a job unless one is willing to work on the Lord's Day. What is the root of the problem?

As a society, we value productivity above everything else. We are restless. We cannot sit still long enough to rest and reflect. We have to be doing something productive even when we are resting. We frantically jog, rush to see a movie, or trim those hedges before another weekend slips by. Most Americans scoff at the idea of taking a day off to do nothing but honor the Creator and rest in His care.

Eighteenth-century French philosopher Voltaire predicted that within 100 years of his life Christianity would be nothing more than history. He admitted, though, that the world would first have to get rid of Sabbath observance. He said, "There is no hope of destroying Christianity so long as the Christian Sabbath is acknowledged and kept as a sacred day." No doubt, Voltaire would be pleased with America's current attitude about the Sabbath.

We can see examples of how people disregard the fourth commandment. The late Cardinal John O'Connor remained committed to his position that the Lord's Day should include rest from recreation as well as work. Not long ago, in protest against the cardinal's stand against Sunday morning children's soccer, parents filled a page of *The New York Times* with letters and comments criticizing him. "The cardinal doesn't understand modern life," they wrote. "The cardinal underestimates how well modern Catholics balance church and family …The cardinal shouldn't undermine sports, for the good of the Church."

But some still remain true to the spirit of the Sabbath rest. Two NCAA-member colleges refuse to hold games on Sunday. They are Campbell University, a North Carolina Baptist school, and Mormon-run Brigham Young University in Utah. The support they received has been appreciated, says Tom Collins, athletic director of Campbell University.

What is all the controversy about? Why should Christians follow a law that was given thousands of years ago to ancient Israel? Let us look at several reasons we should observe the Lord's Day.

All creation requires rest.

God commanded that no one was to work on this sacred day, including livestock. This is because ancient tribes were mainly subsistence farmers, making just enough to feed their families. To them, resting an entire day was not an option. God had to intervene or people would have worked themselves and their animals into an early grave!

The Sabbath rest was also for the protection of the land. Any good farmer knows the principal of crop rotation. If a farmer continues to grow the same crop in the same field year after year, he will permanently damage the soil. But if you allow the soil to rest some years, the nutrients and the moisture in the soil replenish and the field will continue to yield healthy crops. Today, the federal government pays some farmers to set aside certain fields so they will avoid burning out the soil.

Even bowling pins need to rest! I have read that bowling alley operators regularly switch out the pins because too much banging about without a resting period will cut their useful life in half.

According to a Greek legend, a man in ancient Athens noticed the great storyteller Aesop playing childish games with some little boys. He laughed and jeered at Aesop, asking him why he wasted his time in such frivolous activity. Aesop responded by picking up a bow, loosening its string, and placing it on the ground. Then he said to the critical Athenian, "Now, answer the riddle, if you can. Tell us what the unstrung bows implies."

The man looked at it for several moments but had no idea what point Aesop was trying to make.

Aesop explained, "If you keep a bow always bent, it will break eventually; but if you let it go slack, it will be more fit for use when you want it."

People are also like that. That is why we all need to take time to rest. You will be at your best for the Lord if you have taken time to loosen the bow.[2]

We need to follow the advice of Will Rogers, one of the greatest humorists of the 20th century, "I always get up early on Sundays to have a longer day to rest."[3]

The Sabbath sets aside a day to worship God.
To Truett Cathy, Sunday is very special. Cathy, who is a personal friend, has celebrated more than fifty years in the restaurant business. The entrepreneur made up his mind at age eight that he would have his own business.

After their hitch in the military, Truett and his brother pooled their resources to open the Dwarf House restaurant in southwest Atlanta. That was when Truett established that he would not work on Sunday. "Sunday had been a special day for me when I was a child, and I didn't want to be robbed of that day," he says.

As a businessman, his logic was brilliant: "If it takes seven days to make a living, I ought to be doing something else." In the Dwarf House, he developed the Chick-fil-A sandwich, and by 1967 he opened his first restaurant with this single big-seller.

In Truett's book, *It's Easier to Succeed Than to Fail*, he tells the business world that religion and business not only mix, but are a good mix. "I believe that Sunday should be honored and set aside for employees to worship God, to rest, and to spend time with their families. Our track record proves that in the vast majority of malls, we are the food sales leader even though we are open only six days."

Truett Cathy is not at the shop on Sunday. He is working at his church doing what he has done for over thirty years—teaching a Sunday school class for 13-year-old boys. He shares with them that the three most important decisions they will make are: Who will be my Master? Who will be my mate? What will be my mission in life?

As he says, "All of us were created in the image and the likeness of our Creator. It puts a responsibility on us to be our very best at all times."[4]

How can we keep the Sabbath holy if we sleep in late, watch football games, or do any other activity instead of worshiping God? Although I don't see anything wrong with watching decent television programs or reading the newspaper on Sunday, my major attention all day is on God.

Worshiping God on Sunday by attending a Bible-preaching church is part of our responsibility in putting God first in our lives. Not only do Sunday services help us focus on God, they also help us encourage each other to serve Him. Hebrews 10:25 commands believers, "Let us not neglect our meeting together, as some people do, but encourage and warn each other, especially now that the day of His coming back again is drawing near." When we set aside the first day of the week to worship God, we are showing that He has the priority. It helps us develop a healthy awe of God all through the week. Truett Cathy is just one example of how God blesses us when we obey His commandment to rest on the Sabbath.

The Sabbath affords us an opportunity to reflect on all that God has done for us.

The Bible says that God rested after working. "On the seventh day, having finished His task, God rested from all His work" (Genesis 2:2). What does the Bible mean when it says that God rested? Was He tired? Had He strained a muscle? Does the Bible assume that God needed a rest after six days of hard work like anyone else? Of course not.

The Bible says, "Do you not know? Have you not heard? The Everlasting God, the LORD, the Creator of the ends of the earth does not become weary or tired" (Isaiah 40:28, NASB). Creating a universe was nothing for our amazing God. Orthodox Judaism teaches that it involved no more effort for God to create the universe than it takes Him to pronounce a single letter.

God rested in another sense. His rest was more a time of *reflection* about His marvelous creation. Genesis 1:31 says, "God saw all that He had made, and behold, it was very good" (NASB).

When we rest from all our labor, we are afforded an opportunity to reflect on God's goodness to us. Whether we rest in the beauty of His creation or in the way God brings peace and blessing to our lives through Christ, we are surrounded by testimonies to God's matchless goodness. Surely we can take one day to sit back and bask in all that God has done for us.

This commandment is part of God's moral law, which is still in effect. Sabbath-keeping is not exclusively a Jewish institution but a *creation ordinance* that applies to everyone (Genesis 2:2,3). The fourth commandment remains binding until heaven and earth pass away (Matthew 5:17,18). Therefore, it is still to be observed today.

Certainly, the world will pressure us to break the Sabbath. Once, a Christian man was urged by his employer to work on Sunday. The employer said, "Doesn't your Bible say that if your ox falls into a ditch on the Sabbath, you may pull him out?"

The believer replied, "Yes, but if the ox had the habit of falling into the same ditch every Sabbath, I would either fill up the ditch or sell the ox!"[5]

Fortunately, I grew accustomed to resting on Sunday in the home where I was raised. The only person in my family who was a believer was my mother. She was a saint, but she had not yet learned how to introduce her husband and children to the Lord. So she prayed for us. Ultimately, I became a believer and had the privilege of leading most of my siblings as well as my father to Christ. Yet even before my family had received Christ, Sunday was a day of rest in our home due to my mother's godly influence.

We lived on a ranch where we grew crops and food for the cattle.

We worked between ten and fifteen hours a day, six days a week. But as important as work was during the Depression years, we did not work on Sunday. And this was true of America in general at that time.

Nevertheless, beginning in the 1930s through the 1940s, I witnessed a change in society's observance of the Lord's Day. People started to treat it with contempt.

But some remained faithful in their observance. During the 1950s and 1960s, several athletes who became believers through our ministry would not play ball on Sunday. Primo Villanueva and Bob Davenport, both all-Americans, went to Canada to play football rather than remain in the U.S. and be forced to play ball on Sundays. Those young men sacrificed greatly to obey God.

Today, keeping the Sabbath is still vitally important to me. I instruct my associates who arrange my travel not to book a flight that will require me to travel on Sunday unless it's absolutely necessary. I ask them to help me avoid situations where I would go out to eat in restaurants on Sunday because that would cause others to work.

Each time I catch a plane, someone has to fly the plane and take care of the passengers. Each time I go out to a restaurant, someone has to work to prepare my food. Although the planes will fly and the restaurants will be open without my business, I need to obey what God tells me to do in the hope that my example will encourage others.

Resting on the Sabbath is a sign of our trust in God.
There is nothing wrong with hard work. We must use the resources and talents God gave us to earn a living, care for our homes, and provide for the needs of our children. But to work constantly without adequate reflection and worship is a fundamental trust issue. If you truly trust God to provide for you, then you will do as He requires and take time to honor Him on Sundays.

Working constantly may be visible proof that deep inside we do not trust God. You say you trust God, but do you really? Often our actions speak louder than our words. The intoxication with long hours of work on Sunday says: "I trust God, but just in case He doesn't pull through, I need an ace in the hole!"

Our English word "Sabbath" comes from the Hebrew word *Shab-*

bat, which means to cease and desist. Termination of work with accompanying rest is what God requires.

Have you ever noticed that our Lord never overworked or rushed? He didn't frantically hurry to get a job done or run to catch a boat to the other side of the Sea of Galilee. Yet He had the hardest job anyone ever had to do and only three-and-a-half years to do it. But there was very little exertion or strain in His work. Even when people placed huge demands on Him, His pace was deliberate and unhurried. He took time to worship His Father in the temple on the Sabbath.

First Timothy 6:17 records, "Their trust should be in the living God, who richly gives us all we need for our enjoyment." God promises not only to give us our needs, but He even cares about our enjoyment! Time and time again the Bible recounts how God wants us to trust Him for all our needs.

Have you ever heard a person say, "I need 32 hours in a day to get everything done?" God gives us only 24 hours in a day to accomplish all He has given us to do. But did you know that *prayer* is one way we can actually *lengthen* time?

The Bible tells the story of how Joshua led the Israelites to victory over the Amorites. To lengthen the time that Israel could wage war, Joshua did something amazing. He stood and prayed, "O sun, stand still at Gibeon, and O moon in the valley of Aijalon." And the Bible says, "So the sun stood still, and the moon stopped, until the nation avenged themselves of their enemies" (Joshua 10:12,13, NASB). The sun and moon actually stood still, providing the Israelites the additional time needed to make their victory over the Amorites complete.

Did you know that when you pray you are actually saving time? No, God does not make the sun stand still any longer. But prayer is a way to release the miracle-working power of God in your life. Through prayer, God can increase your productivity, eliminate obstacles that slow down your work, and provide resources that will quickly facilitate your objectives. In the end, you will actually find yourself ahead!

Imagine the time you could save each week by praying on the Lord's Day rather than working! Are you behind on a special project or on your bills? It is only natural to think you need to work on Sunday in order to "catch up." But God says to pray. If you rest on the Sabbath, trust God with your needs, and pray, then God will provide for you and your family in a marvelous way.

The Sabbath is a tremendous blessing to all who observe it.
Yes, all the commandments have as their ultimate aim the glory of God. But as I have said repeatedly, the Ten Commandments also exist to bless you and your family. Look at this story from the Book of Luke.

One Sabbath day as Jesus was walking through some grain fields, His disciples began breaking off heads of wheat. The Pharisees who saw them said to Jesus, "They shouldn't be doing that! It's against the law to work by harvesting grain on the Sabbath."

Jesus replied, "Haven't you ever read in the Scriptures what King David did when he and his companions were hungry? He went into the house of God (during the days when Abiathar was high priest), ate the special bread reserved for the priests alone, and then gave some to his companions. That was breaking the law, too."

Then Jesus said to them, "The Sabbath was made to benefit people, and not people to benefit the Sabbath. And I, the Son of Man, am master even of the Sabbath!" (Mark 2:24–28).

Jesus was establishing His authority over the religious leaders. The Pharisees imposed hundreds of silly rules on the people concerning the Sabbath. These laws were a burden to the people. Yet Jesus accused the Pharisees of violating the very laws they attempted to impose on others! In addition, Jesus said that the religious leaders of His day were exercising authority God never gave them. Only Jesus had that right.

Jesus was declaring Himself Master of the Sabbath. Some translations read, "Lord of the Sabbath." In other words, He is saying, "I was there with the Father when the laws were set into place. I know the spirit of the Law and why it was written in stone, so do not presume to lecture Me on My own laws."

The Pharisees completely missed the spirit of the fourth commandment. Jesus said that the Sabbath was instituted to benefit people, not to make people slaves to the Sabbath. It was supposed to be a blessing, not a curse. A time for rest, worship, and reflection, not for watching your every little step. Because the Sabbath was made for man, we must never treat it *legalistically.*

Once a young Dutch pastor confronted a serious situation on a Sunday morning. He lived some distance outside the village where his church was located, and a severe storm had hit during the night, damaging the roads. He could see no way of getting to the church for Sunday worship. But then an idea came to him. He could get to the church if he put on his ice skates and went by way of the canal that ran in front of his church.

When he began to think seriously about his plan, however, he concluded that it might not be such a good idea. The people of his church were fine folk, but they were also very strict about Sabbath observance. Skating was simply not to be done on Sunday. The young pastor thought about the matter and then made up his mind. It was important that worship take place, so he decided to run the risk.

He put on his ice skates and skated to the church. The official board were waiting for him just inside the door. No smiles welcomed him. They were obviously disturbed that their pastor had so clearly violated what they felt to be proper behavior on the Lord's Day.

But if they were displeased, they were also uncomfortable. They were very fond of the young pastor, and they really did not want to cause a rupture in their relationship. After considerable discussion, one of the members asked the pastor, "Did you enjoy the skating?"

"No," said the pastor, "I didn't enjoy it."

A sigh of relief went up from the group. Since there had been no joy in the incident, it was acceptable to the church people![6]

This story shows that the board members had missed the point of observing the Sabbath. They were more interested in keeping the letter of rules they had established than in focusing on joy and worship.

The Sabbath points us to the blessing of eternal life offered in Christ.
Like all the commandments and rituals of the Old Testament, this commandment points to our risen Lord. Living and resting in Christ alone for salvation is the true spiritual meaning of the Sabbath.

The writer of Hebrews says, "So there is a special rest still waiting for the people of God. For all who enter into God's rest will find rest from their labors, just as God rested after creating the world. Let us do our best to enter that place of rest. For anyone who disobeys God, as the people of Israel did, will fall...That is why we have a great High Priest who has gone to heaven, Jesus the Son of God. Let us cling to Him and never stop trusting Him" (Hebrews 4:9–11,14).

In Christ alone we discover perpetual rest from sin and worry. On the first Sabbath, God rested forever, having completed His marvelous work of creation. Likewise, Christ said at the cross, "It is finished." His work of redemption on behalf of the world was completed at Calvary.

What does God require from us in response to Christ's finished work? It is to receive Christ into our hearts by faith. Once we have, God promises to freely pardon all our sins, never to forsake us. The believer has eternal assurance that his sin is forever forgiven and cast as far as the east is from the west. God will remember it no more.

Here are some ways the believer can rest in Christ:

- The sinner's rest—by coming to Christ
  Jesus said, 'Come to Me, all of you who are weary and carry heavy burdens, and I will give you rest'" (Matthew 11:28).

- Redemption rest—secured in Christ
  "The LORD your God has arrived to live among you. He is a mighty savior. He will rejoice over you with great gladness. With His love, He will calm all your fears. He will exult over you by singing a happy song" (Zephaniah 3:17).

- The saint's rest—in communion with Christ
  "Jesus said, 'Let's get away from the crowds for a while and rest.' There were so many people coming and going that Jesus and His apostles didn't even have time to eat" (Mark 6:31).

- Present rest—now
  "We are always confident, even though we know that as long as we live in these bodies we are not at home with the Lord. That is why we live by believing and not by seeing" (2 Corinthians 5:6,7).

- Eternal rest—future

  "There will be no night there—no need for lamps or sun—for the Lord God will shine on them. And they will reign forever and ever" (Revelation 22:5).[7]

The temptation of our busy lives and stressful schedules will always be to compromise one day of rest and worship. After working hard all day on Sunday, a pastor cherished his Monday of rest. When he returned to the office on Tuesday, a church member who claimed to have a pressing need scolded him for relaxing at home. She chided, "The devil never takes a day off!"

The minister calmly replied, "So, if I didn't take a day off I'd be just like him, wouldn't I?"[8]

We honor God when we obey the fourth commandment. And we build up our bodies and minds as we fulfill the pattern of work and rest created by God. We must keep our perspective on God's commandment to take time out to worship Him in our local church.

The first four commandments all have to do with our relationship with God: Worship only God; do not bow down to idols; do not use God's name in vain; and keep the Sabbath holy. We can call them the vertical commandments because they point upward to God. They must be established first.

Now we will go on to the horizontal commandments—those that pertain to our relationships with others. The first horizontal commandment has to do with one of our closest humans ties—that of our parents. It sets the stage for the other horizontal commandments.

LIFE APPLICATION

Set Your Heart's Gauge

Commit the following verses to memory. Then, when you are tempted to turn your spiritual focus away from God to other things, recall these commands from God.

- Exodus 20:8–10—"Remember to observe the Sabbath day by keeping it holy. Six days a week are set apart for your daily duties and regular work, but the seventh day is a day of rest dedicated to the LORD your God."

- Hebrews 4:9–11—"There remains therefore a Sabbath rest for the people of God. For the one who has entered His rest has himself also rested from his works, as God did from His. Let us therefore be diligent to enter that rest, lest anyone fall through following the same example of disobedience" (NASB).

Gauge Your Spiritual Growth

Ask yourself the following questions. If one or more areas pose problems for you, ask God how you can deal with them through the power of the Holy Spirit.

- What is your regular routine on Sunday? Does it honor God?

- What do you think about taking off one day a week to do nothing but honor God and rest in His care? Would this be hard for you? Why?

- How will resting one day a week in obedience to our Lord's command help your schedule? Your family? Your business? Your relationship with God?

- How do your friends, work, or other interests pressure you to break the habit of resting on the Sabbath and keeping it holy?

- Does your work schedule reflect submission to God and trust in His care?

- When you observe the Sabbath, do you have a legalistic, begrudging attitude or are you genuinely happy to honor God in this way?

- Examine your prayer habits. Are you using your daily prayer time to release God's miracle-working power to make your life more productive? How does your prayer life help you to remember the Sabbath day and keep it holy?

Walk in the Power of the Holy Spirit

Use your daily prayer time to deepen your resolve to keep the Sabbath holy. Pray for these things:

- Thank God for the privilege of setting aside one special day a week to honor and worship Him.

- Ask the Holy Spirit to help you use Sunday as a day to focus on eternal rest and eternal perspectives rather than earthly pursuits.

- Ask the Holy Spirit to help you be more productive during the other six days of the week.

- Ask the Holy Spirit to help you rest and trust in God rather than frantically trying to achieve worldly goals through self-effort.

- By faith and in obedience, adjust your schedule so you will honor God with your Sabbath observance.

WRITTEN BY THE HAND of GOD

PART THREE

The Goal of Loving Others

T E N

HONOR YOUR PARENTS

O nce there was a man, his wife, and their four-year-old son who lived in a fine house. In time, the man's father became old and needed care so they brought him into the home to live. But there was a problem. The old father's hands trembled when he ate and many times he missed his mouth and dribbled his food onto the tablecloth.

Putting up with her father-in-law aggravated the wife. She said, "I can't have this. It interferes with a woman's right to happiness." So the couple set the old man on a stool in the corner of the kitchen where they gave him his food in an earthenware bowl. From then on, he ate in the corner, staring at the family with his vacant, old eyes.

Soon his hands trembled so much that he dropped the bowl and it broke. His daughter-in-law was incensed. "If you are a pig," she said, "you must eat out of a trough." So the couple made him a small wooden trough and put all his food in it.

One day at mealtime, the couple noticed their young son playing with some bits of wood. "What are you doing?" they asked.

With a big smile, he said, "I'm making a trough to feed you and Momma out of when I get big."

His words shocked his parents. They cried as they realized what they had done to a beloved member of their family. Then they went to the corner, took the old man by the hand, and led him to the table. From that day on, he was given a comfortable chair at the table and no one got upset when he spilled his food or broke a dish.[1]

This Grimm's tale highlights a problem that has plagued mankind since Adam and Eve—children who do not respect their parents. We can see examples of this throughout our modern culture—kids who talk back to their mothers and fathers, teens who go behind their parents' backs to do exactly what their parents don't want them to do, adults who harbor resentment against actions their parents took long ago. Just as this story illustrates, treating our parents with disrespect will come back to haunt us one day.

The fifth commandment reads, "Honor your father and mother. Then you will live a long, full life in the land the LORD your God will give you" (Exodus 20:12). This law is the first to instruct us how to act toward *each other*, or, as Jesus declared, how to "love your neighbor as yourself" (Matthew 22:39). The very first law concerning our earthly relationships speaks about how to treat our parents, because the way we learn to treat them affects how we behave toward all authority throughout our life.

Modern Life and the Fifth Commandment

Today, changes in culture have affected the family in dramatic ways. In the 21st century, families tend to be smaller and more distant. High divorce rates have resulted in more than 10 million single-parent homes in America.

About 36 percent of children in the U.S. live apart from their biological father. More than 30 percent of births are to unmarried women, and most of these children will always live in mother-only homes. About half of all children in the United States will experience parental divorce.[2] Add to this the homosexual agenda that offers Americans a radical redefinition of family, and you can see the huge amount of stress oppressing the family.

Modern thinking teaches us that parents should be held accountable for all that hinders us or holds us back when we reach adulthood. Many sons and daughters lay everything at their parents' feet —from emotional problems to difficulty holding a job or maintaining a long-term relationship. They look back at their parents' poor parenting skills and bad habits and say, "They are not worthy of honor." Therefore, it is common for children of all ages to disrespect their parents' wishes and disobey on a regular basis. For example, children today are suing their parents for self-custody and winning. Clearly, many child/parent relationships are in great need of the love and healing power of Christ.

Why Honor Parents?

When I was growing up, it never occurred to me to dishonor my parents. But I was raised in a very different culture from the one we have now. Most young people learned, through proper discipline, to be respectful to their parents and elders. They were taught to avoid anything that would dishonor their family.

I enjoyed my relationship with my father and saintly mother. My father was a good man, but he was not a believer. He would drop off my mother at church and he would go to a local café to talk with his friends until the church service was over. My mother and father had been married 35 years before I had the privilege of leading him to the Lord. After that he was always one of the first to suggest to guests that we should read the Bible and pray together.

But in today's dysfunctional families, conflicts reign. Many young people seldom eat a meal with the rest of the family. Family members are busy with so many distractions that family life suffers. Some children live with parents who are alcoholics, drug addicts, or abusive. There is no love, no unity, no harmony. It is hard for these youngsters to imagine loving their father and mother.

But respecting our parents is not optional—no matter what the circumstances are. There are several reasons why God commands us to honor our parents.

Honoring our parents pleases God.

The root meaning of "honor" is "to be heavy or weighty." Thus, we are to treat each parent as a "weighty" person in society, as someone who is important and worthy of respect. So important was parental respect in the Old Testament that a rebellious son was to be stoned to death to protect society. The Law states, "They must declare: 'This son of ours is stubborn and rebellious and refuses to obey...' Then all the men of the town must stone him to death. In this way, you will cleanse this evil from among you, and all Israel will hear about it and be afraid" (Deuteronomy 21:20,21).

The New Testament often speaks of lack of parental respect, but no passage is as direct as this one in Romans: "Their lives became full of every kind of wickedness, sin, greed, hate, envy, murder, fighting, deception, malicious behavior, and gossip. They are backstabbers, haters of God, insolent, proud, and boastful. They are forever inventing new ways of sinning and are disobedient to their parents" (Romans 1:29,30).

The Bible says that disobedience to parents will be prevalent in the days before the return of Christ: "People will love only themselves and their money. They will be boastful and proud, scoffing at God, disobedient to their parents, and ungrateful. They will consider nothing sacred" (2 Timothy 3:2). Doesn't this describe what is happening today?

On the other hand, the Bible celebrates children who honor their parents. Proverbs 10:1 says, "A wise child brings joy to a father." Proverbs 15:5 tells us, "Only a fool despises a parent's discipline; whoever learns from correction is wise."

God gives us examples of children who honored their parents. In good times and bad, Joseph considered his father's welfare and took care of him in his old age by bringing him to Egypt during a time of severe drought. David made provisions for his parents when he was under siege by his enemies (1 Samuel 22:3,4). Jesus took care of His mother—even at the time of His death.

We have no excuse not to honor our parents until their deaths. That is the responsibility God has given us as sons and daughters. We please Him when we obey the fifth commandment.

Honoring our parents maintains God's order.

Why does the Bible place such emphasis on honoring parents? Because as goes the family, so goes society. In fact, the Church has always understood that the word "parents" in the fifth commandment refers to *all* authority. Therefore, we are to show respect, not only to our natural parents, but also, as the Westminster Larger Catechism says, to "all superiors in age and gifts; and especially such as, by God's ordinance, are over us in place of authority, whether in family, church, or commonwealth." When young children are taught to respect parents, they learn habits and attitudes they can apply to other positions of authority.

Parents who disregard God's order for the family, on the other hand, instigate bad behavior in their children. An *Esquire* magazine article claimed that without a father who sets limits, a boy's natural aggression can intensify into a well of pure destructiveness within society. One measure: two-thirds of convicted rapists, three-fourths of adolescent murderers, and three-fourths of long-term prison inmates grew up without a father in the house.

The first and most prominent authority figures in our lives are our parents. If we do not learn to respect, honor, and obey them, we will not learn to honor and esteem any earthly authority. And a society without respect for authority will soon crumble.

Picture a busy intersection with a broken stop light during rush hour. No red, green, or yellow lights flash to instruct you when to stop and go. People get impatient; they race through the intersection without waiting their proper turn. Soon utter chaos reigns. This confusion occurs in countless cultures. Lawlessness breeds lawlessness, resulting in anarchy.

Former presidential candidate and HUD director Jack Kemp says, "People obey the law for one of two reasons: they either love God or fear punishment. When both of these reasons break down, the result is an environment that breeds violence, poverty, and anarchy."[3] This is why it is so important for children to learn to honor their parents. Social order is at stake.

Let me give you two examples. During the 18th century, Max Jukes lived in New York. He did not believe in Christ or in Christian training. He refused to take his children to church, even when they asked to go. By the 1950s, Jukes had produced 1,026 descendants: 300 were sent to prison for an average term of 13 years; 190 were public prostitutes; 680 were admitted alcoholics. His family, thus far, has cost the state in excess of $500,000. They made no great contribution to society.

Jonathan Edwards, a great preacher during the First Great Awakening in America, lived in the same state at the same time as Jukes. He loved the Lord and saw that his children were in church every Sunday. He has had 929 descendants: 430 were ministers; 86 became university professors; 13 became university presidents; 75 authored good books; 5 were elected to the U.S. Congress, and 2 to the Senate. One was vice-president of the United States. Edwards's family never cost the state one cent but has contributed immeasurably to the moral, spiritual, and economic abundance America experiences today.[4] What a difference parents make in the life of a child!

Honoring our parents benefits our own well-being.
Jesus uses the parent-child relationship as the root of many of His parables. The prodigal son is nothing more than a tale of a boy who dishonors his father and brings severe consequences upon his life. The prodigal son fell into ruin. His life was a disaster. He was not mature enough to handle his inheritance. Fortunately, the forgiveness and love of the father overcame the son's lack of respect.

Perhaps you struggle with the idea of honoring your parents because, in some way, one or both failed you. Perhaps a parent has been involved in drugs, alcohol, or crime. We all have imperfect parents. Most of them did the best they could based on what was modeled to them when they were children. But some were neglectful or abusive emotionally or physically. Nevertheless, all of us who are believers are imperfect people who come from imperfect stock—sinners saved by grace.

In his book *More Than a Carpenter*, my dear friend Josh McDowell tells about the difficulty of growing up with an alcoholic father. "My father. I hated his guts. To me he was the town alcoholic . . . I'd go out in the barn and see my mother beaten so badly she couldn't get up, lying in the manure behind the cows. When we had friends over, I would take my father out, tie him up in the barn, and park the car up around the silo. We would tell our friends he'd had to go somewhere. I don't think anyone could have hated anyone more than I hated my father."[5]

What changed Josh's attitude toward his father? Christ. "After I made that decision for Christ—maybe five months later—a love from God through Jesus Christ entered my life and was so strong it took that hatred and turned it upside down. I was able to look my father squarely in the eyes and say, 'Dad, I love you.'"[6] Later, Josh introduced his father to Christ and he became a decent, honorable, sober man before he died.

Josh's story illustrates that parents' imperfections do not nullify the commandment to honor them. Finding the strength and compassion to accomplish this is hard for many people. But as Josh so wonderfully discovered, the love of Christ helps us overcome feelings of bitterness and resentment and provides a beautiful means of reconciliation.

The lack of honor shown to parents often results in a loss of relationship between parent and child. The Spanish have a story about a father and son who became estranged. The son left home and the father later set out to find him. He searched for months with no success. Finally, in desperation, the father turned to the newspaper for help. His ad simply read, "Dear Paco, meet me in front of this newspaper office at noon on Saturday. All is forgiven. I love you. Your father."

On Saturday, eight hundred young men named Paco showed up looking for forgiveness and love from their fathers.[7]

The world is filled with children who desperately long for reconciliation with their parents and with God. If you are not demonstrating proper respect to your parents, you will no doubt want to take appropriate steps to reconcile with them and begin anew.

A young woman who was on our staff experienced conflict with her father through the years until finally it turned into physical abuse. At seventeen, she left home in anger, saying, "I never want to see you again. Don't ever contact me. As far as I am concerned you are dead."

She didn't talk to her father for five years. During this time, she was homeless, so she became a prostitute and a drug addict. Then one day she met a Campus Crusade for Christ staff member who led her to Christ. Soon after, she attended a Christmas conference in Chicago where I was speaking. Present were about 2,000 student conferees.

One evening, I spoke on the importance of loving and honoring your parents. When I concluded I said, "Go to your room, get on the phone, and call your parents and tell them that you love them. Or write them a note and say 'I love you and am grateful for all you have done for me.' Even if they are alcoholics or drug addicts, you are commanded to honor your father and mother. Jesus said to love your enemies, so even if your parents have acted like enemies to you, you must love them."

The next morning, this beautiful, young girl came to see me along with a staff member. She told the story of her severed relationship with her father and how he had affected her life. She described how she had ended up on the streets homeless as a prostitute and finally a drug addict and how she had tried to kill herself several times.

She said, "As you were speaking last night, the Holy Spirit prompted me to call my parents and tell them that I love them. I could hardly wait to get out of the meeting. As soon as I got back to my room, I called my parents. I told them that I love them and that I am so sorry for all I said and did to them. I explained how I received Christ as my Savior and how my life has changed. They treated me so warmly, and they were so happy that I called. Now I can hardly wait to see them."

Honoring our parents is a sacrificial, life-long endeavor. Jesus honored His mother in the last few moments of His life. Even as He hung on the cross, our Lord was more concerned with providing for His mother than with His own grief and suffering. He commanded His beloved disciple John to adopt her as His own.

Tragically, we live in a day when rest homes are filled with millions of deserted elderly people whom nobody seems to care for. They are abandoned by their children and friends. That should not happen to our parents. We must provide the emotional and financial support they need in their golden years. Some of us will have the privilege and responsibility of caring for them when they are physically limited. But no matter how old they are, we should return the generosity, provisions, and sacrifices they made for us.

Honoring our parents leads to God's promise of a long, full life.
The fifth commandment carries a promise that says, "Then you will live a long, full life in the land the LORD your God will give you" (Exodus 20:12). At the time the fifth commandment was given, the Jews had been freed from Egypt and were traveling toward the Promised Land. God wanted them to know that national stability and longevity would result if they honored their parents as a culture. Even today, parents are generally revered and respected in Middle Eastern society.

The blessing is also promised to us as believers who have been grafted into the family tree of God, which makes us "spiritual Jews." Too often we think this promise applies only to individuals. Our nation also can be blessed with great longevity and stability if we respect those whom God has placed in authority over us.

Building anything that results in stability and longevity takes effort and persistence. For example, scattered along five hundred miles of California's northern coastline lie hidden valleys filled with some of nature's most majestic skyscrapers—the redwoods. These valleys provide just the right conditions for phenomenal growth. Many of these mighty monarchs pierce the sky at heights taller than a thirty-story building. Placed side by side, London's Big Ben would be dwarfed by the second tallest redwood and the Leaning Tower of Pisa would rise little higher than the midpoint of the sixth highest woodland colossus.

The longevity and stability of the redwood is incredible. The Grizzly Giant—the largest of the Sequoias in the world—is more than 2,500 years old and may have been a seedling when the prophet Isaiah foretold the virgin birth. Other stately trees were reaching for their destiny as towering pillars when a youthful Christ worked in His family's carpenter shop in Nazareth. Founder's Tree in the Redwood Creek grove of Humboldt County—considered the fifth largest redwood with a circumference at chest level of forty feet—was probably well-developed when the Magna Carta was signed in 1215. Many other redwoods were populating the groves when Columbus discovered America in 1492.

As regal as they appear, these incredible giants of the wilderness sprang from seeds so tiny that twelve can fit on a penny with room left over; more than a million squeezed together would weigh only a pound. Yet each is capable of producing a tree weighing tons.

The right combination of soil, moisture, and sunlight is required for the redwood's proper growth. The soil is crucial.

In the redwood, we see a picture of the blessings of longevity and strength that a nation can enjoy when it affords the family a place of prominence. When children are nurtured in the right environment of loving parents and give parents due respect, our nation will grow and prosper. Respect for parents and authority will stimulate the right kinds of relationships that help society to function as it should for the well-being of its citizens. Disrespect for parents and authority, however, will destroy the climate that makes a culture flourish.

How We Can Honor Our Parents

For some sons and daughters, obeying the fifth commandment is easy because their parents are loving and fair. Other children have more difficulty because their parents do not fulfill their roles in a godly way. But all of us can honor our parents regardless of our circumstances. Let me give you several biblical principles for honoring your parents in positive and negative situations.

We must honor our parents by forgiving them.
No doubt all of us have been hurt and disappointed by our parents at one time or another. It is to be expected because they are human. But for those of us who have our own sons and daughters, we realize that children do not come with instruction manuals.

Vonette and I did our best as parents, but since we are far from perfect, we made mistakes. All parents do. But this is no excuse for disobeying the fifth commandment. We must forgive our parents in these situations because God's Word says we will be forgiven to the extent we forgive others.

In God's eyes, forgiving is essential. John Oglethorpe once commented to John Wesley, founder of the Methodist denomination, "I never forgive."

Mr. Wesley wisely replied, "Then, sir, I hope that you never sin."[8]

According to popular speaker and pastor Gordon Dalbey, many men fail to forgive their fathers. Dalbey says that the "father wound" —man's unfulfilled longing for a father's love—is epidemic today. Many men have fathers who abandoned or abused them in childhood. Since a father is the key to a man's self-identity, these men are desperately confused.

"Christians are terrified to talk to each other about their wounds, so they hide behind religion," Dalbey says. The result is that these men avoid relationships instead of drawing deeper into them.

But Dalbey sees some hopeful signs. "A number of men around the country, broken by drug addiction, divorce, and other traumas, have been forced into the Father's arms, and have received forgiveness and wholeness," he says.[9] With the Father's help, any son or daughter can forgive any hurtful experience at the hands of a parent. The result will always be healing—at least in the heart of the forgiver.

We must honor our parents by respecting their God-given position even if they do not deserve honor.

In the armed services, a good soldier obeys and respects his superior officer whether he leads well or not. The U.S. presidency is the same. Regardless of who is in the White House and what he does, most Americans still honor the office of the president and give it due respect.

The positions of mother or father have even more preeminence. God instituted these positions, so we must honor the position as such. Even when we do not feel like it, we are called to honor parents as the people God put in charge to instruct and enlighten us.

Love Without Hypocrisy

Honoring our parents from our hearts means that our honor must go beyond mere words. Unless we back up our words with actions, we become hypocritical. Jesus chided the Pharisees of His day for honoring God with their lips but not in their deeds. He said, "You hypocrites! Isaiah was prophesying about you when he said, 'These people honor me with their lips, but their hearts are far away'" (Mark 7:6,7).

Perhaps you have heard the story of a little boy who finally sat down after first resisting his parents' command to do so. He said to his parents, "I'm sitting down on the outside, but I'm standing up on the inside!" We do not truly honor our parents unless our attitude is right.

Also, our honor must go beyond deceit. Let us not convince ourselves that we honor our parents when we do not. Again, the Pharisees taught that real and loving care for parents could be achieved through a feeble offering of money to the temple. Jesus said to the religious leaders, "You say, 'You don't need to honor your parents by caring for their needs if you give the money to God instead.' And so, by your own tradition, you nullify the direct commandment of God" (Matthew 15:5,6). Honoring parents is a heartfelt action that often requires direct, hands-on care.

We can honor our parents' position by caring for their needs when they are needy or elderly. According to current estimates by the Congressional Research Service, nearly a quarter of the nation's elderly population—more than 7 million people—have some form of disability for which they require assistance, such as help with bathing, dressing, eating, preparing meals, or taking medicine. As the 76 million baby boomers age, their need for long-term care will increase.[10]

Today, the elderly make up about 13 percent of the population. In 2030 when the first of the baby boomers reach their 85th birthdays, the number of people aged 65 and over will make up about 20 percent of the total population. From 1997 to 2030, individuals 85 and older, the most rapidly growing age group and the group most likely to require long-term care, will more than double—from about 3.9 million to about 8.5 million individuals. By 2050, this population will more than double again—to about 18 million individuals.

Although many parents will live at home until the end of their lives, many will require long-term care. Are you prepared?

Long-term care presents a significant burden for many individuals and for public programs. Long-term care in nursing homes currently costs more than $40,000 annually per resident. A substantial share of nursing home residents pay that out of their own pockets.[11]

Abandonment is one of the biggest fears of the elderly. We need to assure our parents that we will be there for them until the end of their lives. And if nursing home care becomes necessary, elderly parents still need love, care, and regular visits. Our parents cared for us for many years before we could care for ourselves. Care in their older years is an expression of gratitude, as well as an act of obedience.

We must honor our parents by loving them.
The word "honor" carries the idea of prizing something highly, of taking care of someone, showing affection, and making sure that no evil befalls him. God does this for us. The psalmist declares, "He will call upon Me, and I will answer him; I will be with him in trouble; I will rescue him, and honor him" (Psalm 91:15, NASB). We must do the same for our parents.

In spite of all their flaws and faults, most parents have tried, to the best of their abilities, to raise their children right. All that most parents want in return is love and respect. We honor them when we love them, give them emotional and financial support, and talk to them. Loving actions are as necessary as words. Like Eliza Doolittle sings in the famous musical *My Fair Lady*, "If you love me, show me."

Although I travel extensively, I always made every effort to see my parents regularly until they both passed away at age 93. I always tried to help them materially and provide emotional support. As of this writing, they have been gone for almost twenty-five years. Yet I continue to honor them in my memories, and I have a large picture of them in my office. They still mean so much to me.

Have you ever heard someone say, "I wish I had just one more chance to tell my parents I love them"? Do not allow yourself to get caught in this situation. Tell them today and every time you are together. And by all means, show them. As the old saying goes, "When all is said and done, more is said than done."

A Word to Parents

I have said much about honoring parents even when it is difficult; however, this is no excuse for parents to misbehave. The Bible says that parents are to be worthy of respect.

For example, parents are not to exasperate their children. Paul writes, "Now a word to you fathers. Don't make your children angry by the way you treat them. Rather, bring them up with the discipline and instruction approved by the Lord" (Ephesians 6:4).

Also, parents should give their children good things. This includes material things, but also includes nurturing love. "You parents—if your children ask for a loaf of bread, do you give them a stone instead?" (Matthew 7:9).

Ungodly parents exacerbate problems between generations. The percentage of American teens who say they want to be like their parents is only 39 percent.[12] What a terrible tragedy!

What problems cause divisions between parents and teens? When the ten-year-olds in Mrs. Imogene Frost's class at the Brookside, New Jersey, Community Sunday school expressed their views of "what's wrong with grownups," they came up with these complaints:

- Grownups make promises, then they forget all about them or else they say it wasn't really a promise, just a maybe.

- Grownups don't do the things they're always telling the children to do-like pick up their things, or be neat, or always tell the truth.

- Grownups never really listen to what children have to say. They always decide ahead of time what they're going to answer.

- Grownups make mistakes, but they won't admit them. They always pretend that they weren't mistakes at all—or that somebody else made them.

- Grownups interrupt children all the time and think nothing of it. If a child interrupts a grownup, he gets a scolding or something worse.

- Grownups are always talking about what they did and what they knew when they were ten years old—but they never try to think what it's like to be ten years old right now.[13]

Do you see yourself in any of these criticisms? Parenting is hard, particularly in today's culture. But putting Christ at the center of your home will allow Him to guide you into the best decisions for your children. He will fill your heart with love so you will not "exasperate" your young ones.

Susanna Wesley is a godly example of how to love and raise godly children. She spent time each day praying for her seventeen children. In addition, she took each child aside for a full hour every week to discuss spiritual matters. No wonder two of her sons, Charles and John, were used by God to bring blessing to all of England and much of America during the spiritual revivals of the 18th century.

Here are a few rules Susanna Wesley followed in training her children:

1. Subdue self-will in a child and thus work together with God to save his soul.

2. Teach him to pray as soon as he can speak.

3. Give him nothing he cries for and only what is good for him if he asks for it politely.

4. To prevent lying, punish no fault that is freely confessed, but never allow a rebellious, sinful act to go unnoticed.

5. Commend and reward good behavior.

6. Strictly observe all promises you have made to your child.[14]

The fifth commandment can yield incredible blessings to anyone who obeys it. The world is full of earthly relationships—the most important of which is between family members. Yet familial relationships are often the most difficult to nourish. We must continue to make *every* effort to draw our strength from God's Holy Spirit to make our family relationships pleasing to Him. Then He will pour out His abundant blessings upon our families, which will, in turn, bless the world around us in ways we cannot imagine.

Once our hearts are at peace in our homes, we can go on to establish peace in society through the Ten Commandments. One of the most serious problems we see in our culture is the devaluing of the sanctity of life. In our next chapter, we will look at the sixth commandment, which deals with this vital issue.

LIFE APPLICATION

Set Your Heart's Gauge

Commit the following verses to memory. Then, when you are tempted to turn your spiritual focus away from God to other things, recall these commands from God.

- Exodus 20:12—"Honor your father and mother. Then you will live a long, full life in the land the LORD your God will give you."

- Ephesians 6:2—"'Honor your father and mother.' This is the first of the Ten Commandments that ends with a promise."

Gauge Your Spiritual Growth

Ask yourself the following questions. If one or more areas pose problems for you, ask God how you can deal with them through the power of the Holy Spirit.

- What in your life conflicts with your duty to help your parents? Your busy schedule? Your distance from them? What can you do to overcome these obstacles?

- How does your relationship with your parents influence your view of authority?

- How have conflicts with your parents harmed your own well-being?

- How are you supporting your parents emotionally?

- How is your relationship with your parents harming or edifying your relationship with God? With your children? What might you do to change any problems?

- Thinking of the most hurtful situation between you and your parents, have you completely forgiven them whether they deserve it or not?

- In what situation have you honored one of your parents because of their position, even if his or her actions did not earn it? How can this help you in future situations?

- What plans do you have for caring for your parents when they are elderly?

- What have you done in the past few weeks to show your parents that you love them?

Walk in the Power of the Holy Spirit

Commit yourself to honoring your parents in a new way. First, ask God to show you one specific way you can express your love. Then, ask the Holy Spirit to fill you with a renewed love for them. Follow through with your plan.

ELEVEN

DO NOT MURDER

M rs. Gena Foster, a 34-year-old mother of three, entered a freeway in Birmingham, Alabama, on her way to pick up her youngest child from school. As she merged into traffic, she accidentally cut in front of Mrs. Shirley Henson, a company secretary who was hurrying home to walk her two Labradors. Shirley, disturbed by the merging vehicle, flashed her lights.

Then things began to escalate. Gena put on her brakes and an altercation between the two vehicles began that lasted for several miles. Soon, both women pulled off on a side road and stopped at a traffic light.

Gena got out of her sports car and approached the door of Shirley's car. According to police reports, Shirley, a former Cub Scout leader with a teenage son, reached over to her glovebox, took out the gun she kept there, lowered her window, and shot Gena in the face. Gena died at the side of the road. The life of a 34-year-old mother of three was gone in an instant.[1]

This tragic incident illustrates a growing problem facing American drivers: "road rage." The American Automobile Association estimates that between 1991 and 1996 the number of road rage incidents has increased by more than 50 percent and resulted in 218 deaths!

Gena Foster's death is an example of what is happening on America's highways because of the evil that lurks in all our hearts. Most people would adamantly assert, "I am not a murderer, nor am I even capable of murder!" But the apostle John teaches us that *hatred* is a killer, which often leads to overt murder. "Everyone who hates his brother is a murderer; and you know that no murderer has eternal life abiding in him" (1 John 3:15, NASB).

The deaths that too often accompany road rage and other violent incidents prove that deep in each person's heart lies the potential to do great harm to another human being. Murder is not a crime reserved for the dregs of society. Given the right set of circumstances, anyone is capable of it. Shirley Henson was an average middle-class suburbanite. Nevertheless, in a flash, she was responsible for a murder and a precious life was lost.

Only the Creator Has the Right to Take Life

The sixth commandment says, "Do not murder" (Exodus 20:13). Why is murder wrong? Because God is the Creator of all life so only He can take it away. To take life into our own hands is equivalent to "playing God."

Man's attempt to supplant God in matters that pertain to life always results in disaster. For example, left unchallenged, godless trends in science result in Satan having full control over life issues. Eugenics and fetal tissue research are but natural outgrowths of the world's current devaluation of human life and its deification of science.

To understand these moral issues, we must make a distinction between "killing" and "murder." Not all killing is murder. The narrow scope of the sixth commandment focuses on the taking of an "innocent" human life by another human, often with premeditation. According to the great biblical scholar Charles Ryrie, the word "kill" is used 49 times in the Old Testament. In each case, the word in the original Hebrew language means "to murder with premeditation." Furthermore, each time the sixth commandment is repeated in the New Testament, a word is always used that means "to murder" in the sense of taking innocent life.

At first glance, this command looks extremely clear. But there are many contemporary questions related to the taking of a life. To begin to understand God's perspective on murder, let's ask, "What is it not?"

Capital punishment is not murder.
According to Genesis 9:5,6, capital punishment is the penalty for murder. God said to Noah and his family, "Murder is forbidden. Animals that kill people must die, and any person who murders must be killed. Yes, you must execute anyone who murders another person, for to kill a person is to kill a living being made in God's image."

Why the death penalty for murder? Because man was created in the very image of God; therefore, taking the life of a person is to attack the Creator God. Imagine that someone destroyed something you made and cherished. Would you not feel as though you had been personally attacked? This simple analogy, however, does not approach the seriousness of murder. God values life, and humans are the pinnacle of His creation. There is no clearer way to assault the Creator than to destroy a living person—His finest creation.

Many people argue that capital punishment is state-sanctioned murder and is therefore against the sixth commandment. However, these people are mistaken. Capital punishment is not about harming the innocent, but is executing justice upon the guilty who have taken a human life with forethought. Therefore, this form of "killing" is acceptable in God's eyes.

All my life I have been in favor of capital punishment. But with the erosion of our judicial system in recent years, I have come to question its administration. Illinois Governor George Ryan, citing a "shameful record of convicting innocent people and putting them on death row," placed a moratorium on all executions in the state. "I cannot support a system, which, in its administration, has proven so fraught with error," the governor said, "and has come so close to the ultimate nightmare: the state's taking of innocent life."[2]

I agree with Governor Ryan's concern. Until we can be certain that the death penalty is being administered fairly, I will continue to support it with the qualification that states enforce capital punishment only after the guilt of the condemned has been proven through DNA profiling or through other proven irrefutable means.

Military defense of a nation is not murder.
Sergeant Alvin C. York was the most celebrated soldier of World War I. To this day, his story remains a testimony of one man's heroic faith and bravery. But those who knew York as a young man would never have guessed he would become the most decorated soldier of his time.

Born in rural Tennessee in 1887, York was the third of eleven children. His deadly accurate shooting ability became evident early in his life. But York was also a troublemaker. He spent much of his early years drinking liquor and gambling. Then following the death of a close friend in a bar fight, he gave his life to Christ.

By the time he was drafted for military service, one of the best marksmen in the South did not believe he could kill another man, even in war. York came from a long line of men who had fought for their country since the American Revolution, yet he had difficulty reconciling his patriotic duty with his faith. "I wanted to be a good Christian and a good American too," he said. "My religion and my experience told me not to go to war, and the memory of my ancestors ...told me to get my gun and go fight. I didn't know what to do... There was a war going on inside me, and I didn't know which side to lean to."

York was soon sent overseas. After seeking the counsel of some of his superiors and praying to God, York was eventually convinced that there is such a thing as a "moral war."

The dramatic events of October 8, 1918, at the battle of Argonne etched the name of Alvin York in history. York's patrol was ordered to take out German machine-gun fire. With only a rifle and a pistol, York helped kill more than twenty Germans. His actions led to the surrender of 132 enemy soldiers.

York would never see great wealth from his daring feat. Rather, the southern gentleman went back to his Tennessee home and spent what little money he earned from lecturing to enhance educational standards for the youth of Fentress County, Tennessee, and to start a small Bible school.[3]

What changed Alvin C. York from a passivist to one of America's greatest war heroes? He realized that freedom often comes with a price tag. Man is a sinner. When evil men ascend to power within a nation, their insidious thirst for more power is usually too much for one nation to satisfy. Soon other nations are threatened, which inevitably leads to war.

King Solomon wrote that there is "a time for war, and a time for peace" (Ecclesiastes 3:8, NASB). His father, King David, spent many years fighting wars against enemies of their people. During King Solomon's time, the people experienced a time of peace. That could not have happened if David had not paved the way. During this peace, Solomon built a magnificent temple to the glory of God. Those who had fought and killed the enemy during David's reign were doing what God led them to do to assure the future of the Hebrew nation.

Self-defense is not murder.

Although warfare is often a form of self-defense, the two are not identical. Warfare is a collective act of the citizens of a nation whereas self-defense is an individual act not related to military action.

Sir William Blackstone (1723–1780), a devout Christian, English jurist, and professor of common law at Oxford, said that self-defense is one of the "absolute rights of individuals." John Dryden (1631–1700), English poet and dramatist, said, "Self-defense is nature's eldest law."

Self-defense is not something that people need to learn. It is instinctive, a part of nature. In fact, all animals and even some plants defend themselves when threatened. Thus, God never needed to teach His people that it is permissible to defend ourselves. But He did lay down laws for the nation of Israel that limited the use of self-defense. (See Exodus 21:12–22:3.)

Our laws today also restrict self-defense. According to Randall Watters, a former Jehovah's Witness who now ministers to members of cults, "Self-defense is generally justified only when a reasonable person would find it necessary to avoid grievous or serious bodily injury or death that is otherwise unavoidable. In some states, the law requires you to make every reasonable attempt to retreat before you can use any self-defense measure . . . unless an attempt at retreat would be futile or would put you in harm's way.

"For instance, if the assault is on the side of a highway and your only means of retreat is to cross the busy highway, you would not be required to put yourself in that situation. If the assailant has a contact weapon such as a knife, the assailant must be within twenty-one feet of the defender in order for the defender to be availed the right of self-defense. You cannot shoot at someone who threatens you with a knife from 50 feet away."[4]

To be certain about your rights, check the laws on self-defense in your state.

Killing an animal is not murder.

Many years ago when I was growing up on a ranch in Oklahoma, I loved to hunt game. A great influence on my adult life was my father-in-law, who was one of the leading hunters in our area. Back then, I killed for pleasure. But after I became a Christian, my enthusiasm for hunting waned. I soon realized that killing animals for pleasure was wrong. We are to never misuse our position as "caretakers of the earth." All creatures great and small are to be respected and treated with kindness.

But does God permit us to kill for food? In Genesis 1:28–30, God gave plant life to man as food, but it is also clear that God permitted meat eating after the fall of man. God said to Noah and his family, "Be fruitful and multiply, and fill the earth…Every moving thing that is alive shall be food for you; I give all to you, as I gave the green plant" (Genesis 9:1,3, NASB).

The New Testament tells us that Jesus ate meat. Mark records, "On the first day of the Festival of Unleavened Bread (the day the Passover lambs were sacrificed), Jesus' disciples asked him, 'Where do you want us to go to prepare the Passover supper?'" (Mark 14:12). The disciples and Jesus observed the Passover. Clearly, a lamb was killed for this celebration.

In Romans 14:2,3, Paul views vegetarianism as a spiritual weakness. In 1 Timothy 4:1–3, Paul warns Timothy about those who heed "deceitful spirits" and "doctrines of demons," and who "forbid marriage and advocate abstaining from foods" (NASB). Paul then says that all animals are permissible for food as long it is gratefully received (vv. 4,5).

While Paul does not condemn vegetarianism as a dietary choice, he denounces it as a doctrine. Paul makes it quite clear that vegetarianism is not a Christian philosophy and that those who practice vegetarianism should not think of themselves as better believers than those who do not. Therefore, if we argue that vegetarianism is a Christian philosophy, we reject the authority of Paul and the example of Christ. In our senior years Vonette and I have become vegetarians for health reasons, not because of spiritual convictions.

Sanctity of Life

We have seen that the Bible does not consider all killing to be morally wrong. Yet the Bible is clear that we are to consider all human life as sacred. From the most vulnerable to the most hardy, God considers every person as precious.

Yet our culture devalues the sanctity of life. We have called murder by other names and made it seem acceptable. Taking into account all that the Bible has to say about life, we should always stand for the sanctity of human life and defend those who are helpless to defend themselves. That includes the unborn, adults with handicaps or incurable diseases, and the world's oppressed. As believers in the God of life, we must always affirm life and even defend it. Let's look at several social issues that God calls murder.

Abortion is murder.

Many people do not realize that abortion is murder. Abortion is murder because it takes the life of the most innocent and defenseless in our society. Life begins from the very moment of conception. The fetus is not just a blob of flesh; it is a human being created in the image of God. When we take the life of that embryo or child, we violate the sixth commandment.

Since *Roe v. Wade*, the infamous landmark Supreme Court decision in 1973, approximately 40 million babies have been aborted—an average of 4,000 each day! The right to abort is nothing less than infanticide! The overwhelming majority of all abortions, 95 percent, are done as a means of birth control. Of the remaining 5 percent, only 1 percent are performed because of rape or incest, 1 percent because of fetal abnormalities, and 3 percent due to the mother's health problems.[5] How tragic that in the fight over abortion, some Christian denominations accept abortion as a right! It is incomprehensible that people can be so determined to kill unborn babies.

But many believers are standing up for the lives of the unborn. They are bringing the plight of these innocent lives to our national consciousness.

Norma McCorvey is such a person. She is at the center of a ministry called Roe No More. What is so amazing about her stance against abortion is that she is the woman known as "Jane Roe" in the *Roe v. Wade* decision. She campaigned for abortion rights, although she has never had an abortion herself. She says, "I could out-cuss the most crass of men and women; I could out-drink many of the Dallas taverns' regulars; and I was known for my hot temper. When pro-lifers called me a murderer, I called them worse. When people held up signs of aborted fetuses, I spit in their face."

She adds about her involvement with the abortion controversy, "This issue is the only thing I live for. I live, eat, breathe, think everything about abortion."[6]

Then in 1995, she met Jesus Christ and He changed her life. It all began when Operation Rescue, a pro-life group, moved into the same office center in north Dallas. Clashes between pro-abortion and pro-life advocates became a frequent occurrence.

But Flip Benham of Operation Rescue reached out to Norma in friendship. Also, a 7-year-old girl named Emily, whose mother worked for the pro-life group, showed love to Norma. Eventually, Norma found that Emily's mother had once considered abortion when she was pregnant. Norma says, "I was forever changed by this experience. Abortion was no longer an 'abstract right.' It had a face now, in a little girl named Emily."[7]

The love of Flip and Emily won Norma's heart, and she received Christ as her Savior. Now she is a woman full of incredible joy who treasures the sanctity of life. In fact, Roe No More Ministry helps post-abortion women.

If you, or someone you know, is considering an abortion, take a stand for life and reject death. Adoption is the courageous alternative for an unplanned pregnancy. That child is so precious. Contact your local pro-life group for help in doing what's right.

Euthanasia is murder.

Euthanasia is murder because it takes life rather than supports those who need physical, emotional, or financial help. It advocates abandonment rather than compassion. The following excerpt from *The New York Times* is chilling.

> The Department of Justice, in a detailed memorandum explaining the government's aims regarding the American legal code, has announced its intention to authorize physicians to end the sufferings of incurable patients. The memorandum, still lacking the force of law, proposed that "it shall be made possible for physicians to end the intractable pain of incurable patients, upon request, in the interests of true humanity."[8]

This planned legal recognition of euthanasia has raised a number of religious questions and ethical concerns. The Catholic newspaper *The Wanderer* observes: "The Catholic faith binds the conscience of its followers not to accept this method of shortening the sufferings of incurables who are tormented by pain."[9] In Protestant circles as well, life is regarded as something that God alone has authority to take.

Nevertheless, the Department of Justice is still hard at work in its attempt to legalize killing at the federal level. With passage of the Death with Dignity Act, Oregon has already legally sanctioned assisted-suicide at the state level. The Oregon law is a terrible precedent. The Church must pray that this trend goes no further in American public policy and that current law in support of euthanasia is soon reversed. The Church must also take the lead in ministering to those who suffer so much pain that they despair of life.

Genocide is murder.

Genocide is a total disregard for God's value in the lives of a group of people He created. It is murder on a grand scale. Genocide is crime on a different scale from all other types of murder. It is an effort to completely exterminate a national, ethnic, racial, or religious group. Genocide is therefore a "crime against humanity." When we hear the word "genocide," we naturally think about the killing of 6 million Jews by Adolf Hitler during World War II. However, there are many more cases of this horrible crime.

The following is only a partial listing of those who have suffered from genocide in the 20th century: 1.5 million Armenians, 3 million Ukrainians, 6 million Gypsies and Slavs, 5 million Russians, 5 million Chinese, 1 million Ibos, 1.5 million Bengalis, 1.7 million Cambodians, 500,000 Ugandans, 250,000 Burundians (continuing), 1 million Sudanese (continuing), 800,000 Rwandans (continuing), 1 million North Koreans (continuing), and 10,000 Kosovars.[10]

Genocide is proof that, without God, man is absolutely inhumane. Rather than civilization advancing morally, we are plummeting into a moral abyss. Our sinfulness shows that we cannot survive without God's standards, the Ten Commandments, and the life-giving power of the Holy Spirit.

Suicide is murder.

Abortion, euthanasia, and genocide are premeditated forms of murder that stem from a diminished view of the sanctity of life. Nevertheless, another premeditated form of killing also results from a low valuation of life. It is suicide. Those who contemplate this action are placing a low value on something that God values very highly—their own life.

In 1997, suicide was the eighth leading cause of death in the United States. The total number of suicide deaths was 30,535. Suicides outnumbered homicides (19,846) by 3 to 2. There were twice as many deaths due to suicide than deaths due to AIDS (16,516).

Suicide by firearms was the most common method for both men and women, accounting for 58 percent of all suicides. The highest suicide rates were for white men over 85. But what is especially sad is that suicide is not uncommon among America's youth. Suicide was the third leading cause of death among young people 15 to 24 years of age. There were even 303 suicides among children ages 10 to 14.[11]

Clearly suicide is a sign that Satan has managed to convince a person that all hope is lost. But the Bible says that Satan is a liar. He has come to "steal and kill and destroy" (John 10:10). But Jesus came to give abundant life! If the thought of harming yourself enters your mind, please pray, quote Scripture, and listen to praise and worship music. This way your mind will be filled with hope. As you meditate on God and His Word, Satan and his evil schemes will be defeated.

Domestic violence may lead to murder.

In addition to the forms of murder we have already reviewed, the problem of domestic violence is also a front-page issue. Domestic violence, when it turns to murder, is somewhat different from the other forms of killing we have looked at. It is typically not premeditated. It often happens in the heat of passion.

One of the startling statistics now surfacing is this: "During the Vietnam era 58,000 American service persons died from combat-related injuries. During those same years, 54,000 women in the United States were murdered by their husbands, ex-husbands, or boyfriends." Court records reveal that men who murder their female partners receive a prison sentence of only two to six years. Women who kill their partners get an average prison sentence of 15 years.[12] The inequity reflects badly on our judicial system.

Like all the other social problems we have looked at thus far, the root of domestic violence is the absence of Christ's Spirit in the heart of the murderer. Paul remarks, "As the church submits to Christ, so you wives must submit to your husbands in everything. And you husbands must love your wives with the same love Christ showed the church. He gave up His life for her...In the same way, husbands ought to love their wives as they love their own bodies. For a man is actually loving himself when he loves his wife. No one hates his own body but lovingly cares for it, just as Christ cares for His body, which is the church" (Ephesians 5:24,25,28,29). If we follow the biblical guideline for marriage relationships, domestic violence will not occur.

Anger can be murder of the heart.

Do you remember this old saying: "Sticks and stones may break my bones, but words will never hurt me"? It is wrong. Words can cut very deeply and leave a wound that festers long after skin and bones are healed. Jesus was acutely aware of this. He knew the power of words to heal and to harm, and He warns us about it in the Sermon on the Mount. "You have heard that the law of Moses says, 'Do not murder. If you commit murder, you are subject to judgment.' But I say, if you are angry with someone, you are subject to judgment! If you call someone an idiot, you are in danger of being brought before the high council. And if you curse someone, you are in danger of the fires of hell'" (Matthew 5:21,22).

Jesus knew many of His followers obeyed the letter of the law but had allowed their hatred and contempt for others to ferment in their hearts and spill out of their mouths. Once anger stews, it turns to bitterness. Once bitterness takes root it grows into hatred. And once hatred is allowed to grow, it may become an act of violence. But Jesus knew that even if it never leads to violence, words can still kill.

The New Testament says, "The tongue is a small thing, but what enormous damage it can do...People can tame all kinds of animals and birds and reptiles and fish, but no one can tame the tongue. It is an uncontrollable evil, full of deadly poison" (James 3:5,7,8).

Careless words spoken in haste can damage a relationship beyond repair. But more than that, they can also damage a soul beyond repair, and according to the words of our Lord, you could be guilty of violating the sacred commandment to honor life by not watching your tongue. God gave us two ears and one mouth. We should listen twice as much as we speak. Our tongues can be either a blessing or a curse. The choice is ours. We can choose to uplift or to degrade, abuse, or kill with our words. Those who uplift will form deep lifelong friendships, nurture a family life that respects and adores each member, and develop bonds with people who remember the words of kindness spoken to them.

Television and Murder

As sinful humans, we do not need much influence to do the things that we abhor. Are you surprised that murder statistics are escalating? Americans are becoming more and more desensitized to murder through the influence of television.

Forty years ago, former FCC chairman Newton Minow made his famous speech in which he classified television as a "vast wasteland." He was definitely ahead of his time. Through the medium of television, the average child in America today will view 25,000 murders by the age of 18!

Minow, who is now a lawyer based in Chicago, feels as though things are only getting worse. "In 1961 I worried that my children would not benefit much from television," he told an audience at Columbia University in 1991. "[Now] I worry that my grandchildren actually will be harmed by it."[13]

Television is a neutral tool. What we do with it determines its benefit or harm. Today's benefit may best be found in turning the TV off more often and utilizing that time to write a network and tell the directors what types of entertainment you would like to see and support. Who knows—the silent box may even inspire you to engage in a little daytime drama with your own family.

Amazing Grace

Society has a way of ranking sin in order of importance. We think, *A lie is bad, but not too bad. Adultery is worse, but permitted if you can get away with it. But murder is unquestionably wrong, particularly if the murderer is a serial killer. There is no way that a multiple murderer could ever be redeemed.*

But did you know that it is no harder for God to forgive a murderer than it is for Him to pardon a person who cheated on his taxes? Just look at these real-life examples of brutal killers who found favor with God.

Convicted killer David Berkowitz, known as "Son of Sam," went on a notorious murder spree in the 1970s that left six dead and terrorized thousands of New Yorkers. Berkowitz planted cryptic letters at murder scenes which he signed "Son of Sam." They were filled with satanic symbolism used to bait police and panic the public. He said a satanic cult was behind the murders, which he called "sacrifices to the devil."

Berkowitz is now serving six 25-year sentences in a Sullivan County prison in New York. The *New York Daily News* reports that today

Berkowitz is a mild-mannered prison preacher and model inmate. He uses the 16 cents an hour he earns as a jail janitor to send Bibles overseas. Berkowitz said he became a believer in 1988 when a fellow inmate gave him a Bible, which changed his life.

Berkowitz said about his crimes in an interview, "I am so very sorry that it happened. People who didn't deserve to die have lost their lives."[14]

Westley Allan Dodd, a brutal child torturer and rapist, was executed on January 5, 1989, for three murders in Washington State. Before he died, Dodd requested that he be killed in the same way he had killed one victim. When he first waived all appeals, he said he knew he must be killed. His hanging, the first in the country in twenty-eight years, spurred a national debate on the cruelty of that method of capital punishment.

Can you imagine a man beating, raping, and killing children? How could God ever forgive such a man?

Dodd testified that he became a Christian shortly before his execution. In his final statements, he said there was a way to stop sex offenders. "Turn to the Lord and you will find peace."[15]

"It's all right. I'll see you in heaven," murderer John Sterling Gardner told friends before he was executed by lethal injection in North Carolina. Gardner was convicted in 1982 for armed robberies and three murders he committed in a six-week crime spree. In 1991 he received Christ as his Savior when he considered a Christian friend's execution. Soon after, he met Raleigh businessman C. A. Dillon at a Prison Fellowship death row seminar. Dillon became Gardner's Bible study leader and close friend.

Dillon told the *Greensboro Daily News & Record* that Gardner accepted punishment for his crimes as God's will and that the two men held a communion service on the day before the execution. Gardner regularly said, "I'm grateful that I got put in prison. If I were not here, I would not have found Jesus."[16]

Karla Faye Tucker was executed in Texas on February 3, 1998. She was the first woman since the Civil War to be executed in the Texas prison system. Her crime? Along with Daniel Garrett, she killed Dean and Deborah Thornton. She swung the pickax.

But something miraculous happened to Karla Faye during her fourteen years on death row. Soon after her arrest, she learned the truth that God loves even the vilest sinner and that He pardons completely the person who asks Him for forgiveness. Karla Faye said in an interview a month before her execution, "I asked [God] to forgive me and I knew I needed forgiveness. And I knew I had done something really horrible. But I think right at that moment what mostly hit me was His love. His love. It just surrounded me."[17] In that moment, the murderer became a child of God.

Evangelist Mordecai Ham was a great preacher who was responsible for leading Dr. Billy Graham to the Lord. In 1910 during a Texas revival meeting led by Ham, a man in the congregation was overcome by the love and mercy of God. He had killed four men and never dreamed God could care for him. This man was so touched by the gospel that he stood up during that revival and shouted, "Saved! Saved! Saved!"

Jack Scofield, the musician for the revival, was so moved by this joyful outburst that he used those words to write a popular hymn with that name the next afternoon. The inspiration for this widely sung hymn came from the enthusiastic gratitude of a four-time murderer who found the grace of God.[18]

These stories are testimonies to God's amazing grace! We read in Colossians 1:13,14, "[God] has rescued us from the one who rules in the kingdom of darkness, and He has brought us into the Kingdom of His dear Son. God has purchased our freedom with His blood and has forgiven all our sins." Who wrote these words? Paul, who once was a murderer himself! Yet his words apply to all people, regardless of their sin. Jesus paid the full penalty for all our sins. He took upon Himself our guilt and condemnation so we can know blessed forgiveness and peace with God.

You may be reading this book and wondering if God can pardon the things you have done. If God through Jesus Christ can show grace to the types of people I have just mentioned, certainly He can forgive you. If you have not made a decision to receive Christ as your Lord and Savior, do so before you put down this book. Then live a life of faithful obedience to Him and you will experience His forgiveness, love, peace, joy, freedom, and a life worth living.

In our modern world, everyone considers murder a deep wrong. But we do not feel such a great consensus about the subject of the next commandment—adultery. Once again, God's Word is clear about His standard for our attitudes and actions regarding marital fidelity.

LIFE APPLICATION

Set Your Heart's Gauge

Commit the following verses to memory. Then, when you are tempted to turn your spiritual focus away from God to other things, recall these commands from God.

- Exodus 20:13—"Do not murder."

- 1 John 3:15—"Anyone who hates another Christian is really a murderer at heart. And you know that murderers don't have eternal life within them."

Gauge Your Spiritual Growth

Ask yourself the following questions. If one or more areas pose problems for you, ask God how you can deal with them through the power of the Holy Spirit.

- Who in your circle of acquaintances do you hate? What would God want you to do about your feelings?

- What are your beliefs about abortion? Do they reflect God's value for every person He has created in His own image?

- What do you believe about capital punishment and wartime killing? Have you ever searched the Scriptures to check out your beliefs?

- Where do you stand on euthanasia? Could you explain to someone why it is murder rather than compassionate killing?

- Have you ever had thoughts of suicide? If so, what plans do you have to circumvent these feelings?

Walk in the Power of the Holy Spirit

From the questions above, consider the areas that are out of control in your life. Only God can give peace and victory over thoughts and words of anger and hate. Read Colossians 1:13,14. Claim God's promise of victory over Satan's dark kingdom. Then, in prayer commit yourself to handling in God's power your temptations to be angry and hate others. Whenever thoughts or words come up that are contrary to what God commands, immediately reaffirm your commitment to walk by faith rather than by emotions.

TWELVE

DO NOT COMMIT ADULTERY

I t can never happen to me!" Have you ever said this to yourself about committing adultery? But marital unfaithfulness can happen to anyone. It has been said that adultery is more often the sin of a fool than that of the wicked. Many men and women fall into this sin because they are foolish enough to think they are immune to sexual temptation. Christian or non-Christian, weak or strong, anyone who thinks he can never fall is merely fooling himself.

Not too many years ago, a best-selling author and president of a major Christian organization was admired and respected by many believers throughout the world. While visiting a college campus to give the commencement speech, he struck up a conversation with a member of that school board. After some pleasantries, the new acquaintance asked, "If Satan were to blow you out of the water, how do you think he would do it?"

"I'm not sure I know. All sorts of ways, I suppose; but I know there's one way he wouldn't get me."

"What's that?" asked the board member.

"He'd never get me in the area of my personal relationships. That's one place where I have no doubt I'm as strong as you can get," replied the Christian leader.

Yet just a few years later, he was involved in an adulterous relationship that shattered his ministry, his marriage, and his life.[1]

This is a reminder of Satan's cunning ability to tear down and destroy the most effective Christian leaders. Satan is crafty and powerful. That is why Paul wrote, "Let him who thinks he stands take heed lest he fall" (1 Corinthians 10:12, NASB).

Satan knows how to use our God-given sex drives to lead us astray. He is a master manipulator whose purpose is to kill, hurt, and destroy. There is nothing he would like more than for us to violate our sacred marriage vows of fidelity.

Even at nearly eighty years of age, I must be aware of my own weaknesses and tendency toward depravity. I know I am capable of any sin and must not relax my vigil. Since the beginning of Campus Crusade for Christ, it has been my policy never to be alone with a woman other than Vonette. It is not that I fear women, but rather I fear my own potential to fall into sin. In addition, I am aware that the picture of meeting privately with a woman can convey something improper. Far too many people look to me for spiritual leadership to permit that to happen.

Over my fifty-five years of following our Lord, I have prayed, "God, if there is even a chance I might be unfaithful to Vonette, break her heart, and bring dishonor to your holy name, please take my life before it happens." Then I claim the promise of 1 Corinthians 10:13 about receiving strength from God to resist temptation: "Remember that the temptations that come into your life are no different from what others experience. And God is faithful. He will keep the temptation from becoming so strong that you can't stand up against it. When you are tempted, he will show you a way out so that you will not give in to it."

Even though I have been married since 1948 to the most wonderful woman in the world to me, whom I love dearly, I dare not underestimate the power of Satan to deceive me if I cease even for a moment to abide in Christ.

But what about sex before marriage? People tend to view adultery and fornication as wholly distinct sins. Adultery is an act of sexual intercourse with someone other than one's own spouse. Fornication, on the other hand, is an act of illicit sexual intercourse between unmarried persons. Thus, many people feel that they are not in violation of the sixth commandment against adultery if they commit fornication. Unfortunately, these people are splitting hairs.

While it is true that adultery and fornication represent different sins, more unites them than separates them.

In the Bible, the Greek word used for adultery, adulterer, and adulterous is *moichos*. It stands for one who has sexual intercourse with the spouse of another. Hebrews 13:4 uses this word: "Let marriage be held in honor among all, and let the marriage bed be undefiled; for fornicators and adulterers God will judge" (NASB).

The Greek word used for fornicator or fornication, which denotes illicit sexual intercourse, is *porneia*. The word, which also appears in Hebrews 13:4, refers equally to immoral sexual behavior for either married or unmarried couples. Clearly, every act of adultery includes fornication. But does every act of fornication include adultery?

Note that Hebrews 13:4 refers to both "fornicators and adulterers" when issuing a command to keep the marriage bed undefiled. The point is that both fornication and adultery are outside of marriage and are therefore viewed by God as an attack upon His intended design. The intention of the sixth commandment is to protect the institution of marriage. Fornication breaks the spirit of the sixth commandment because it represents sex outside the marriage covenant. Therefore, the sixth commandment is an all-inclusive directive to avoid *all* sexual immorality, including homosexuality, lesbianism, sodomy, pornography, and any other distortion of God's sexual plan for marriage.

Reasons to Avoid Adultery

The seventh commandment is very simple and straightforward. It reads, "Do not commit adultery" (Exodus 20:14). No flowery words or poetry, just a clear directive from God Almighty. Do not do it. Period.

But why is God so concerned about our sexual purity? After all, He gave us our desires and passions. Why does a prohibition against marital infidelity make the top ten of moral laws? There are many reasons, but let me share several important ones with you.

Adultery is dangerous because it is a sin against our bodies.
God designed us to leave our parents and "cleave" to one another in marriage: "As the Scriptures say, 'A man leaves his father and mother and is joined to his wife, and the two are united into one.' This is a great mystery, but it is an illustration of the way Christ and the church are one" (Ephesians 5:31,32). In marriage, this means that two people become *one flesh.* Adultery causes a severing of this one-flesh relationship, resulting in great harm to our bodies.

The Bible explains why adultery is so damaging, "Don't you realize that your bodies are actually parts of Christ? Should a man take his body, which belongs to Christ, and join it to a prostitute? Never! And don't you know that if a man joins himself to a prostitute, he becomes one body with her? For as the Scriptures say, 'The two are united into one.' But the person who is joined to the Lord becomes one spirit with Him. Run away from sexual sin! No other sin so clearly affects the body as this one does. For sexual immorality is sin against your own body" (1 Corinthians 6:15–18).

To illustrate the effect of adultery upon the body, just imagine what you would have to do to give your arm to another person. Naturally, you would need to sever it from your body. In a similar way, when you give your body to another man or woman in adultery, you must sever the one-flesh relationship you share with your spouse. The Bible says that this always brings great suffering to our bodies.

One way adultery physically harms our bodies is through disease. Today the rate of sexually transmitted diseases is alarming. Although the number of newly reported cases of AIDS has gone down slightly, the overall number of AIDS cases is significant. As of December 1999, the total number of adults and adolescents diagnosed with AIDS was 733,374. The total number of deaths from AIDS in the U.S. was 430,441.[2]

More than twenty Sexually Transmitted Diseases (STDs) have now been identified, and each year they affect more than 13 million men and women in this country. The annual comprehensive cost of STDs in the United States is estimated to be well in excess of $10 billion.

Genital herpes affects an estimated 60 million Americans. Approximately 500,000 new cases of this incurable viral infection develop annually. Approximately 400,000 cases of gonorrhea are reported each year.[3]

These frightening statistics are proof that a man reaps what he sows! What is the message? Flee from adultery!

Adultery is dangerous because marriage is an earthly reflection of the relationship Christ has with His Church.

Christ has made a covenant relationship with the Church—a blood oath—something He is incapable of breaking. That is why the Church is often referred to as "the bride of Christ." Christ woos us like a man woos a woman to be His bride. He treats the Church with the highest regard because it is *His* body.

Paul writes, "Husbands ought to love their wives as they love their own bodies. For a man is actually loving himself when he loves his wife. No one hates his own body but lovingly cares for it, just as Christ cares for His body, which is the church. And we are His body" (Ephesians 5:28–30).

Nevertheless, not all men love their wives as they should. Ted Engstrom tells the story of a disgruntled husband named Joe. He was ready to divorce his wife of three years but was so angry with her that he wanted to not only leave her but hurt her as well. Joe was so serious about his intent to inflict emotional damage that he visited a psychologist and sought his professional opinion as to how he could most severely hurt his wife.

The wise counselor sized up the situation and gave the following advice. "This is the perfect solution. Go home and start treating your wife like a goddess. Give her your undivided attention, take her out to eat, help around the house, compliment her every move, and just treat her like a queen. Do this for two months, then just pack your bags and walk out. When you leave her after treating her so well, she will literally crumble."

Joe thought it was a wonderful scheme so he put it into practice as soon as he got home. For two months he gave his wife the best he had to offer. After this eight-week setup, the marriage counselor gave

Joe a call. He asked, "Well, did she crumble when you left?"

Joe shot back, "Are you kidding? I wouldn't leave this woman for the world. I now have the best marriage a man could want. My wife is a goddess!"

The counselor hung up the phone with the deep satisfaction that he had accomplished what he set out to achieve.[4]

When we treat our spouse like a prized treasure, the result is a beautiful and fulfilling marriage. This marriage relationship then serves as a picture to our children and our friends and neighbors of how much Christ loves us.

Adultery is dangerous because of its consequences.

Adultery does tremendous harm to a marriage. It tears husband and wife apart. To illustrate, glue two pieces of paper together. These pieces of paper represent two people who get married—they have become one. Then one spouse decides to leave the other for someone else. To show the result, pull the two pieces of paper apart. What happens? Both pieces rip and are destroyed. No matter how much care is taken in removing them from each other, they are both damaged. This is a vivid picture of the consequences of adultery.

The aftermath of adultery includes broken trust, devastating pain, divorce, and children caught in the crossfire between feuding parents! The list goes on and on from one single act of infidelity. Some of these hurts may never heal.

Divorce also affects the children in a large way. According to an article in *USA Today*, "The statistics on the fallout of divorce are sobering: Kids in single-parent homes do far worse on a variety of measures of well-being than kids in intact families. The children of divorce also run greater risks of dropping out of school, having behavior problems and becoming single parents themselves."[5] These children are the innocent victims of their parents breaking the eighth commandment. The harm is so great that it is impossible to fully evaluate the damage.

So we must heed the Bible's warning: Run from adultery! Flee! Do not even entertain thoughts of unfaithfulness. Although God's forgiveness will be available to anyone who repents of adultery (just as with all sins), Scripture warns that once we head down the path of sin, the consequences are still inescapable. This unique physical and spiritual bond was designed by God to belong only to a husband and wife. Betraying it leads to broken families, heartache, and disease.

A Culture of Immorality

I do not have to tell you what our society says about the seventh commandment. Many spouses treat their marriage like a pair of old shoes. After they are broken in and comfortable, it is time for a new, exciting pair. Explore. Look around. Do not confine yourself to one sexual partner. In art, literature, film, television, and almost every form of human expression today, adultery is presented as a simple change of heart between two consenting adults. This is a diabolical trick of Satan.

Television has greatly influenced America's growing tolerance of infidelity. The following findings are from a study conducted by a team from the University of California at Santa Barbara. The study is said to be the most comprehensive survey yet on television's sexual messages. The programs evaluated were broadcast between October 1997 and March 1998 on ABC, CBS, Fox, NBC, PBS, HBO, Lifetime, TNT, and USA.[6] According to a study of 1,351 shows, excluding newscasts and children's shows, 56 percent feature sexual references or behavior.

- The risks and responsibilities of sex are infrequently shown with fewer than one show in 10, or 9 percent of all shows with sexual content, including any mention of contraception, AIDS prevention, or related matters. Comedies score lowest with only 3 percent mentioning such matters.

- Soap operas (85 percent contain sexual content), movies (83 percent), and talk shows (78 percent) dwell on sex more insistently than other genres.

- Among dramas and newsmagazines, 58 percent feature sexual content, followed by comedies at 56 percent, and reality shows at 23 percent.

These statistics reveal a troubling trend toward cheapening the important role of sex in marriage. Giving ourselves to one another sexually implies a very deep trust. It is God's way of giving us the ultimate form of touch, an intimate connection that takes great vulnerability. Adultery breaks that trust. And one single act of infidelity is all it takes. For some, once that trust is broken, it may never return.

The Curse of No-Fault Divorce

Unfortunately, the world has an "answer" for adultery—to make separating easier through no-fault divorce. But no-fault divorce is now being fought in many states because of its disastrous effect. Intended to provide options to both couples facing divorce, no-fault divorce only empowers the spouse who wishes to leave and has the resources to do so, leaving the other spouse helpless, overwhelmed, and facing hardship.

These laws are very lenient. "It is easier to divorce my wife of 26 years than to fire someone I hired one week ago," said Randall Hekman, former president of the Michigan Family Forum and a former judge. Before no-fault laws, any spouse who wanted a divorce had to prove the other was to blame through adultery or some form of destructive behavior. Today, no-fault divorce laws allow a marriage to be dissolved for almost any reason, even if only one party wants a divorce. According to a study in *Journal of Marriage and the Family*, the divorce rate has increased in 45 states since no-fault laws passed.[7]

An Old Law for the Common Good

Although American culture is becoming more lenient in its views on adultery, the fact remains that adultery is still a federal crime. Consensual or not, adultery is illegal in the U.S. military. For example, Major General David Hale, a two-star general, was accused of committing adultery with four officers' wives while in command of a NATO base in Turkey. Rather than face court-martial, General Hale, who denies any wrongdoing, took early retirement.

Rear Admiral John Scudi, a 54-year-old married admiral serving at the U.S. Navy's headquarters in the Pentagon, was charged with having two mistresses. According to naval officials, one of the Admiral's jilted lovers exposed a back-door business deal involving government contracts he had with her. Scudi, a Navy man for 32 years, was relieved of his duties and was charged with two counts of adultery as well as violating ethics rules.

Although rarely enforced, adultery is also illegal in many U.S. states. Here are two examples:

- California: "Adultery [is] a felony... punishable by imprisonment in the state prison not exceeding 5 years."

- Colorado: "Any sexual intercourse by a married person other than with that person's spouse is adultery, which is prohibited."

These laws reflect a time in this nation when the seventh commandment was considered so important that people believed its enforcement ensured public safety. Legislators knew that adultery carried the power to destroy the family, which is the basic building block of society. They realized that without offering protections to the family, a society simply cannot prosper.

Are Christians Exempt?

Perhaps you believe that adultery is a problem for unbelievers, but that surely Christians obey the seventh commandment. Not so. According to author Kirby Anderson, "There is growing evidence that adultery is equally a problem in Christian circles. An article in a 1997 issue of *Newsweek* magazine noted that various surveys suggest that as many as 30 percent of male Protestant ministers have had sexual relationships with women other than their wives.

Anderson, editor of *Marriage, Family & Sexuality*, writes, "The *Journal of Pastoral Care* in 1993 reported a survey of Southern Baptist pastors in which 14 percent acknowledged they had engaged in 'sexual behavior inappropriate to a minister.' It also reported that 70 percent had counseled at least one woman who had had intercourse with a minister.

"A 1988 survey of nearly 1,000 Protestant clergy by *Leadership* magazine found that 12 percent admitted to sexual intercourse outside of marriage, and that 23 percent had done something sexually inappropriate with someone other than their spouse. The researchers also interviewed nearly 1,000 lay-subscribers to *Christianity Today* who were not pastors. They found the numbers were nearly double: 45 percent indicated having done something sexually inappropriate, and 23 percent having extramarital intercourse."[8]

How tragic that the Christian community is not leading the charge for preserving a safe, wholesome atmosphere for the family and reflecting Christ's love through marital bonds!

The Anatomy of a Sin

What is there about adultery that makes so many people so susceptible? Next to eating and self-preservation, sexual desire is our strongest impulse. Most often, adultery is not just a slip-up, but a series of bad decisions that can lead to ruin. Adultery, like most sins, starts in the mind, and slowly that small voice within urges us to step just a little closer to the line until we have crossed it.

The story of King David, in 2 Samuel 11, is an example of the anatomy of adultery. Here are the steps:

The first step toward adultery is idleness. David's adultery took place in the spring during the time when kings and nations were accustomed to waging war. But rather than personally leading the army into battle, David sent his trusted Commander of the Army, Joab, in his place. Verse 1 says, "But David stayed behind in Jerusalem." King David should have been involved in the battle, but instead his unwillingness left him with time on his hands.

The old saying is "idle hands are the devil's playground." Never allow yourself to be caught in a situation where your mind is allowed to wander for long. Occupy it with the things of God. Stand firm in the battle against all evil. As much as possible, keep His business in the front of your mind.

The second step toward adultery is lust. Verse 2 says that while David was on the roof of the palace enjoying the cool of the evening, he spotted a woman bathing. The second David saw Bathsheba, he should have turned his eyes away from her.

Job writes, "I made a covenant with my eyes not to look with lust upon a young woman" (Job 31:1). It is not wrong to look at a woman, but it is wrong to look at her lustfully. This is where David failed. His look turned to a stare, which quickly led him into temptation.

The third step toward adultery is temptation. Unbridled lust leads to temptation. The apostle James warns, "Each one is tempted when he is carried away and enticed by his own lust" (James 1:14, NASB). The words "carried away" convey the sense of being "taken captive." The fact that lust easily leads to temptation is also seen in James 1:15, "Then when lust has conceived..." What does lust conceive? Verse 14 says it conceives temptation.

The fourth step toward adultery is the birth of sin. James says, "Then when lust has conceived, it gives birth to sin" (James 1:15, NASB). Sin is born the moment temptation prompts us to take some form of action. Taking action is what David did. "David sent messengers and took her" (2 Samuel 11:4, NASB).

Could David have stopped himself from taking action? By step four, it is highly unlikely David could have regained control. Notice James does not say lust "might" give birth to sin, rather he says, "It gives birth to sin." This means David's opportunity to save himself was back at step two—before lust turned to temptation and temptation gave birth to sin.

Let me repeat. James says that once lust conceives temptation, it *will* give birth to sin! How many men and women have wandered too far down sin's path unable to find their way back?

The fifth step related to adultery is the fullness of sin. Some people wonder if there is a difference between thoughts of adultery and the act itself. There is a difference. Although lust is sinful, James 1:15 distinguishes *lust* from the *act* of adultery. In other words, there are *degrees* of sin. Once David committed adultery, his sin was complete. Sin is not complete until adultery has been accomplished.

Paul makes a clear distinction between the "desire of the flesh" and carrying it out. Paul writes, "But I say, walk by the Spirit, and you will not carry out the desire of the flesh" (Galatians 5:16, NASB).

The sixth and final step related to adultery is death. James says, "And when sin is accomplished, it brings forth death" (James 1:15, NASB). Not only did David commit adultery, but also he conspired to kill Bathsheba's husband, Uriah the Hittite. David himself also suffered greatly as a consequence of his sin. Bathsheba became pregnant. Soon the prophet Nathan confronted the king, telling him that the child would die. He also warned David that his own son, Absalom, would attempt to overthrow his reign. David's life was never the same. The experience of David is a grim reminder that "the wages of sin is death, but the free gift of God is eternal life through Christ Jesus our Lord" (Romans 6:23).

Avoiding Adultery

Now that we have examined the devastating progression of adultery, we know more clearly how important it is to avoid this sin. Keeping in mind the following facts can help us resist temptation and remain faithful to our partner.

Guard the attitude of your heart.

As with all Ten Commandments, the real issue is what goes on in our hearts. Jesus said, "You have heard that it was said, 'You shall not commit adultery'; but I say to you, that everyone who looks on a woman to lust for her has committed adultery with her already in his heart" (Matthew 5:27,28, NASB). It is our heart attitude that directs our actions.

When spouses allow their hearts to wander away into lust, they become like the dog who was trying to dig under the stove. When his owner searched under the appliance, he found that the dog had been digging for one piece of old dog food that had somehow rolled under there. What was so amazing was that the dog dish, full of fresh food, was just inches away from the dog's nose. Yet the dog still went after that morsel under the dirty stove.

Anytime you are tempted and your heart is drawn away from your spouse, Satan is trying to influence you. Do not allow yourself to dwell on sexual thoughts that do not glorify God. They are like the morsel of food that rolled under the dirty stove—not worth entertaining.

Sometimes married people can find themselves obsessively attracted to a person other than their spouse. It starts with what can seem like an uncontrollable desire just to be near the other person. The feelings can be so strong that the married person can mistakenly assume he or she has fallen in love with someone else. But in reality, the person has been overtaken by the temptation of obsession which Satan hopes will lead to adultery and divorce. If you are experiencing something like this, do not allow yourself to be deceived into believing your feelings are genuine. Ask God to free you from the alluring attraction.

Adultery is more than a physical act; it is also a spiritual state of mind. Never look at another man or woman and ask, "Did I marry the wrong person?" and then think your inclination is of God. It is not. It is *always* of the devil!

Do not rationalize your sin.

One of the biggest mistakes we make is to think that we are immune from adultery. But given the right circumstances, we are capable of almost anything. Most adulterous relationships begin as friendships. A friendship may start as a result of one person offering comfort to someone of the opposite sex during a time of trial. Or perhaps it began due to similar interests or hobbies.

Work environments are good places for friendships to develop. Friendships are all right. The problem is when people begin to see each other in a different light. This is why it is important to create "boundaries" for ourselves to make sure that friendships remain less than intimate. Emotional attachments can quickly lead to more, especially when our needs at home are not being met.

Do not underestimate the power of your sexuality.

We are sexual beings, so there is nothing wrong with the feelings we have. We have a deep, innate desire to procreate and God put it there to accomplish His purpose that we "fill the earth and subdue it" (Genesis 1:28). Sexual desires are a beautiful gift of God, but they can be distorted by Satan. Do not dismiss them. They are only evil when we dwell on them in a wrong way and eventually act upon them outside of marriage.

Do not discount Satan's desire to destroy your marriage.

Satan knows your weaknesses and will play every trick in the book to get you to stray from your vows. But where there is temptation, there is always a way out. As I said earlier, 1 Corinthians 10:13 holds the key to avoiding temptation: "Remember that the temptations that come into your life are no different from what others experience. And God is faithful. He will keep the temptation from becoming so strong that you can't stand up against it. When you are tempted, He will show you a way out so that you will not give in to it." As a new Christian I memorized this wonderful promise from God. Whenever I am tempted I claim God's promise. On thousands of occasions He has kept His promise and by His grace I have never been unfaithful to my beloved Vonette, after 52 years of marriage.

God gives us to each other in marriage to love with our whole bodies. The Word says, "Do not deprive each other of sexual relations" (1 Corinthians 7:5). Use this gift that God gave you and you will have a fruitful, loving relationship. Deny it, and one of the marriage partners will start looking for other ways to satisfy their deep need for intimate connection.

Heed the warning signs about inappropriate relationships.
Because your mate knows you better than anyone else, listen when he or she warns you of an inappropriate relationship. If your wife or husband senses that a relationship you have with a person of the opposite sex is not right, end it. God gives this early warning sign to guard against adultery. Your mate's sensitivity should be one loud signal.

Another sign is if you notice that you look forward to seeing a coworker in a meeting or if you are intentionally running into a certain person to whom you are attracted. Realize the Holy Spirit is saying to you, "This could be leading to something very inappropriate." When you find yourself doing this, flee, run away, and do not look back. It will save your marriage.

The Way Back

Let me say a word to the person who has already broken the seventh commandment. Many Christian couples who are experiencing the aftermath of adultery ask, "Must we be divorced because of adultery?" The answer is no. Dr. Paul D. Meier, a noted Christian psychiatrist, writes, "Divorce is never necessary—not even in cases where adultery is involved."

He gives the options for this situation. "There are only three choices for a person in an unhappy marriage. The distressed partner can: 1. divorce—America's greatest cop-out (and by far the most immature choice); 2. tough out the marriage without working to improve it (another immature decision but not quite as irresponsible as divorce); 3. maturely face up to personal hang-ups and choose to build an intimate marriage out of the existing one (the really mature choice to make)."

He continues, "In those cases where a couple takes the easy way out, they run away from facing their own hang-ups by divorcing and remarrying. Then there are four miserable people instead of just two." He then concludes, "In all the cases where both marriage partners were willing to come together for at least four sessions of counseling (even if they had already filed for divorce), *not a single couple ended up getting a divorce.*"[9]

Not a single one! Divorce is not the only alternative; it is only the poorest one! Healing can take place as long as we are willing to commit ourselves into God's care and to confess our sins. God offers grace to those who have already committed adultery.

The results of healing an improper sexual relationship are incredible. Mary had rebelled against the preaching and strict lifestyle of her Nazarene father, a godly pastor. She lived with her boyfriend in open defiance of her biblical training. Now God was disciplining her because of her disobedience. She was miserable and filled with hate and resentment when a mutual friend brought her to my office for counsel.

I shared with Mary that just as a loving father disciplines a disobedient child, so God in His love for us disciplines us when we are disobedient. Through tears, she sobbed, "I want to get right with God!"

We cried together for thirty minutes while her boyfriend waited outside my open office. Then we prayed together and Mary found God's grace in a time of desperate need. As you have been reading this chapter, perhaps God has been speaking to you. If you are like Mary—personally miserable due to an improper relationship—realize that God is using His discipline as a way to restore you. What if God permitted you to enjoy your sin? That would show that you are not His child because God disciplines His children. Discipline is a sure sign that God cares for your welfare and still wants His very best for you. If you are enjoying your sin, you are not a true believer.

If you are enmeshed in some stage of adultery, take time right now to confess your sin. God will forgive you. Next, go to your spouse with the confidence that he or she truly loves you and share your failure. Then together go to Christ and ask Him to heal the fracture in your marriage and to help both of you see what went wrong that led to the problem. Immediately seek counsel as a couple. A competent, trained counselor can advise you on practical steps to take that will strengthen your marriage. You may want to investigate FamilyLife, a ministry of Campus Crusade for Christ, led by Dennis Rainey and his fine staff. Plan today to attend a FamilyLife Marriage Conference in your area.[10] Your marriage will be so much better for it. Thousands of marriages headed toward divorce and disaster have been saved and healed.

Without question, breaking the seventh commandment reaps devastating consequences. It destroys the most intimate relationship we will ever have.

Breaking the eighth commandment also leads to painful results—but in a much different way. Yet many people excuse themselves in their failure to keep it. As we will see in the next chapter, we must guard carefully against the temptation to steal.

LIFE APPLICATION

Set Your Heart's Gauge

Commit the following verses to memory. Then, when you are tempted to turn your spiritual focus away from God to other things, recall these commands from God.

- Exodus 20:14—"Do not commit adultery."

- 1 Corinthians 6:18—"Run away from sexual sin! No other sin so clearly affects the body as this one does. For sexual immorality is sin against your own body."

- Proverbs 6:32—"The man who commits adultery is an utter fool, for he destroys his own soul."

Gauge Your Spiritual Growth

Ask yourself the following questions. If one or more areas pose problems for you, ask God how you can deal with them through the power of the Holy Spirit.

- Does your commitment to marriage reflect that of Christ to His Church? What practical examples can you give?

- When considering your actions toward your spouse over the past week, are you taking care of him or her as well as you do your own body?

- When you have thoughts that could lead to adultery, what do you do to counteract them?

- Are you watching questionable films and TV programs? Are you reading books that affirm or undermine marriage?

- What are your views on divorce? Do they match God's perspective?

- Do you sometimes allow yourself to view pornographic material? What could you do to avoid that temptation?

- Are you nurturing a relationship that could lead to adultery? What boundaries do you need to set for yourself so you will not put your-self in temptation's path?

- If you have committed adultery, have you resolved the issue through confession to God and to your spouse?

- When thinking about adultery, have you ever shrugged your shoulders and said, "That could never happen to me"? Are you too complacent about the power of your own sexuality?

- Do you ever look forward to meeting with someone of the opposite sex to whom you are attracted? Do you "unintentionally" run into this person frequently?

- Do you have a close relationship with someone of the same sex who can alert you to possible problems with inappropriate relationships of the opposite sex?

Walk in the Power of the Holy Spirit

This chapter gives several ways to avoid adultery. Spend some extra quiet time with God. Ask Him to reveal any problems in the following areas:

- Having a wrong attitude of heart toward sexual temptations you experience

- Rationalizing the sin of inappropriate relationships

- Underestimating your own sexual drive

- Heeding warning signs about inappropriate relationships

Ask God to help you change any area that is not pleasing to Him.

THIRTEEN

DO NOT STEAL

Many years ago after one of my lectures on how to be filled with the Holy Spirit, a businessman approached me and shared his deep desire to experience the wonderful blessing of the Spirit-filled life. But every time he got down on his knees to pray to be filled with the Spirit, he was convicted about what he had stolen from his employer.

I immediately told him to confess his sin to God, then go to his employer and make restitution. He was terribly concerned that although he wanted to make things right, his employer would probably fire him. But he agreed to go.

When the man shared his dishonesty with his employer, he was absolutely shocked by his boss's response. His boss actually congratulated him for his honesty. Then his employer offered a plan that would take a small amount of what he had stolen out of the man's paycheck each week until all had been repaid. The result was that not only did the formerly dishonest man learn a valuable lesson through paying restitution, but also two days later he was by faith filled with the Holy Spirit!

The eighth commandment says, "Do not steal" (Exodus 20:15).

Interestingly, American culture has conflicting views on the topic. People do not want others stealing from them. In that way, they favor God's law because it serves them. Legislatures allocate millions each year to make sure the eighth commandment is enforced and thieves are punished.

But other forms of stealing are considered acceptable to many Americans. We agree that stealing someone's personal property and embezzling millions in a scam is wrong, but what about sending your insurance company an inflated claim or filing dishonest tax returns? Look at these statistics.

- Government figures show that $20 billion in taxes go uncollected every year from people who have underreported their incomes. According to a survey done for U.S. News & World Report, almost a quarter of American adults cheat on their income taxes.

- The auto insurance industry reports that fraudulent claims account for as much as $20 billion each year.

- Time magazine reported that American workers steal $40 billion per year from their employers by doing such things as lying about their hours, making personal long-distance calls, and taking home office supplies. That sum is ten times the cost of street crime.

- Companies lose up to $350 billion annually from employees taking dishonest sick days.[1]

- In 1995, retailers lost an estimated $30 billion to theft by employees and customers. Such shoplifting increases the cost of goods by as much as 15 percent.[2]

We can see only the obvious, but God knows our hearts and requires purity even when no one is watching. Subtle, unseen dishonesty is the real test of character.

What about Christians? Do we have higher standards in our honesty? Sadly, Christians are included among these crimes. Doug Sherman and William Hendricks write in Keeping Your Ethical Edge Sharp, "A growing body of research suggests that religious beliefs and convictions make little difference in the behavior of people on the job."[3]

But we often give mixed messages about honesty. A little boy got caught stealing pencils from school. When his father found out, he was enraged. He said, "Why'd you go and do something like that? If you need pencils just tell me . . . I can bring some home from work."

Why do we steal, defraud, and manipulate to our advantage? I think there are three basic reasons.

Stealing shows a lack of trust in God.
God is our Provider. If we truly trust Him to meet our needs, we do not need to cut corners, withhold our true income from the IRS, or steal anything. Jesus assures us, "So don't worry about having enough food or drink or clothing. Why be like the pagans who are so deeply concerned about these things? Your heavenly Father already knows all your needs, and He will give you all you need from day to day if you live for Him and make the Kingdom of God your primary concern" (Matthew 6:31–33).

Over the years, my staff and I have seen God's all-sufficiency and faithfulness displayed countless times. In the beginning years of this ministry when Campus Crusade for Christ was quite small, I was informed that we had an urgent need for $485. Since we never had any surplus funds—then or now, fifty years later—I began to pray about this need.

I was alone in the office praying on a Saturday morning when the mailman knocked. I reached the door just as he was leaving. He said, "It's a good thing you were here, or I wouldn't have been able to leave this letter." Then he handed me a registered letter.

I signed for the letter and went back into my office to continue praying. But first, I felt impressed to open the letter.

Inside, I discovered a bank note for $500 sent by a friend from Zurich, Switzerland, whose entire family had become followers of Christ through my personal ministry. I had prayed in faith, expecting God to answer my request for $485, and He did!

Through the years on thousands of occasions I have seen God provide finances in the midst of trying circumstances—in response to faith. Today, Campus Crusade for Christ has a yearly budget of more than $500 million, but there is not a penny left at the end of the day. God is always faithful to provide for our daily needs. He will do the same for you. Trust Him rather than taking what does not belong to you.

Stealing shows a lack of respect for others.

Jesus said, "'You must love the Lord your God with all your heart, all your soul, and all your mind.' This is the first and greatest commandment. A second is equally important: 'Love your neighbor as yourself'" (Matthew 22:37–39). Clearly, if you love your fellow human beings as God commands, you will not steal from them.

The eighth commandment applies to strangers and extends to corporations and governmental taxing authorities. You may think these are faceless, nameless entities, but they are actually made up of people like you with families, hopes, dreams, and fears. Do not be deceived into thinking they have such deep pockets that they will not miss the little bit you defraud from them.

God will not be mocked. His moral laws are as absolute and inviolate as the laws of physics. We will not escape God's notice if we steal in secret. Yet many people steal and cover up their theft. I once read about a developer who drained an old gravel pit before starting construction on that site. What he found was astonishing. At the bottom of the pit were a dozen almost-new cars in perfect condition. The local police traced the tags back to the owners and discovered all of them had claimed the cars had been stolen to collect on the insurance. The owners were prosecuted and jailed.

Stealing will result in consequences that you do not like. Hidden sin many times brings public shame.

Stealing shows we are feeling panic.

People do many unwise things when they get impatient or panicked. They feel as if they have no choice but to cut corners to make ends meet. But God always honors those who are patient and believe He will provide.

I know a young man in Texas who struggled for years until finally he had modest financial success. At the end of the year, he faced a rather large tax bill, so he scrimped and saved all he could to pay his taxes that April. But days before they were due, he discovered $3,000 he had forgotten to report. It was contract labor and the firm had not sent him any forms so if he did not report it, the IRS would be none the wiser.

He calculated that the extra income would mean another $750 in taxes. It would break him! He would have to borrow the money from family or friends who were not very supportive of his career choice. At that point, he could give in to his fears or he could trust God to help him solve the problem. He was tempted to just let it slide. But after he prayed, he concluded, "I have no choice but to pay it." He swallowed hard and reported the full amount.

The very next day, this faithful young man received a check for $750 from an old debt he had long forgotten. God does provide, if we let Him.

But perhaps you are thinking, *I would never steal. That temptation is not a problem for me!* Many of the things we do are other actions disguised as stealing. In our next section, we will examine some overt and some subtle ways of taking things from others.

How Do We Steal?

We can steal in many ways. Some are obvious, while others are not as apparent. Yet all of them are breaking God's moral laws. Let us look at several ways we can steal.

We steal by taking something that does not belong to us.
Years after becoming a Christian, St. Augustine realized his youthful in-discretions as a thief were wrong. He wrote in the *Confessions of St. Augustine:*

> Near our vineyard there was a pear tree, loaded with fruit, though the fruit was not particularly attractive either in color or in taste. I and some other wretched youth conceived the idea of shaking the pears off this tree and carrying them away. We set out late that night (having, as we usually did in our depraved way, gone on playing in the streets till that hour) and stole all the fruit that we could carry. And this was not to feed ourselves; we only tasted a few, then we threw the rest to the pigs. I had no wish to enjoy what I tried to get by theft; all my enjoyment was in the theft itself and in sin. Our real pleasure was in doing something that was not allowed.[4]

Today, many teenagers steal for the same reasons. An Ohio State University study measured moral development among adolescents. Psychology professor John Gibbs said more than 90 percent of the 323 teens studied, about half of whom were incarcerated delinquents, said stealing is wrong.

The most common reason they gave for not stealing was that they might get caught and punished. Other reasons included "the other person might get even" and "you might not need the item." A more mature perspective would be that stealing is wrong because it is against the law of God and hurts other people.[5]

Stealing is an unlawful attempt to gain wealth. There are many ways to steal besides shoplifting or taking towels from the hotel where you are staying. A few years ago a young Christian songwriter sent a song he had written to a well-known Christian singer/songwriter in hopes that he would perform it. Within weeks a letter arrived at his home from the artist thanking him for the submission, but also stating he had no need for the music.

Several months later, the young songwriter went to hear the Christian artist in concert. Just before the intermission, the artist performed a song he claimed to have written himself. To the astonishment of the young songwriter seated in the audience, it was *his song* that was performed!

Stealing is taking anything that does not belong to you or that you did not pay for—and that includes nonmaterial things like someone's reputation or copyrighted material. Taking the credit for someone else's work is stealing. Using "crib notes" during an important exam is stealing a grade. Ordering inferior materials for a job someone is paying top dollar for is stealing. Theft comes in many forms and is always wrong. But God asks the question, "What will a man be profited, if he gains the whole world, and forfeits his soul?" (Matthew 16:26, NASB). There is nothing in this world worth gaining that interferes with our future in heaven.

We steal by not paying our bills.
When Campus Crusade for Christ moved its headquarters from Arrowhead Springs in San Bernardino, California, to Orlando, Florida, we

were unable to lease or sell some of our property in San Bernardino. The buildings remained empty, yet every month we still had to make our mortgage payments.

I was counseled by some successful Christian businessmen to default the payments and allow the bank to repossess the property. After all, many businesses had done this during the economic downturn. Financially, we would be far better off, but that would be wrong since we had signed a contract with the bank. We purposed to trust God to help us pay the bills and sell the property in a way that would bring honor and glory to Him.

Of course, I was concerned over what might happen to the ministry's credit rating if we had walked away from our contractual responsibility. But the One I feared most was the Lord. I was convinced that there was no way God would continue to bless our labor for Him if we took the easy way out. We needed to do the right thing and God provided for our financial obligations. In fact, God blessed us abundantly. Campus Crusade for Christ prospered not only financially, but in many other ways. I honestly believe that if we had evaded our responsibility, God would have found a way to chasten us, and it would have taken many years to prove our integrity and regain our reputation.

Today, people think that paying what they owe is optional in some situations. Some illegally hook up cable television in their homes, rationalizing that it hurts no one. Others run up credit card bills and then neglect to pay when meeting the payments becomes difficult. Some allow their homes to go into foreclosure when, with sacrifice and perseverance, they could have repaid the loan. Bankruptcy and other financial loss programs were developed for people going through disastrous circumstances that cannot be solved any other way. As believers, we should trust God for our finances rather than defaulting on our bills.

We steal by not paying our tithe to God.
God said to disobedient Israel:

> "Should people cheat God? Yet you have cheated Me! But you ask, 'What do You mean? When did we ever cheat You?' You have cheated Me of the tithes and offerings due to Me. You are under a curse, for

your whole nation has been cheating Me. Bring all the tithes into the storehouse so there will be enough food in My Temple. If you do," says the LORD Almighty, "I will open the windows of heaven for you. I will pour out a blessing so great you won't have enough room to take it in! Try it! Let Me prove it to you!" (Malachi 3:8–10).

The word *tithe* comes from the old English word meaning "a tenth." Paying tithes means giving one-tenth of your earned income back to God. Now someone might ask, "How can I be robbing God by not paying my tithes? It is my money." But the Bible teaches that God is the one who owns all the world's wealth. David declared, "The earth is the LORD's, and everything in it. The world and all its people belong to Him" (Psalm 24:1).

Elsewhere, the Bible teaches that God owns all the gold and silver in the world: "The silver is mine, and the gold is mine, says the LORD Almighty" (Haggai 2:8). We think we own 100 percent of our money and are giving God 10 percent in tithes. However, the truth is that God owns 100 percent of the money in our possession and claims the return of only 10 percent. We are stewards; God is the owner. Failure to pay our tithes to God is nothing less than robbery.

Tom and Marti were newlyweds. They were just getting started in business and had all the expenses of setting up housekeeping. Soon they found their budget severely strained. In fact, the bills were piling up. Then they were challenged to tithe their gross income. Their first response was, "Impossible! We can't even pay our present bills, let alone take 10 percent off the top."

As they prayed together, they felt led that tithing was God's will. Since they wanted to please Him by obeying His command, they began systematically and faithfully giving priority to their tithe. At first, it was nip and tuck, and some of the other obligations had to wait. But after a few months, they were amazed to see how they were able to accomplish more with the nine-tenths than they had previously been able to accomplish with the total amount.

Today, they are enthusiastic over the privilege of laying up treasures in heaven, seeking first the kingdom of God. Tithing was only the beginning. Now they are giving 40 percent off the top because God has prospered them abundantly.

I began to tithe as a new believer when I was made aware of the scriptural principle that everything belongs to God and that we are stewards during our brief time on earth. As a believer, I also have the privilege of giving "offerings." This is the amount we can give after we pay our tithes. Not only do we support the work of the gospel in the world through sacrificial giving, but we also lay up treasures in heaven.

Our responsibility to pay tithes is seen in the fact that God is responsible for the means we have to make a living (John 3:27). Are you a dentist? The gold used in the crowns you fit comes from the ground God created. Are you an auto mechanic? If you were to take all the metal, rubber, oil, plastic, and gasoline products you work with and boil them down to their basic elements, you would find they have the earth as their source, which the Lord created. Are you a teacher? God has blessed you with the ability to think and communicate to help you accomplish your job.

Even the paper currency we use for money comes from trees that are part of the created order. It is not too much that God requires us to return to Him at least 10 percent of what is His anyway.

Paul Harvey tells a true story that shows how we many times give our least to the Lord. A woman called the Butterball Turkey Hotline with a very unusual dilemma. She had a turkey that had been in the freezer for twenty-three years and wanted to know if the turkey was safe to eat.

The Butterball specialist said the old bird would be edible only if it had remained at zero degrees all these years. He quickly added that the turkey would have probably lost its flavor, and he would not recommend eating it.

The caller responded, "That's what we thought. We'll just give it to the church."

What a terrible attitude: If it is of value, keep it. But if it is worthless, give it to the church. This mindset involves a lot more than old, frozen turkeys. This may explain why 75 percent of adult Americans gave less than $500 to both churches and charities in 1995. The Southern Baptist Convention estimates that only 10.25 percent of its 15.4 million members give a tenth or more of their income.[6]

God is calling you to test Him. Pay your tithes and see if He does not pour out a blessing (Malachi 3:10). It may come in the form of a financial blessing or perhaps an answer to prayer that has been on your heart for a while. Sometimes, the blessing will come immediately to those who honor God in their tithes. Other times, it comes in the form of a subtle blessing that endures for a lifetime. Regardless, Malachi 3 is the only place in Scripture where God says we may test Him. Try Him on this. I have never met a believer yet who tithed to God and felt betrayed. Vonette and I have given our tithes and offerings for 52 years and God has faithfully fulfilled His promise to meet our needs.

We steal by not working as we should for our employers.
The Bible says, "If you are a thief, stop stealing. Begin using your hands for honest work, and then give generously to others in need" (Ephesians 4:28).

Notice that a person is to not only steal no more, but rather is to become a hard-working employee. Why? So he can give his surplus to those who are in need. In fact, Paul writes, "Even while we were with you, we gave you this rule: 'Whoever does not work should not eat'" (2 Thessalonians 3:10).

Every year many people file workmen's compensation claims because of job-related injuries. But soon after, some dishonest people were caught on videotape doing hard, manual labor in their yards and some had even taken on side jobs. They were sent to prison for a long, long time. If you are doing something like this, your dishonesty will eventually catch up to you.

Paul's strong words about work, together with many similar passages, provide the foundation for what is called the "Protestant work ethic." Paul is addressing the problem of people panhandling food and money from hard-working people. He says that if they are physically able to work, but refuse to do so, they should not eat. Instead, people should be diligent by working with the talents God has given them.

We can change our attitude about work. The gospel is changing the way people in Brazil view themselves and their work. A poll of 2,000 Brazilians found that they see themselves as more optimistic and hard-working than in the past. Churches are a key component in the new spirit, which stresses organization, savings, and personal improvement.[7]

We steal by adopting a "get something for nothing" mentality.

Under the new American approach to work, the Protestant work ethic is being replaced by a "get something for nothing" mentality. This attitude is seen in two basic ways: the welfare system and government-sponsored gambling.

Joanna Elachi is a research assistant for the California-based Pacific Research Institute's Center for Enterprise and Opportunity. In "The Rise of Welfare," she writes,

> In the economically insecure times following the Great Depression, Americans gratefully allowed the federal government to step into the role of problem-solver and social caretaker.
>
> Public entitlement programs burgeoned with the onset of Roosevelt's New Deal and, later, Johnson's Great Society. Individual responsibility and community support were lost in a swamp of federal "anti-poverty" programs.
>
> But nearly 35 years after the War on Poverty began, we are far from being poverty free. The redistribution of almost $7 trillion in taxpayer money has produced a poverty rate that is actually higher today than in 1965.[8]

In "What Went Wrong With Welfare?" Michael Bauman points out that you get what you pay for. "When you tax something, you get less of it. When you subsidize something, you get more of it. Poverty is not always about money—if it were, it wouldn't exist $7 trillion later. Chronic poverty is at least partly about behavior, and welfare teaches the wrong lessons."[9] Giving people government subsidies when they are able to work defrauds the taxpayer and harms the person who is shirking work.

Naturally, Jesus wants the Church to reach out in Christian love to people who are unable to work. However, many others take advantage of welfare in America. It has become increasingly clear that those who are more than able to make a living are grossly abusing the program.

Even most welfare recipients agree with this view. An early 1990s survey in Wisconsin asked welfare recipients why they were on welfare. Eighty-two percent blamed circumstances beyond their control, 6 percent claimed sole responsibility, and 12 percent chose a combination of the two.

But when these welfare recipients were asked, "Why are people on welfare?", 90 percent said that those on welfare are partly or fully to blame for their problems.[10]

Therefore, as Michael Bauman rightly points out, "The recipients of Christian charity ought to be either diligent workers or else unable. The unwilling and the slothful must get nothing from us but exhortation. To give something else is to do them moral injury, something Christian love does not do."[11]

Gambling is another way people try to get something for nothing. Dr. Phil Stringer, Executive Vice President of Landmark Baptist College, remarks, "Gambling does not create any wealth; it only redistributes it. And, it usually redistributes it in a way that harms society in general."

A recent survey estimated that as many as 4.2 million Americans may be addicted to gambling. One study reported that gambling institutions brought in an average income of $4.35 per adult in the community. But a Maryland study indicated that increased crime, higher welfare costs, and dealing with gambling addicts cost the average adult between $13 and $23 in taxes every year![12]

Compulsive gambling is a serious mental addiction that endangers both the compulsive gambler and those around him. It involves the ultimate self-delusion—the belief that something for nothing is possible, which, of course, is a totally false perception of reality and brings about negative results.

Nevertheless, legislators remain extremely reluctant to give up revenues from state-sponsored gambling. The immediate financial benefits are too compelling. *New York Times* columnist William Safire remarks,

> Gambling promotion has become a key to state budget balancing. Card-carrying right-wingers are not supposed to mind taxing the poor, but really soaking the poor—as this excessively regressive taxation does —sticks in my craw. Why? Because it is wrong for the state to exploit the weakness of its citizens. It is the most unfair and painful form of "painless" taxation. The money isn't coming from a few big bookies and croupiers, but from the pockets of millions.
>
> And gambling taxation feeds on itself. "We cannot give up the state income from betting," say legislators who feel guilty about pre-

tending that gambling is good, because the states have become dependent on the money, or because other states will use casinos to lure their tourism. They have become as hooked on gambling as a source of revenue as any compulsive gambler betting the milk money.[13]

We clearly need to return to a time when government rewarded work. Today several conservative think tanks and foundations are developing workable strategies designed to pair faith-based organizations and local governments for the purpose of reestablishing the unemployed in the workforce. Welfare-to-work programs are showing progress. We need to pray that these programs continue to bear fruit and that work becomes the priority for the unemployed.

We steal by oppressing our employees.
The eighth commandment also applies to employers. When they refuse to pay a fair wage or force their workers into longer hours for the same pay, they are guilty of theft. But the Bible promises *judgment* upon the one who oppresses his employees:

- "Then I will draw near to you for judgment . . . against those who oppress the wage earner in his wages" (Malachi 3:5, NASB).

- "Do not withhold good from those to whom it is due, when it is in your power to do it" (Proverbs 3:27, NASB).

- "Scripture says, 'You shall not muzzle the ox while he is threshing,' and 'The laborer is worthy of his wages'" (1 Timothy 5:18, NASB).

Perhaps the best example of breaking the eighth commandment's requirement to pay a fair wage is found in China. Today an estimated 50 million Chinese men and women have passed through forced labor camps. Fifteen million have perished. Anywhere from 6 to 8 million people are captive in the 1,100 camps of the Laogai. These prisoners are forced to work under grossly inhumane conditions.[14] Fortunately, the United States has a ban on all products that come from Chinese slave-labor camps, although some still get through.

What does God promise to those who deal righteously with their employees? "The generous prosper and are satisfied; those who refresh others will themselves be refreshed" (Proverbs 11:25,26). Paying people what they are worth and rewarding hard work pleases God. An employer will be blessed to the degree he treats his workers well.

We steal by taking advantage of the legal system.
With 70 percent of the world's lawyers practicing in America, you would think justice should prevail. However, it does not appear that this is the case. Consider these examples:

- A burglar fell through a skylight while robbing a school. His attorneys charged the school with negligence and won $260,000 in damages.

- A man in Massachusetts stole a car from a parking lot, then died in a traffic accident. His estate sued the parking lot for letting him steal the car.

- In San Francisco, a cab driver corralled a mugger by pinning him to a wall with his taxi. The thief ended up with a broken leg, so a jury ordered the cabbie to pay the crook $24,595 for using "excessive force."

- One lady claimed she lost her psychic powers after being injected with dye during a CAT scan. She was awarded nearly $1 million in damages. Charles Colson says, "One wonders why she didn't foresee her problems and avoid the scan altogether."[15]

God is the only One who understands true justice: "Your throne is founded on two strong pillars—righteousness and justice" (Psalm 89:14). Whenever stealing occurs, God knows about it. In due time, He will make all things right. Those who are honest will be rewarded and those who are dishonest will suffer the consequences.

But as with all sin, Jesus Christ has the answer for those who have broken the eighth commandment!

The Solution for Stealing

The Gospel according to Luke says that Jesus was crucified between two criminals. While Jesus was suspended between heaven and earth in the final throes of His agony, one of the criminals said, "Are You not the Christ? Save Yourself and us!" (Luke 23:39, NASB).

But the other criminal, who was being executed as a thief, rebuked the man, saying, "Do you not even fear God, since you are under the same sentence of condemnation?" (v. 40). Then, turning to Jesus, he said, "Jesus, remember me when You come in Your kingdom!" (v. 42).

Jesus responded, "Truly I say to you, today you shall be with Me in Paradise" (v. 43).

These words, some of the very last Jesus spoke in His earthly body, demonstrate His power to forgive right up to the last seconds of His life. But what is equally interesting is that the last person to receive forgiveness from Christ, and the promise of eternal life, was a thief. When we put our lives in His hands, we will experience forgiveness and abundant life we do not deserve.

Richard O'Neal Jones is a former thief who now teaches people how to prevent crime. He always wanted a career as a hustler. He spent two years in prison for running a welfare-fraud ring that made several hundred thousand dollars. In prison, at age 41, Jones became a Christian.

When he read the Bible, he realized God could use his past for good. Jones interviewed dozens of fellow inmates about their "specialties"—such as robbery, car theft, and rape—and documented in his book, *Tips Against Crime*, their suggestions about how individuals could make themselves safe.

Jones produced the cable television show *Tips Against Crime*. He now speaks to neighborhood groups, churches, and senior citizens. He also counsels African-American youth and is on the board of a prison after-care program.[16]

Jesus still forgives thieves, providing them life abundant and life eternal! There is no life so corrupt that God cannot use it. If you have a habit of stealing in some way and need forgiveness, come to Christ right now and confess your sin. God will forgive you completely. Then ask Him to begin to use you in a new and honest way to bring glory to His name. You will be amazed at what God can do with a broken vessel that is His to heal and shape. He will mold you into someone who will bring others into His kingdom!

The ninth commandment, which we will learn about in the next chapter, deals with another aspect of honesty—telling the truth. This is a sin that most of us have struggled with many times.

LIFE APPLICATION

Set Your Heart's Gauge

Commit the following verses to memory. Then, when you are tempted to turn your spiritual focus away from God to other things, recall these commands from God.

- Exodus 20:15—"Do not steal."

- Ephesians 4:28—"If you are a thief, stop stealing. Begin using your hands for honest work, and then give generously to others in need."

- Malachi 3:8—"Will a man rob God? Yet you have robbed Me! But you say, 'In what way have we robbed You?' In tithes and offerings" (NKJ).

Gauge Your Spiritual Growth

Ask yourself the following questions. If one or more areas pose problems for you, ask God how you can deal with them through the power of the Holy Spirit.

- On your tax return last year, did you fail to report your accurate income?

- Have you ever made a fraudulent insurance claim?

- Do you pad your timecard at work, make personal phone calls on your employer's lines, or take office supplies home with you?

- Do you ever deceitfully call in sick when you want to take a day off?

- Are you ever tempted to shoplift?

- Have you ever taken something from a friend or relative without permission?

- Have you ever taken something because you were in a pinch or needed to hide what you were doing?

- Do you find yourself wanting something so badly that you would steal to get it?

- Are you honest about fully paying back all your debts?

- Have you ever illegally hooked up television cable?

- Have you claimed bankruptcy for reasons other than an unexpected calamity such as permanent disability?

- Do you like to get "something for nothing"? Does this desire get out of hand?

- To satisfy a desire for more wealth, are you tempted to buy into get-rich-quick schemes or to gamble?

- If you are an employer, are you paying fair wages? Is your concern mainly for your bottom-line or do you also compassionately consider those who depend on you for wages?

- Have you ever filed a lawsuit you knew was frivolous?

Walk in the Power of the Holy Spirit

Examine your giving record to your church and other Christian organizations. Are you tithing or are you robbing God? Do you give offerings above your tithe? Take special time to dedicate your finances to God. Set the amount you should tithe and ask God to help you follow through with your giving plan. Then, plan to set aside some income for giving to causes or needs above your tithe. Thank God that you are able to give back to Him a portion of what He has given to you.

FOURTEEN

DO NOT BEAR FALSE WITNESS

For many months, America and the world watched as events surrounding then-President Bill Clinton and White House intern Monica Lewinsky unfolded. Although almost all Americans believed Mr. Clinton's behavior was despicable, a majority did not find the president's conduct worthy of impeachment. But among those who did believe the president had committed a removable offense, it was not his adultery, but his perjury that they considered unacceptable.

In a CNN/*USA Today*/Gallup poll of 550 adult Americans, a significant number believed Bill Clinton lied under oath.

- Did Clinton commit perjury before the Starr grand jury?
  Yes 71%   No 23%

- Did Clinton commit perjury in the Paula Jones lawsuit?
  Yes 64%   No 27%
  (Sampling error: +/- 5% pts)

The article also reports: "Clinton faces the threat of impeachment because of his relationship with ex-White House intern Monica Lewinsky, but he has denied he committed perjury or obstruction of justice in trying to conceal their relationship . . . Most Americans agree with Republicans on the House Judiciary Committee that President Bill Clinton committed perjury and abused his office, but they still do not want him impeached."[1]

The ninth commandment reads, "Do not testify falsely against your neighbor" (Exodus 20:16). Any statement that does not represent the whole truth, whether or not it harms another person, is forbidden by the ninth commandment. In other words, not only does the ninth commandment forbid making false statements *about* our neighbor, but also statements that are made *to* our neighbor. Paul writes, "So put away all falsehood and 'tell your neighbor the truth' because we belong to each other" (Ephesians 4:25). How do we break the ninth commandment?

We lie by committing perjury.

Where does the idea of perjury come from? It is rooted in the Bible's prohibition against bearing false witness found in the ninth commandment. The historical significance of perjury as a civil crime dates to 15th-century England when lawmakers stressed that unless truth was supported and enforced by law, the court system would be rendered useless. Truth and justice are inseparable. Justice cannot exist where false testimony is permitted. Unless we enforce the truth in our public proceedings, we cannot possibly expect to secure justice for those who are entitled to the court's protections. The person who perjures himself commits a grave crime because in most cases the perjurer is as intent on bringing harm to someone else as he is in protecting himself from prosecution. Therefore, under our current system of justice, a person can receive jail time if found guilty of perjury—bearing false witness against a neighbor. Since the president did lie before a federal grand jury, he was quite fortunate to escape removal from office by Congress.

Because perjury threatens the welfare of another, it is clearly a crime against that other person. But perjury is also a crime against society because it is the highest form of disrespect for a civilized people who provide courts of justice where truth should be held in high esteem.

The courts should not allow anyone to break the sacred oath to "tell the truth, the whole truth, and nothing but the truth" with impunity. The future of justice in America depends on ensuring that courts are places where grievances of citizens are addressed and truth is enforced according to the law.

We lie by telling a "white lie."

Let me give you an example of three white lies wrapped in one. A prospective Harvard student was taking a campus tour when the guide stopped before a statue in Harvard Yard. On the pedestal was this inscription: "John Harvard, Founder, 1638." The guide informed the people that this was known as the statue of the three lies.

First of all, the artist commissioned to do the sculpture could not find a clear picture of John Harvard after which to model his work, so he just chose a picture of a respectable-looking gentleman from the proper era.

Second, John Harvard was not the founder of Harvard University. He was simply a contributor to the college in its early days.

Third, the date on the statue's base represents, not the date of John Harvard's death as might be supposed, but the year he donated his library and half his fortune to the college.

The irony lies in the fact that on the side of the statue is the Harvard emblem emblazoned with the school's motto: *Veritas*, meaning "truth."[2]

Have you ever heard a person say, "Yes, I lied, but it was only a little white lie"? Perhaps you have either said or thought this too.

Unfortunately, there is a major problem with the "white lie" theory. It has no support in Scripture. You say it was only a little white lie? Then perhaps you are equally comfortable with the idea of a little white adultery, or a little white murder.

C. S. Lewis observed, "A little lie is like a little pregnancy, it doesn't take long before everyone knows." Austin O'Malley said, "Those that think it permissible to tell white lies soon grow colorblind." Little white lies are an attempt to rationalize God's standards, and that all too often gets us into *big* trouble.

We lie by fudging the truth.

In England nearly 300 years ago lived a merchant commander named Captain Fudge. This historical figure became famous for his lies and exaggerations about adventures on the high seas. His crewmembers were so accustomed to his tales that they would call each other "Fudge" when one was straying from the truth.

By the mid-1800s, children in America were referring to lying as "fudging." Today many people still use the phrase "fudging the truth" when talking about deception.[3]

As this letter to Ann Landers reveals, fudging the truth to impress people can lead to ruin:

> Dear Ann Landers:
>
> I was a compulsive liar who started young. Although my parents did all they could to stop it, I kept lying. My problem was I was trying to impress people. My life never seemed glamorous enough.
>
> Here is a short history of what happens to a liar. I went through school lying to my friends, trying to look like a big shot. When I got out of high school, I had no friends, so I started to look for new ones. By then lying was a way of life. In order to support the lies, I needed more money than I had so I wrote checks I couldn't cover. I also impersonated a naval officer and later a successful businessman. My wife found out that I had totally misrepresented myself and invented friends and businesses I never had. She left me. The same thing happened with my second wife. I decided I had to change. Shortly after I married my third wife, I went to prison for passing bad checks. She divorced me while I was in prison.
>
> This advice is for the kid who lies. Please think about the future. A lie not only hurts you, but it poisons all your relationships. I'll get out of prison some day, and when I do, I vow to tell the truth. I will probably still be called a liar, but after a while people will find out that they can trust me.
>
> I'm now 26 years old, and by the time I'm 50, I will have built a good reputation. A kind teacher once told me that a person's word is worth more than gold. It's too bad that it took me so long to wake up to that fact. If you are a liar, stop while you still have friends. I hope my letter will help somebody who is where I was about 15 years ago.[4]

Certainly it is wrong to shade or exaggerate the truth to impress others or to improve your standing or to make a point. Many success-oriented people tend to exaggerate the truth out of sheer frustration with their lack of success. But creating a false reality to build up yourself in the eyes of others is not glorifying to God.

The right thing to do when you are tempted to embellish the truth is to remember Paul's counsel not to think more highly of yourself than you ought to think. He writes, "Be honest in your estimate of yourselves, measuring your value by how much faith God has given you" (Romans 12:3). If our thoughts conform to God's estimation of our gifts and talents, this will be reflected in our words.

We lie by fibbing.
What is a fib? Although the dictionary does not make hard and fast distinctions between a fib, a fudge, and a white lie, there are nuances that distinguish the three. Culturally speaking, "fibbing" is broader in meaning than fudging, but is more restrictive than a white lie. We fib when we want to make people feel we are making life easier for them, when in reality we are making it easier for ourselves. Here is a brief list of famous American fibs:

> The check is in the mail.
> I'll take care of it right away.
> Give me your number and the doctor will call you right back.
> Money cheerfully refunded.
> One size fits all.
> Your luggage isn't lost; it's only misplaced.
> Leave your resumé and we'll keep it on file.
> This hurts me more than it hurts you.
> I just need five minutes of your time.
> Your table will be ready in a few minutes.
> Open wide, it won't hurt a bit.
> Let's have lunch sometime.[5]

Many people consider fibbing to be harmless. But look at each of these fibs. They all create a lack of trust and elevate the fibber's interest over those of another. If you find yourself at the wrong end of a fib, you know how it hurts.

When we fib, we face the threat of getting caught in an untruth. We become like the four high school boys who caught spring fever and skipped their morning classes. When they showed up for class after lunch, they reported to their teacher that the car had a flat tire.

Much to their relief, she just smiled and said, "Well, you missed a quiz this morning so take your seats and get out a pencil and paper."

Still smiling, the teacher waited as the boys settled down and got ready for her questions. Then she said, "First question. Which tire was flat?"

We may chuckle at the antics of these boys and how their fib was exposed. But we too will be exposed as liars when we try to get by with just a little fib.

We lie by gossiping and slandering others.

The ninth commandment also speaks to our very human tendency to damage others by defaming their character. The "rumor mill" is usually the place where a false witness against a neighbor is born and where an innocent person's reputation is assailed. The Word of God warns us many times that gossip and slanderous words spoken with malicious intent or in careless disregard for the truth will not go unpunished.

A young pastor of a church in a small Texas town was the victim of vicious gossip started by a man and his wife. Like the dry grasslands in August, once the ugly rumor caught fire, there was no stopping it until it had spread throughout the entire community. After a few days, the man and wife who set the rumor mill in motion went to the pastor to ask his forgiveness, and asked what they could do to correct their wrong toward him.

The pastor said to them, "Here's what you can do. Go and get a chicken and bring it to me."

So they did, not knowing what to expect.

When they returned, he said, "Pluck all its feathers and spread them all over town from the top of the water tower."

They thought he was a little crazy, but the couple did as he asked.

When they returned, the pastor said, "I have one more thing I want you to do to make right the damage you've caused." When they agreed, this wise young pastor said to them, "Go and collect all the feathers and put them back on the chicken."

They just stood there, ashamed, seeing that it was impossible to undo what they had done.[6]

Mark Twain commented, "A lie can travel half way around the world while truth is still lacing up her boots." There is not a worse feeling in the world than to be caught passing on vicious rumors. Our careless, idle talk hurts people, and we should be held accountable for it. When we make misleading statements and gossip, or even just exaggerate some choice details for a more colorful story, we tear our neighbors down. This displeases God.

The Bible says, "It is foolish to belittle a neighbor; a person with good sense remains silent. A gossip goes around revealing secrets, but those who are trustworthy can keep a confidence" (Proverbs 11:12,13).

A scientist with the National Institutes of Health has found out that "poison from the skin of the tiny South American tree frog is far more toxic than any other known venom...Rain forest Indians use the venom from the skin of the kokoi frog to poison their blowgun arrows." Permit me to suggest a poison even more deadly—the poison from an evil tongue. "With their tongues they keep deceiving, the poison of asps is under their lips; whose mouth is full of cursing and bitterness" (Romans 3:13,14, NASB).[7]

We lie by telling a half-truth.

Have you ever been the recipient of a half-truth? If so, you know a half-truth can still be damaging and is always misleading.

An old Yiddish proverb says, "A half truth is a whole lie." What is a half-truth? It is a statement or explanation that reflects well on the person making it, but often casts aspersions on someone else. Like a whole lie, a half-truth has self-protection as its goal.

A half-truth is highly deceptive. By it we deceive ourselves into thinking we are giving out the truth because we have told a portion of the truth. We deceive others when in our self-seeking indifference to the real story we hold back the part that indicts us. A half-truth is every bit as selfish and conceited as a whole lie—perhaps more so—because it lacks the courage it takes to make a lie complete.

We lie by saying harmful words.

The Bible has much to say on the subjects of truth and falsehood. But of all the biblical writers, Paul provides the broadest definitions of these twin concepts. For Paul, speaking a truth involves more than making a statement that is factually accurate, but also includes speaking words that encourage and build up. Likewise, a falsehood is more than saying what is untrue, but also includes speaking words that hurt and tear down.

Paul writes, "Let no unwholesome word proceed from your mouth, but only such a word as is good for edification according to the need of the moment, that it may give grace to those who hear" (Ephesians 4:29, NASB).

Once, a woman approached the great preacher and biblical commentator Dr. Harry Ironside after his sermon. As the woman stood glaring at the famed preacher with a look of dismay, he said, "Ma'am, what is it?"

She responded, "Dr. Ironside, I have enjoyed your preaching for many years, but quite frankly, sir, that is the most hideous red tie I have ever seen worn by a man."

"Is that right?" he responded. "My red tie offends you?"

"I'm quite offended," blurted the woman.

Without a moment's hesitation, the preacher motioned to his assistant and said, "Bring me a pair of scissors." The assistant hurried and brought the scissors as he had been instructed. Dr. Ironside took the scissors and placed them in the woman's hand and said, "Cut it off."

"What do you mean, cut it off?" asked the woman.

"If my tie has offended you, then take the scissors and cut it off," he replied.

"Oh, Dr. Ironside," the woman exclaimed, "I could never cut your tie off!"

"Ma'am, I insist," he contended. "If the tie has offended you, cut it off!"

The woman hesitated for a moment, raised the scissors, and with one eye closed, cut the tie below the knot.

Dr. Ironside asked, "So do you feel better now that you have cut off the thing that so offended you?"

Trembling, the woman responded, "Yes, Dr. Ironside, I do."

He took the scissors from her hand and said, "Now stick out your tongue!"

This story illustrates the importance of speaking words that edify others and how a critical tongue can get us into trouble. James observes, "The tongue is a fire, the very world of iniquity" (James 3:6, NASB).

What exactly does it mean to edify? Many assume that to edify merely means to instruct or enlighten someone on any given subject. But this definition is too intellectual and misses the deeper, spiritual intent of the word.

Grace Notes, a ministry of Village Missions International, says the word edification is "the process of spiritual growth in a believer who is living according to the plan of God and who is fulfilling the command to 'grow in grace and in the knowledge' of Jesus Christ."

The Greek word that is translated "edification" is *oikodome*, a noun found in a number of New Testament passages: Romans 14:19; 1 Corinthians 14:5,12; 2 Corinthians 10:8; 13:10; and Ephesians 4:12,16,19. In all these passages, edification has two meanings:

1. Collectively, it refers to the building up of the body of Christ. In Ephesians 4:16, you can see that the edification of individuals results in the building up of the church.

2. For individual believers, edification refers to the spiritual growth and momentum in the Christian way of life, resulting in the glorification of God.

When the collective connotation is used, *oikodome* should be translated as "construction, building up," or "building process." When the individual connotation is used, *oikodome* should be translated as "edification." To grow in Christ, a Christian must have a consistent, daily fellowship with the Lord through confession of sin and learning and applying Bible teaching. Edification is the means of advancement and productivity in the Christian way of life."[8]

By speaking the truth in love, we help to build the body of Christ in a practical way. Words that give grace to the hearer help people grow in the knowledge of Christ. They encourage others and motivate them to discover more about Christ and the abundant life He offers.

We lie by saying we speak for God when we really do not speak for Him. Have you ever heard a Christian brother or sister say, "God told me," when in fact He did not? Many Christians use the mighty name of our sovereign Lord simply to impress others, win a theological argument, or to get their way. But to evoke the name of God has serious consequences, and to take it lightly breaks both the third commandment against taking God's name in vain and the eighth commandment against lying.

In the 13th chapter of Ezekiel, God sternly warns people not to say, "My message is from the Lord," when, in truth, it is not. Be careful. I do believe that God can impress things upon our hearts. If it were not for the fact that God told me to help fulfill the Great Commission and help reach the world for Christ, beginning on the college campuses, Campus Crusade for Christ would not be making the worldwide impact it is today. But we must be careful not to be flippant about the way we claim God is speaking to us, when it may be the flesh that is talking.

Unfortunately, one place we see this problem is on TV. Today the airwaves are full of quick-sales artists and hucksters who all too often are motivated by selfish gain. Some Christian hucksters tell people that God has spoken to them, saying that you should send them money or buy trinkets from their ministry. A watching world looks upon some religious charlatans and crooks with cynicism and disdain, questioning whether the gospel has any real credibility at all. This is most unfortunate for most of the Christian leaders on the TV whom I know are honorable and authentic.

Beloved, always be truthful with people. The phrases "God told me" or "God says" when used in a discussion are generally appropriate only when quoting the Bible. Peter underscores the integrity and inspiration of the Holy Scriptures when he writes, "Know this first of all, that no prophecy of Scripture is a matter of one's own interpretation, for no prophecy was ever made by an act of human will, but men moved by the Holy Spirit spoke from God" (2 Peter 1:20,21, NASB). Speaking for God was a singular role played by the biblical writers and should not be treated in a cavalier or self-centered fashion.

Is It Ever Right to Lie?

In Holland during World War II, Corrie ten Boom hid Dutch Jews in a "hiding place" in her family home to save them from the Nazis. If a Nazi soldier came to the door and asked her, "Are you harboring Jews in this house?" would she have been wrong to lie? Is lying always wrong? Or is it sometimes justified?

What if you see a man running into an alley to escape someone who is trying to kill him and the attacker asks, "Where is he?" What would you say? Would you lie and send the attacker on a wild goose chase to protect the pursued man's life? Or would you tell the truth?

These examples demonstrate that at times we must lie to protect a "higher good." This is a consideration only when we are faced with a *moral dilemma*. For example, if it comes down to a choice between endangering a human life or lying, the higher good of protecting the sanctity of life becomes the governing principle in this decision.

The problem addressed by the ninth commandment is the *immoral aspect* of lying. Although all lies are deceptive, not all deception is immoral. There are times when the dictates of morality demand we lie, as in the case of Rahab the harlot who, in faith, hid the Hebrew spies and lied concerning their whereabouts to protect them from harm. (See Joshua 2 and Hebrews 11:31.)

Nonetheless, the times we are called upon to make critical decisions of this nature should be considered rare and are to be approached in much wisdom and prayer. A way to decide if you are facing a moral dilemma that requires you to lie is to follow a principle revealed in the story of Rahab. Notice that Rahab did not lie to cover her own sin. Rather, her lie was motivated by her desire to protect others from mortal danger—those who were about to be sinned against. It is never right to invoke a "higher good" to justify lying when it is your own sin you are attempting to hide. Rahab, Corrie ten Boom, and many other godly people lied only when the physical safety of others was at stake.

Breaking Free to the Truth

The breakdown of truth in America and the ease with which so many people lie is alarming. Research shows 91 percent of Americans lie routinely; 36 percent confess to dark, important lies; 86 percent lie regularly to parents; 75 percent lie to friends; 73 percent to siblings; 69 percent lie to spouses; 81 percent lie about feelings; 43 percent concerning income; and 40 percent about sex.

Psychologist Michael Lewis, of Rutgers University, says there are three types of lies.

First, people lie to protect others' feelings. An example of this is saying a gift is nice when you actually hate it.

Second, people lie to avoid punishment. A little boy gets caught with his hand in the cookie jar, and says, "I was just counting them to make sure they were all still there!"

Third, people lie from self-deception. We sin and offend others, but we lie to ourselves about our responsibility and blame the offense on something or someone else. Lewis feels these lies of self-deception may be the most frequently used.[9] Self-deception could explain why so many people reject Christ. They have lied to themselves about their need to confess their wrongdoing and to receive God's forgiveness.

In this age of obsessive lying, we must remember who is the "father of lies." Jesus said to the Pharisees, "You are the children of your father the Devil, and you love to do the evil things he does. He was a murderer from the beginning and has always hated the truth. There is no truth in him. When he lies, it is consistent with his character; for he is a liar and the father of lies" (John 8:44). It does not matter if it is perjury, a white lie, a fib, a half-truth, or any other variation of lying; the source of all lies is Satan.

We must also remember who has promised to set us free from the devil's power. Jesus said, "You are truly My disciples if you keep obeying My teachings. And you will know the truth, and the truth will set you free" (John 8:32). An ancient prayer says, "Deliver me from the cowardice that shrinks from the truth, from the laziness that is content with half truths, from the arrogance that thinks it knows all truth, O God of truth deliver me."

In our own wisdom, we cannot know the truth. Our culture and our sinful nature both influence us to deceive ourselves and to lie. But as we focus on Jesus, who is the Truth, and on His Word, we will be able to know and reflect the truth of God. His Spirit will convict us of our lies and lead us into all truth.

LIFE APPLICATION

Set Your Heart's Gauge

Commit the following verses to memory. Then, when you are tempted to turn your spiritual focus away from God to other things, recall these commands from God.

- Exodus 20:16—"Do not testify falsely against your neighbor."

- Ephesians 4:25—"Put away all falsehood and 'tell your neighbor the truth.'"

Gauge Your Spiritual Growth

Ask yourself the following questions. If one or more areas pose problems for you, ask God how you can deal with them through the power of the Holy Spirit.

- If you have testified in court or in another area such as before a tax auditor, were you committed to telling the truth even if it hurt your cause?

- Do you have a habit of telling white lies or fudging the truth or fibbing?

- Do you embellish the truth when telling others something about yourself?

- When you are tempted to tell a lie, what vain motives underlie your sin? A desire to make yourself look better, to keep peace, or to get what you want at any cost?

- Do you have a problem with gossip? In what situations do you find yourself saying things about others behind their back?

- When facing a difficult situation, do you tell a half-truth to get yourself out of trouble?

- Do you tear others down with your words?

- When talking about spiritual matters, do you use God's name glibly to impress others?

- In your relationships, do you lie to protect the feelings of others?

- Do you lie to avoid bad consequences?

- At work, do you lie to put the blame for your actions on someone else?

Walk in the Power of the Holy Spirit

Memorize the ancient prayer, "Deliver me from the cowardice that shrinks from the truth, from the laziness that is content with half truths, from the arrogance that thinks it knows all truth, O God of truth deliver me." Whenever you find yourself tempted to fudge the truth in any way, pray a prayer similar to this one, asking God to help you reflect the nature of Jesus Christ, who is the Truth.

FIFTEEN

DO NOT COVET

n his short story "The Window," author G. W. Target tells of two seriously ill men who occupied the same hospital room. The old man by the window was propped up for an hour each day to drain fluid from his lungs. The younger man spent his entire time on his back. The two men enjoyed each other's company and talked for hours about all different types of subjects.

During the hour he was propped up in his bed, the older man would describe all the things he saw to his bedfast roommate, just to entertain him. Each day he would give great detail about the activities going on outside. He described the park with its lovely lake and grand old trees. He would tell of children playing and lovers walking through the park.

One day, a beautiful parade went by. Even though he couldn't hear the music, the man on his back could see it all in his mind as his roommate gave the details. But somehow, it didn't seem quite fair. Although he enjoyed listening to his friend describe the sights, he began to crave the view of his comrade. His desire for the bed by the window became a consuming thought. It even kept him awake at night.

Then in the darkness of one sleepless night, his roommate began to cough. He was choking on the fluid in his lungs and was desperately groping for the button to call for help. The covetous roommate could have easily pushed his button to summon a nurse, but instead, he watched the old man die.

The following morning, the nurse discovered the old man's death. The standard procedure was carried out and the body was removed. The surviving man then asked that his bed be switched so he could see out the window. At last, he would have what he felt he deserved.

Painfully and slowly he struggled to prop himself up for that first look at the park. To his chagrin, the window looked out to a blank wall. The truth was his old roommate had pictured the scenes he described only in his mind. The younger man learned an important lesson: Fulfillment in life is never achieved by the venom of covetousness.[1]

The Meaning of Coveting

This story brings us to the tenth and final commandment, which says, "Do not covet your neighbor's house. Do not covet your neighbor's wife, male or female servant, ox or donkey, or anything else your neighbor owns" (Exodus 20:17).

What is coveting? It means two things.

First, coveting is an inappropriate desire for something that belongs to someone else.

Coveting is an improper craving for something another person possesses to such an extent that you cannot be happy unless you have it. It is a sinful desire for things that belong to your neighbor.

It can be a new car your neighbor purchased. Now, there is nothing wrong with desiring a new car. The problem comes when you desire another person's automobile.

Marriage is a wonderful gift from God. Desiring to be married is natural and God expects it. It is when you want someone else's husband or wife that you violate the tenth commandment.

Over the centuries, many people have misinterpreted the tenth commandment to simply read, "Do not covet." In other words, they take it to mean they should not desire anything at all. But the commandment does not say, "Do not covet," but rather says, "Do not covet your *neighbor's* possessions." Having a balanced desire for material things to better oneself or one's station in life is not wrong. We need a certain number of things to accomplish certain goals and to facilitate our daily living. The Lord encourages us, "Ask, and it shall be given to you; seek, and you shall find; knock, and it shall be opened to you" (Matthew 7:7, NASB). To balance acquiring things with a godly perspective, He also emphasized, "Seek first His Kingdom and His righteousness; and all these things shall be added to you" (Matthew 6:33, NASB).

Second, coveting is an ungodly desire for anything that could take God's place in our lives.
The fact that we are not to covet what rightfully belongs to someone else does not mean we are free to excessively crave things that belong to no one. The tenth commandment would be violated if we were to become obsessed with sports, hobbies, or work.

God knows us. He knows how easily we can become captivated with things we desire. Ungodly coveting means we spend an inordinate amount of time and energy planning to acquire something. It means we allow our lust for material things to substitute for our true love for God. Our desire becomes an obsession.

The tenth commandment clearly prohibits us from desiring anything in our neighbor's possession. Nevertheless, in light of this commandment, our *principle duty* is to never let our desire for things and people surpass our love for God. Covetousness, in any form, turns our hearts and minds away from God as our heavenly Provider toward lusting after other things that we believe will bring joy and peace.

Contentment—the Antidote to Covetousness

There is an antidote for covetousness. It is contentment. What is contentment?

Contentment is being happy with what you have.
Once a rich industrialist was disturbed to find a fisherman sitting lazily beside his boat. "Why aren't you out there fishing?" he asked.

"Because I've caught enough fish for today," said the fisherman.

"Why don't you catch more fish than you need?" the rich man asked.

"What would I do with them?"

"You could earn more money," came the impatient reply, "and buy a better boat so you could go deeper and catch more fish. You could purchase nylon nets, catch even more fish, and make more money. Soon you'd have a fleet of boats and be rich like me."

The fisherman asked, "Then what would I do?"

"You could sit down and enjoy life," said the industrialist.

"What do you think I'm doing now?" the fisherman replied as he looked placidly out to sea.[2]

Now there is a contented soul! However, many people are not content with what they have. To them, the grass always looks greener on the other side of the fence. These people are dissatisfied even when their circumstances are favorable and their needs are met. Instead of doing their duty cheerfully and conscientiously as unto the Lord, they yield to a spirit of covetousness. As a result, they miss God's best for their lives and fail to see the blessings God has bestowed on them.

William Randolph Hearst invested a fortune collecting art treasures from around the world. One day Mr. Hearst read the description of a valuable art item, which he then sent his agent abroad to locate. After months of searching, the agent reported that he had finally found the treasure.

To the surprise of Hearst, the priceless masterpiece was stored in the warehouse of none other than William Randolph Hearst. The multi-millionaire had been searching all over the world for a treasure he already possessed. Had he read the catalog of his treasures, he would have saved himself a lot of time and money.[3]

Contentment doesn't depend on how much we have or don't have. Contentment is a state of mind that celebrates what we have at the moment.

Contentment is being happy in every circumstance.
In the Bible, we find a true example of contentment. As a missionary, Paul journeyed throughout the Mediterranean world. Paul's commitment to suffer for Christ and His gospel took him into extremely dif-

ficult circumstances.

In writing about his own life and ministry, Paul remarks, "Five times I received from the Jews thirty-nine lashes. Three times I was beaten with rods, once I was stoned, three times I was shipwrecked, a night and a day I have spent in the deep. I have been on frequent journeys, in dangers from rivers, dangers from robbers, dangers from my countrymen, dangers from the Gentiles, dangers in the city, dangers in the wilderness, dangers on the sea, dangers among false brethren; I have been in labor and hardship, through many sleepless nights, in hunger and thirst, often without food, in cold and exposure. Apart from such external things, there is the daily pressure upon me of concern for all the churches" (2 Corinthians 11:24–28, NASB).

What was Paul's attitude throughout his suffering? Even when Paul's ministry landed him in a Roman prison, he found no reason to complain, but was fully content: "I know what it is to be in need, and I know what it is to have plenty. I have learned the secret of being content in any and every situation, whether well fed or hungry, whether living in plenty or in want. I can do everything through Him who gives me strength" (Philippians 4:12,13, NIV). He did not have a burning desire to change his circumstances or to have more. Instead, he was content to follow God's leading in all his situations.

In *The Art of Contentment*, Puritan Thomas Watson offers one of the best definitions of contentment: "It is a sweet temper of spirit, whereby a Christian carries himself in an equal poise in every condition."[4]

Does the fact that we are to be content in every circumstance mean we cannot carry a concern? Not at all. Thomas Watson observes of Hannah in the Old Testament, "Hannah's spirit was burdened; 'I am' says she, 'a woman of a sorrowful spirit.' Now having prayed, and wept, she went away, and was no more sad; only here is the difference between a holy complaint and a discontented complaint; in the one we complain to God, in the other we complain of God."[5] Hannah brought her deep sorrow to God and entrusted Him with her burden. She didn't complain, "God, why haven't You done what I want You to do?" Instead, she cried out, "God, I have a heartfelt need. You are the only One who understands and can help me deal with my desire to have a child." She left her problem in God's hands and He answered her prayer.

It is when we "complain of God" rather than "complain to God" that we create conditions in our hearts that lead to ungodly covetousness. When this sinful desire is birthed on the inside, it soon leads to sinful action.

Greed—the Source of Coveting

In combating the inner craving for those things we should not have, it is important to know that covetousness is an outgrowth of *greed*. Greed is an excessive appetite for possessions. Greed is a big, broad acquisitiveness that simply wants more. In the words of Henry Fairlie, "Greed loves not possessions so much as possessing. Coveting, on the other hand, is interested in one or two specific things that belong to your neighbor."

Greed is a dangerous emotion. We become like the stinging ants who were busy accumulating storehouses of food. The landowner put a small circle of poison around their hill. Thinking the tiny grains of poison were food, the ants picked them up and carried them throughout the colony. Soon hundreds of ants were busily carting poison into their hill.

The landowner noticed a hole in the circle of poison. Some smaller, nonstinging ants had discovered this "food" and were stealing it from their neighbors, moving it away from the anthill to their own colony. Thinking they were getting the other ants' treasure, the smaller ants were unwittingly poisoning themselves.

In Luke 12:15, Jesus warned against greed, saying, "Be on your guard against every form of greed; for not even when one has an abundance does his life consist of his possessions" (NASB). Here Christ's reference to "all kinds of greed" includes covetousness.

This is another fact: Because covetousness is an outgrowth of greed, it is not surprising that "greed" is mentioned twice as often in the Bible as "covet." God clearly wants us to avoid all kinds of greed. Let us look at several types of greed and covetousness that we practice.

Planned Obsolescence

Have you noticed that as soon as you buy the most recent version of something, a few months later the manufacturer produces a newer version? Or that your new electronic gadget, which comes with a 12-month warranty, happens to break on the day *after* your warranty expires? The cost to repair the gadget is usually so high that it is cheaper to purchase a replacement.

If this sounds familiar, it should. It is called "planned obsolescence." This theory says that our national economy is best served when people are buying. Modeled on the federal subsidy for farmers, this theory was codified into law by Congress in 1959. We pay farmers not to farm. Why not pay fixers not to fix? And if repairmen do need to fix, why not permit them to quote such exorbitant prices that people will be forced to buy, buy, buy?

Madeline Begun Kane, who writes for *Midwest Today*, offers this explanation: "In the '50s, skillful repairmen were so good at their jobs and so reasonably priced that a manufacturer couldn't even make a sale to his mother. After all, why purchase a replacement when someone was willing and able to fix your appliance without demanding to be named in your will?

"The solution was simple: Encourage fixers to either bungle the job or to quote such ludicrous repair estimates that even a miser would opt to buy rather than repair. How do you accomplish this? Easily. Just pay repairmen a healthy percentage of the profits on replacement appliances. The idea was swiftly adopted and, unlike our appliances, the scheme functions flawlessly."[6]

Planned obsolescence is one way that the world's system simply does not permit the average American to remain content with many consumer items. I honestly believe many people would learn to be content if the things they bought simply lasted longer. But because things have such a way of breaking down all the time, the repeated *need* to buy can easily lead to covetousness once the habit has been established. The solution lies in smart buying and learning how to do our own repairs whenever possible.

Consumer Debt

The spiral of buying that has resulted from planned obsolescence has led many Americans into debt. If that were not enough, we are constantly bombarded with advertisements that make us feel like second-rate citizens unless we have the latest thingamajig. The world we live in says, "Never be happy with what you have. Go for what you want and never mind the costs. Just keep rolling over your debt load." The result is that we have become a nation living beyond its means.

Joining the advertisers in the "buying frenzy" are the credit card companies. Credit cards are easily obtained and leave us virtually enslaved to the massive debt we quickly acquire. If you have good credit, you can receive an approved credit card application each week in the mail. But the effect of "keeping up with the Joneses" has led to more covetousness and has devastated many households. Rising consumer debt is spiraling out of control for many medium-income families.

According to consumer debt indicators, "Household debt of all types has increased rapidly throughout the 1990s. For example, mortgage debt has grown more than 50 percent since the beginning of the decade to $3.75 trillion by the first quarter of 1996, while revolving credit has increased a whopping 127 percent to $456 billion by September 1996.

"Perhaps more troubling, however, is that the ratio of consumer debt to personal income has risen dramatically over the last several years, from a low of 14.10 percent in December 1992 to a high of 18.11 percent in July of 1996. High ratios of debt to personal income can foreshadow future defaults.

"Indeed, the rate of credit card delinquencies, although highly volatile, typically follows the debt-to-income ratio with a lag. Considering that we have yet to see a decrease in this ratio, we may reasonably expect the consumer delinquency rate to continue rising in the near future."[7]

Benjamin Franklin could not have said it better: "Contentment makes poor men rich; discontentment makes rich men poor."

Tragically, most Christians have also accumulated too much debt. When they do, they lose their joyful freedom in serving Christ because they are worrying about how to pay their bills. Being consumed with how to meet obligations robs us of our creative energy in serving the Lord. Christ promises to meet all our needs—not our wants—according to His riches in glory. But He can't when we disobey God's commandments.

If you have too much debt, I encourage you to meet with a financial counselor who can help you set up a budget. Then in prayer, trust God to help you be a better steward of what He has entrusted to you financially.

Ambition

The world deceives many people into thinking they can practice covetousness as long as they call it ambition. A godly ambition, in and of itself, is not a bad thing. Since 1945, I have been ambitious to help spread the gospel of Jesus Christ throughout the world. Praise God, today Campus Crusade for Christ, in cooperation with scores of mission agencies and tens of thousands of churches, has helped to reach over 6 billion people in 186 countries with the most joyful news ever announced. Nevertheless, an *ungodly* ambition teaches that the desire for my neighbor's job, house, car, or boat is part of a natural desire to succeed. This is a lie of Satan.

God put a desire in us to serve Him and to provide for our families, but Satan attempts to distort this truth. He wants you to believe you will not be satisfied until you have reached the level that others have. But like everything with the father of lies, reaching this goal only stretches your finances to the very limit and leaves you empty in the end.

One of the ways people express their ambition is through gaining titles. During the Middle Ages everyone sought status in their titles. Not only was it an "in" thing to be a baron or a knight or a member of nobility, but even farm workers coveted more exalted titles for their work. The lowly lad who cleaned out the horses' stalls was called the "Count of the Stable" from which we get "constable," a name still given to police officers in Canada.

Even the lowliest job on the estate had its titular reward. The serf who was in charge of the pigs was called "The Sty Warden" or "Steward." From this humble origin we get the word "stewardship." Today, this word is used to encourage people to share more of their time, talents, and treasure for the work of the church.[8]

Tragically, unless we remember our humble beginnings, titles can easily go to our heads. Throughout the years I have been truly blessed to receive numerous awards from many prestigious organizations, including the Templeton Prize for Progress in Religion, which carried over a $1 million prize (all of which was given to promote fasting and prayer throughout the world). Additionally, I have been privileged to receive six honorary doctorates. The titles bestowed upon me through these degrees are important and have been used by the Lord to open doors to the gospel. But I must never forget that even with all the honor bestowed upon me, I am still Bill Bright. I am just a man, like any other, who is prone to the same weaknesses that plague all men. My ambition has never been to seek titles, but only the One who has been given the "name above all names"—Jesus Christ. He is my Lord, Master, Savior, and King—my everything. For more than fifty years, I have chosen to give up all worldly desires and to be his slave.

The Tenth Commandment Summarizes the Law

Perhaps the most outstanding aspect of the tenth commandment is that it summarizes all ten of the commandments. There is absolutely no way a person can break any one of the other nine commandments without first breaking the tenth. The tenth commandment lies at the root of all sin.

Paul remarked, "What shall we say then? Is the Law sin? May it never be! On the contrary, I would not have come to know sin except through the Law; for I would not have known about coveting if the Law had not said, 'You shall not covet'" (Romans 7:7, NASB). Why does Paul reference the tenth commandment when commenting on the Law? For Paul, coveting was the source of every evil desire. Matthew Henry, the great biblical commentator, observes, "St. Paul, when the grace of God caused the scales to fall from his eyes, perceived that this law, 'Thou shalt not covet,' forbade all those irregular appetites and desires which are the first-born of the corrupt nature, the first risings of the sin that dwelleth in us, and the beginnings of all the sin that is committed by us."[9]

Think about it. Is it possible to tell a lie without first dishonoring your parents? Yes. Is it possible to steal without first committing adultery? Yes again. But is it possible to lie, steal, commit adultery, or even worship other gods without first being dissatisfied with your present estate? No.

Here are some examples of how breaking the tenth commandment leads to breaking other laws:

- Jacob coveted Esau's blessing as the first-born. He then deceived his father, Isaac, and took the blessing for himself. Jacob's coveting led him to violate the fifth commandment (honor your father and mother) and the eighth commandment (do not steal).

- The tribe of Dan was not content with the size of the land apportioned them so they coveted land to the north and planned to take it by force. To ensure the overthrow of the inhabitants of the area, they took Micah's idols, which they believed had the power to provide victory. This act led the Danites to break the first commandment (do not have any other gods besides Me) and the second commandment (do not worship idols).

- Saul coveted David's immense popularity with the people and as a result attempted to take David's life, breaking the sixth commandment (do not murder).

- David coveted Uriah's wife, Bathsheba, and committed adultery, thus violating the seventh commandment (do not commit adultery), which led to murder when David arranged to have Uriah killed, breaking the sixth commandment (do not murder).

- Ahab coveted Naboth's vineyard. To get it, he hired two men to lie about Naboth, breaking the ninth commandment (do not bear false witness) and had him killed, breaking the sixth commandment (do not murder). Then he stole the vineyard from Naboth's family, breaking the eighth commandment (do not steal). In this case, coveting led to the violation of four commandments.

In addition to these biblical examples, coveting has been the source of most wars throughout history: Hitler coveted the wealth, land, and prestige of the European nations and attempted to enslave them beneath his fascist military might. The current struggle between the Indians and the Pakistanis—a struggle that dates back many centuries —stems from each one coveting the other's land.

These examples demonstrate that coveting is a sinful desire for particular things that belong to others. If this desire is not surrendered to Christ, it will lead to outward sin, which in turn creates a snowball effect causing us to violate more of God's laws.

Knowing Christ—the Key to Contentment

In *The Wizard of Oz*, young Dorothy learned a valuable lesson: "There's no place like home." Like Dorothy, many people today live dissatisfied with their "Kansas," seeking instead the glamour and excitement they believe lies somewhere over the rainbow. But no matter where they live, what job they have, or what possessions they own, true and lasting satisfaction is never theirs. Little do they realize that real peace, joy, and satisfaction could have been theirs all along through a deep and loving relationship with our Lord Jesus Christ.

An ancient Persian legend tells of a wealthy man by the name of Al Haffed who owned a large farm. One evening a visitor related to him tales of fabulous amounts of diamonds that could be found in other parts of the world and of the great riches they could bring him. The vision of all this wealth made him feel poor by comparison. So instead of caring for his own prosperous farm, he sold it and set out to find these treasures. But the search proved to be fruitless.

Finally, penniless and in despair, he committed suicide by jumping into the sea.

Meanwhile, the man who had purchased his farm noticed the glint of an unusual stone in a shallow stream on the property. He reached into the water, and to his amazement, he pulled out a huge diamond. Later when working in his garden, he uncovered many more valuable gems.

Poor Al Haffed had spent his life traveling to distant lands seeking jewels when on the farm he had left behind were all the precious stones his heart could have ever desired.

The real challenge the tenth commandment lays before us is to discover the "jewel" that has been near us all along—a treasure that surpasses all the earthly wealth of all the kings and princes of the world.

It is Christ. When Christ fills your heart and mind as Lord and Master, you can be at peace and content with the things, people, and circumstances that our Sovereign God has placed in your life.

The only thing that truly satisfies is seeking Jesus Christ and His heavenly riches. Striving, coveting, and spending our time wanting what is not available to us can leave us broken and bitter. J. Paul Getty, one of the richest men to have ever lived, was once asked, "How much is enough money?" His answer was, "Just a little bit more." The worst part is getting those things we wanted so badly and still feeling empty inside. The satisfaction we thought would fill us does not exist apart from Christ.

How can we defeat greed and covetousness in our lives? Through *love*. Love is a key principle of the covenant between God and His people. Love is also about valuing a fellow human being the way God values us. If we are to love people the way we love ourselves, we must value their life, marriage, possessions, and reputation. We should do everything in our power to help protect their goods and belongings.

Coveting is the first step toward breaking relationship with your neighbor, but God wants you to love your neighbor. To love and value another person means not taking what belongs to them and disciplining your thought life so that you will not even think about wanting what they have.

If ever you should find yourself lacking in peace and contentment, the Bible offers this solution: "Don't worry about anything; instead, pray about everything. Tell God what you need, and thank Him for all He has done. If you do this, you will experience God's peace, which is far more wonderful than the human mind can understand. His peace will guard your hearts and minds as you live in Christ Jesus" (Philippians 4:6,7).

We have now seen how important it is to keep each of the Ten Commandments. We will each have difficulty obeying some more than others. But one biblical principle explains our responsibility to obey them all. We will study this principle in our next section.

LIFE APPLICATION

Set Your Heart's Gauge

Commit the following verses to memory. Then, when you are tempted to turn your spiritual focus away from God to other things, recall these commands from God.

- Exodus 20:17—"Do not covet your neighbor's house. Do not covet your neighbor's wife, male or female servant, ox or donkey, or anything else that your neighbor owns."

- Matthew 6:33—"Seek first His kingdom and His righteousness; and all these things shall be added to you" (NASB).

Gauge Your Spiritual Growth

Ask yourself the following questions. If one or more areas pose problems for you, ask God how you can deal with them through the power of the Holy Spirit.

- What is it that you covet? Material possessions that someone else owns? A colleague's position at work? Recognition that someone else receives?

- What is it that you desire above God or that turns your heart away from God?

- Are you content with what you have? Are you happy in all your circumstances—even the ones that are very difficult to bear?

- Do you always want the newest "thing" on the market?

- Is your desire for things leading you into debt?

- Do you sometimes have "buying frenzies"?

- In your effort to climb the work ladder, do you hurt others in the process?

- Is there a title that you would like to have above anything else?

- Do you want things just to make yourself look or feel better?

- Do you pick your friends according to what you can gain by your relationship with them?

- What have you done this past week to show your neighbor that you love him or her?

Walk in the Power of the Holy Spirit

Having a thankful attitude combats discontent and covetousness. As soon as you feel those sinful thoughts coming, thank God for the situation that has caused these feelings. For example, if you wish you had a bigger income like your friend has, thank God that He has given you what you have now. Tell Him the financial problems you have and leave those problems in His hands. Repeat Matthew 6:33 whenever your thoughts turn away from God and onto other things.

WRITTEN BY THE HAND of GOD

PART 4

Living
by the Ten
Commandments

THE PRINCIPLE
OF SOWING
AND REAPING

I t had been a winter of heavy snow and the ski slopes were in magnificent shape. Skiers from all over the country flocked to Breckenridge, Colorado, to fly down the powder-filled hills.

But the slopes also held a threat of danger. The snow had piled so high that the possibility of an avalanche hung over many wilderness cliffs. Officials at the resort posted huge, distinct signs at the edges of the well-traveled areas that said, "DANGER! OUT OF BOUNDS!"

In spite of the warnings, several adventurers skied past the signs onto the pristine slopes. The lure of untouched powder drew them past the point of safety.

As the skiers flew down the slopes, there was a low rumble. The unstable snow pack groaned as it began to slip down the steep cliffs. Within seconds, too quickly for the skiers to tumble out of harm's way, four of the trespassers were buried under a half-mile-wide avalanche.

Tons of snow and rock snuffed out their lives. For the next few days, rescue teams dug into the white tomb to extricate the bodies.[1] What had begun as an adventure turned into tragedy.

We all understand the significance of disregarding physical laws. Yet sometimes we take chances, believing that we won't get hurt. Usually, we learn the bitter fact that we can't break the rules without suffering the consequences.

Spiritual laws are just as binding as physical ones. They are written by the hand of God. But sometimes we forget this fact because the consequences aren't as immediate as when we break physical laws.

The Bible tells us that *everything* we say and do is being recorded in heaven, and that someday our "file" will be opened and we will be judged accordingly. The apostle John writes about a coming day of judgment: "I saw the dead, the great and the small, standing before the throne, and books were opened; and another book was opened, which is the book of life; and the dead were judged from the things which were written in the books, according to their deeds" (Revelation 20:12, NASB). Although many people would like to alter the contents of these books in their favor, that is impossible. The books cannot be changed.

Today, too many people, including believers, do not take seriously the record they are writing in life. Everyone knows you cannot stick your hand in a fire without getting burned. Yet when it comes to spiritual matters, many people disregard the consequences of their sin. But they get burned just as surely when they lie to their boss or cheat on their spouse.

Up to this point, we have seen that the Ten Commandments are far more than a simple set of do's and don'ts. They are a tremendous source of peace, joy, blessing, and liberation when obeyed in the power of the Holy Spirit. But if disobeyed, the Ten Commandments become the standard God uses to judge our lives. They are like the fulcrum in the center of a seesaw. They don't bend or change, but the seesaw tilts according to the amount of weight placed at each end.

Where are you building the greatest weight—on the side of obedience or disobedience?

Sowing and Reaping for Eternity

The dual ability of God's Law to act as either a source of blessings or curses is summarized by Paul in his letter to the church at Galatia. "Do not be deceived, God is not mocked; for whatever a man sows, this he will also reap. For the one who sows to his own flesh will from the flesh reap corruption, but the one who sows to the Spirit will from the Spirit reap eternal life" (Galatians 6:7,8, NASB). This is called *the principle of sowing and reaping*.

This principle comes from nature. Every year, America's hardworking farmers harvest billions of bushels of barley, corn, oats, wheat, and rye. They reap in the fall what they sowed in the spring, and, assuming proper soil and weather conditions, they reap bountifully—many times more than what was sown.

To reap a plentiful harvest, a farmer must also be aware of the wild animals and the cunning devises they use to destroy his crop. A flock of wild ducks can strip a field of wheat in the fall, leaving only pieces of straw. Rabbits can raid a garden until all the vegetables are ruined.

In a similar way, the principle of sowing and reaping relates to every area of Christian living: If you sow adultery, you will reap a broken marriage. If you sow thievery, you will go to jail. If you sow a heart of worship to God, you will reap joy and peace. If you sow honesty, you will reap trust.

The law of sowing and reaping in our actions is as fixed as the law of gravity and as sure as the sunrise and sunset. Godly conditions govern a plentiful, spiritual harvest, and ungodly acts reap destruction and ruin.

What we do now will deeply affect our future. I want to share with you four spiritual truths that will enable you to reap a bountiful, spiritual harvest.

First, reaping a spiritual harvest means turning from self-deception.
For fifteen years, Jim Fixx, author of the 1978 bestseller *The Complete Book of Running*, ran eighty miles a week. He appeared to be in tiptop shape. It did not seem possible that a man his age could be in better condition. Yet at age fifty-two, Fixx died of a massive heart attack while running alone on a Vermont road. His wife, Alice, said she was certain that Fixx had no idea he suffered from a heart problem. Why?

Jim Fixx refused to get regular checkups for fear of what they might reveal. After Fixx's death, doctors speculated that his heart muscles were so strong that he may not have felt the telltale chest pains or shortness of breath that usually signal arterial heart disease.[2]

In a similar way, many people practice avoidance in their spiritual lives. They do not want to know the real spiritual condition of their heart so they refuse to look into God's Word to measure their behavior. They stubbornly convince themselves that as long as their actions are righteous in their own eyes, they have God's approval, which will shield them from any real consequences. This self-deception is a powerful lie.

The *Penguin Dictionary of Psychology* defines self-deception this way: "the deceiving of oneself in the sense of the inability to have accurate insights into one's limitations."[3] This definition is wholly inadequate. It limits self-deception to a person's ability to convince himself that he is more gifted and versatile than he is. But clearly, self-deception extends to other things, such as ignoring God's resolve and ability to punish human rebellion.

Who is the source of all kinds of deception in our world? It is Satan. The Bible says, "This great dragon—the ancient serpent called the Devil, or Satan, the one deceiving the whole world—was thrown down to the earth with all his angels" (Revelation 12:9). Satan opposes everything that is true and righteous.

Here are some biblical examples of self-deception:

- The builders of the Tower of Babel deceived themselves by thinking their mutiny against a holy God would go unnoticed. "Let's build a great city with a tower that reaches to the skies—a monument to our greatness! This will bring us together and keep us from scattering all over the world" (Genesis 11:4). But the God whom the builders had written off as an insignificant tribal deity responded with great fury. He destroyed the tower and confused their language, causing them to scatter all over the world—just what they were trying to avoid.

- King Saul deceived himself by believing he could usurp the role of priest and offer spiritual sacrifices in the place of Samuel the priest. Soon Samuel confronted the King with the true nature of his rebellious act. "'How foolish!' Samuel exclaimed. 'You have disobeyed the command of the LORD your God. Had you obeyed, the LORD would have established your kingdom over Israel forever. But now your dynasty must end, for the LORD has sought out a man after His own heart. The LORD has already chosen him to be king over His people, for you have not obeyed the LORD's command'" (1 Samuel 13:13,14). Saul's sin was so serious that he squandered not only his own reign as king, but also his legacy as the first in a long line of kings.

- Peter deceived himself when he said to Jesus, "Even if everyone else deserts you, I never will" (Matthew 26:33). Jesus replied, "The truth is, this very night, before the rooster crows, you will deny Me three times" (v. 34). Peter thought he could stand against adversity when he was really weak, so he failed Jesus at a most critical moment. He denied Jesus three times.

What insidious evil lurks deep in the human heart! The prophet Jeremiah observes, "The heart is more deceitful than all else and is desperately sick; who can understand it?" (Jeremiah 17:9, NASB). Often, people suppress the truth about themselves, going about their lives as though God will never catch up to them. But sooner or later, the all-knowing God will even the balances. God will not overlook what you are sowing. The psalmist declares, "O LORD, You have examined my heart and know everything about me" (Psalm 139:1). Remember, the Lord does not close His books at the end of the year.

Many people fail to see that given the right set of circumstances, we are capable of the very things we criticize in others. The moment we feel we can understand our own inner thoughts without the illumination of God's Holy Spirit, we deceive ourselves. And in practicing self-deception, we reap a whirlwind of consequences.

The only solution to self-deception is to adopt a standard that is above our own ideas and thought patterns from which we can measure our thoughts and actions. When we use the Ten Commandments as our guide, we prevent ourselves from straying off a righteous path and into faulty human reasoning.

*Second, reaping a spiritual harvest means seeing
our behavior from God's perspective.*

Satan wants us to rationalize that our wicked behavior is compatible with God's Law. For example, using a theory called "victimless crimes," Satan tries to convince us that breaking God's Law is not so wrong. In their book *Victimless Crimes?: Prostitution, Drugs, Homosexuality, Abortion*, authors Robert F. Meier and Gilbert Geis do not measure sinful actions by God's Law. Instead, the authors argue that some crimes should be viewed in the context of a social consensus regarding the wrongfulness of such acts and whether the consequences that arise are against criminal law. They ignore the fact that prostitution, drug addiction, homosexuality, and abortion break the Ten Commandments.

Perhaps you have heard someone say in defense of sexual immorality, "What does it matter what two consenting adults do as long as they are not hurting others?" Today, people argue that because prostitution is between two consenting adults, it should not be seen differently than any other sexual act. Proponents of legalized prostitution further argue that the government can regulate prostitution and indeed profit from it through a modest tax.

What is happening here? People are attempting to erase the concept of "sin" from our civil laws. The victimless-crime theory totally opposes God's Word, which recognizes that such sins are an offense to God and therefore should be avoided at all costs. And not only does the sinner break the most obvious commandment, breaking others soon follows. For example, prostitution will surely break the commandments "do not covet" and "do not lie," among others.

Not too many years ago, our society understood that criminal acts were first sinful acts. We knew that robbing a bank or murdering a store clerk first of all violated the Law of God, then the laws of government. We also understood that even in cases where sinful acts did not bring harm or injury upon others, permitting unrestrained sin to penetrate society invites the decline of culture and the eventual downfall of a nation.

What was the basis for this understanding? Deeply embedded in the American consciousness was the notion that God's Law was the standard simply because it was instituted by God. What God commands is the final authority for everyone.

You may wonder why it is so important to obey God's Law—even when we do not think it will hurt someone else. Because God's Law enables us to see things from His view rather than from man's flawed reasoning.

Let me give you an example from the life of a teenager. Carrie, a high school girl, came home excited after learning that an unmarried teen friend was pregnant.

When hearing the news, her mother exclaimed, "But she's too young to be a mother! It's impossible for her to do a good job!"

Carrie shook her head confidently. "No, my friend wants to be a mother. She's excited about having her baby. She'll be a good mother."

Of course, Carrie's mother understood how much more was involved in being a parent than cuddling a newborn. Not only would the young teenage girl be hurt through early parenthood, but the baby's life would also be harmed from not having a mature mother and would suffer from not having a father in the home.

Carrie's mother taught her children the biblical concept of abstinence before marriage. Yet the daughter had accepted the prevalent thinking on her high school campus that being a teenage mother was a glorious event.

A year later, Carrie, who by then had witnessed the tragedy of her friend's young life as an inadequate single teen mother, adopted her family's views about abstinence before marriage. She was so glad that she had followed the command to be sexually pure even when it didn't make sense to her at the time. Today, she is engaged to a wonderful Christian young man and is looking forward to starting a family when the time is right.

We can see how the Ten Commandments protected Carrie from behavior that would have hurt her and others—even when she didn't realize the significance of her obedience. In a similar way, we don't always have good insights into our own lives and problems. That's why we must follow the Ten Commandments even when we don't understand why. When we do, we are trusting God and His eternal perspective.

Third, reaping a spiritual harvest means knowing that God sees everything. Paul's warning against self-deception is based on a truth that has supplied the foundation for every individual or nation that has ever sought true prosperity and blessing. No one can fool the almighty God who sees all. Sin *will* be punished and good works *will* be rewarded.

Indeed, one of the names of God revealed in the Old Testament is *El-Roi*, the God who sees. The psalmist declares, "From His throne He observes all who live on the earth" (Psalm 33:14). The Book of Hebrews says, "Nothing in all creation can hide from Him. Everything is naked and exposed before His eyes" (Hebrews 4:13).

We often forget that God is omniscient. We act like the thief who took along his young son to steal vegetables from a neighbor's garden late one evening. The man looked first to the left, then to the right, then to the front and back to make sure that no one could see his crime. When he was sure no one was looking, he began filling his sack with choice vegetables.

To his surprise, his young son wisely said, "Daddy, you forgot to look up!"

We may be able to hide our wrongdoing from family, friends, and associates, but we can never hide it from the all-knowing, all-seeing God! He sees our sin both in the brightness of the day and in the blackness of the night, standing atop the highest mountain, or hiding beneath the sea in an underwater cave.

To think that we can sin without God noticing is to mock the living God. To mock God means to ridicule Him. Mock also carries the sense of throwing down a challenge or daring someone to engage in formal combat. But God does see our sin—and He will repay.

Both meanings of the word *mock* are illustrated by the actions of Goliath, the Philistine giant who mocked the armies of Israel. Goliath shouted, "'Do you need a whole army to settle this? Choose someone to fight for you, and I will represent the Philistines. We will settle this dispute in single combat! If your man is able to kill me, then we will be your slaves! But if I kill him, you will be our slaves! I defy the armies of Israel! Send me a man who will fight with me!' When Saul and the Israelite heard this, they were terrified and deeply shaken" (1 Samuel 17:8–11).

In this story, Goliath is a picture of sin. When Goliath challenged the Israelite army, he was mocking God because the Israelite army was no ordinary force. They were the "armies of the living God." Yet they allowed a single, uncircumcised Philistine to terrorize them.

If we permit the Goliaths of sin to control our lives, we mock the living God in the same way. We must never compromise with sin or yield to its temptation. Sin must be defeated through the power of the Holy Spirit, who enables us to live righteously according to the Ten Commandments.

If we continue to live in sin, we set ourselves against an immovable force—almighty God. We become like the ship captain who looked into the dark night and saw faint lights in the distance. Immediately he told his signalman to send a message. "Alter your course 10 degrees south."

Promptly, a return message was received, "Alter *your* course 10 degrees north."

The captain was angered; his command had been ignored. So he sent a second message: "Alter your course 10 degrees south—I am the *captain!*"

Soon another message was received: "Alter your course 10 degrees north—I am seaman third class Jones."

Immediately the captain sent a third message, knowing the fear it would evoke: "Alter your course 10 degrees south—I am a battleship."

Then the reply came, "Alter your course 10 degrees north—I am a lighthouse!"

Just as the captain of the battleship should have followed the seaman's directions, we must take our directions for living from God's holy Law. If not, like the lighthouse that proved to be an inalterable force capable of destroying the captain's vessel, God's immutable laws will serve to judge us and ultimately destroy us. But if we look to God's Law for our direction, it will serve as a lighthouse to help us avoid rocky consequences.

Fourth, reaping a spiritual harvest means
understanding the law of cause and effect.
Remember, Paul says, "The one who sows to his own flesh will from the

flesh reap corruption, but the one who sows to the Spirit will from the Spirit reap eternal life" (Galatians 6:8, NASB). The law of cause and effect is one of the basic rules of life. In his teaching series entitled "Living a Life of Integrity," Reverend George Munzing says, "If you cheat in practice, you'll cheat in the game. If you cheat in your head, you'll cheat on the test. You'll cheat on the girl. You'll cheat on your mate. Compromise of God's laws leads to dishonesty in business and other similar acts. Sow a thought, reap an act. Sow an act, reap a habit. Sow a habit, reap a character. Sow a character, reap a destiny."[4]

Many people use the principle of cause and effect to their advantage in everything from business planning to how hard they should hit a tennis ball cross court. Nevertheless, many of the same people appear oblivious to how this truth relates to their relationship with God.

When God tells us that life is a series of decisions with real consequences, He is not using scare tactics, but is communicating to us the ways of life. For example, if a person smokes five packs of cigarettes a day, he most likely will develop a serious lung disease.

The same applies in the realm of the Spirit. Those who ignore God face a dark future. Those who do not know Jesus as Lord and Savior probably spent more time last year preparing for their summer vacation than they have spent their whole life preparing for eternity. But the Bible says the decision an individual makes in this life either for or against Jesus will determine his eternal future. James, the brother of Jesus, urges, "Draw near to God and He will draw near to you. Cleanse your hands, you sinners; and purify your hearts, you double-minded" (James 4:8, NASB). On the other hand, believers who pray, fast, share their faith, devote themselves to the study of God's Word, and apply its truths to their lives each day grow in the grace of God and inherit an eternity of joy and blessing.

In an old tale, a wise man always gave right answers to the difficult questions of life. One day, an arrogant young man sought to stump the older sage. He concealed a live bird in his hands, then asked, "Sir, is the bird in my hands alive or dead?"

His deceitful plan was simple. If the wise senior guessed that the bird was dead, then the younger man would open his hands and let the bird fly away. If the sage guessed that the bird was alive, the young

THE PRINCIPLE OF SOWING AND REAPING

man would give his hands a quick squeeze and open them to reveal a dead bird.

Surprisingly, the old man never looked at the younger man's hands. Instead, he looked deep into his eyes and quietly said, "My son, it is whatever you wish it to be."[5]

Many seek to escape the effects of sin through trickery and deceit. But God is far wiser than that. He places the responsibility for choosing life or death squarely in our laps. The life we live is the one we wish to live—God's way or the way of death. The choice is in our own hands.

Fifth, reaping a spiritual harvest means
looking ahead to the final judgment.

Someone once asked Daniel Webster, one of the greatest minds to grace America, "What is the most brilliant thought you have ever had?"

Daniel Webster replied, "My greatest thought is my accountability to God."

The unassailable truth of the Bible is that someday every man, woman, and child will stand before almighty God to give an account of the deeds they have performed. Yet people ignore this fact. While the world lives in open defiance to this truth, the attitude within the Church is that a gracious God would never cause His children to stand before Him to account for their lives. But He will! By faith, the believer must live in the full conviction that just as there is now no condemnation to those who are in Christ Jesus, we shall also all be called to account for the deeds we have performed in the flesh. Thankfully, although we will give an account for our deeds, it will be Christ's blood and righteousness that will cover the sins of His people.

To the Athenian philosophers, Paul proclaimed, "Therefore having overlooked the times of ignorance, God is now declaring to men that all people everywhere should repent, because He has fixed a day in which He will judge the world in righteousness through a Man whom He has appointed, having furnished proof to all men by raising Him from the dead" (Acts 17:30,31, NASB).

Throughout the many years I have been in Christian service, I have stressed that the abundant life Christ offers is possible only when we are filled with the Holy Spirit and live a life of obedience and surrender. The lack of joy, peace, and effectiveness in so many Christians' lives is largely a result of unconfessed sin and a failure to appropriate the fullness of God's Spirit.

But there is far more at stake in failing to reap a spiritual harvest than missing out on the abundant life Christ offers in this lifetime. Remember that you can't ignore God and get away with it. You will always reap what you sow! Those who live only to satisfy their own sinful desires will harvest the consequences of decay and death. But those who live to please the Spirit will harvest everlasting life from the Spirit. Although eternal life is clearly a gift, this particular passage emphasizes that eternal life is a *reward* to those who live in righteousness. Thankfully, those of us who have trusted Christ will not appear before the Great White Throne judgment of sinners (Revelation 20:11–15). But all believers will appear before Christ's judgment seat (2 Corinthians 5:10). This is not a judgment of sin, but of how faithfully we have served our Savior with the opportunities and talents He gave us. Then we will receive rewards for what we have done for Christ.

Dear beloved, if ever there was a motivation to live your life according to God's holy standards, it is that a day is coming when the "books" will be opened and God will inventory your life. What those books reveal will determine your position in God's kingdom for eternity.

We cannot escape this final accounting of our faith in action. The uselessness of faith without action applies to every part of life. To illustrate, when John Wesley was six years old, the parsonage in which he lived with his family caught fire. When the alarm sounded, his parents thought everyone was out of the house, including the children. But it soon became painfully obvious that John was still trapped inside. At this point, everyone believed that John was in danger of losing his life, but that did not help him. Then his mother, who was not only a person of great faith but also a very practical woman, ran next door, got a neighbor with a ladder, and working with the neighbor, rescued her young son from the flaming house. She believed her son was in danger, but her faith wasn't of any use to her until she took action.

James writes, "Faith without works is dead" (James 2:26, NASB).

Unless our faith is matched by our willingness to act in accordance with our belief, our faith is useless. Saving faith always results in action. It is our actions—the way we conduct ourselves ethically in light of God's holy Law—which Christ will review at the final judgment. That Day will also mark that momentous occasion when Christ will *reward* the righteous according to what they have done.

Don't be lulled into thinking that just because you are a believer, you will automatically earn rewards. Not all farmers reap the same size crop. Those who work hard at sowing reap a greater harvest. Likewise, not all believers will reap the same rewards in heaven. Paul writes, "Now he who plants and he who waters are one; but each will receive his own reward according to his own labor" (1 Corinthians 3:8, NASB). We receive these rewards in relationship to the nature and the amount of good works we bring to Jesus.

Although service for Christ should never be motivated by the prospect of heavenly rewards, we should all be eager to receive them if it pleases Christ to bestow them to us. Meredith Wilson, composer of the delightful musical *The Music Man*, entitled his autobiography *And There I Stood With My Piccolo*, from a story told him by an old Moravian flute player:

> A very important king hired a whole orchestra to play for him one night during his supper, just because he felt lonesome. This orchestra played great and the king was so delighted that before going to bed, he said, "Boys, your playing gave me whips and jingles, and just for that you can all go to my countinghouse and fill your instruments with gold pieces."
>
> I can still hear that happy clatter as sack after sack of golden delights streamed into the tuba and slithered down the neck of the bassoon and spilled out over the bells of the French horns. And there I stood with my piccolo!
>
> When the heavenly King honors our efforts for Him at the final judgment, I want to be standing there with more than a piccolo. I want to serve my Lord faithfully on earth because I know the Lord will reward everyone according to what he has done.[6]

You might be thinking, *I don't head a large Christian organization like you. I'm limited in what I can accomplish for Christ.*

If so, you are missing the point. Jesus did not say, "If you love Me, build a massive ministry." He said, "If you love Me, you will keep My commandments" (John 14:15, NASB).

If you love Jesus, seek Him with your whole heart, mind, soul, and strength, obey His commandments, and share His gospel with others. These are the priceless gifts of good works you perform for our Lord. In return, Christ will lavish His choicest rewards upon you in glory!

The principle of sowing and reaping, then, is not just a whip to keep us in line. Viewed from the platform of righteous living, it is a liberating promise to those who obey God. The Ten Commandments truly are keys that unlock blessings both now on earth and later for all eternity. They are God's gift to us, so let us practice them out of gratitude and love for our gracious heavenly Father and loving, compassionate Savior!

LIFE APPLICATION

Set Your Heart's Gauge

Commit the following verses to memory. Then, when you are tempted to turn your spiritual focus away from God to other things, recall these commands from God.

- Galatians 6:7,8—"Do not be deceived, God is not mocked; for whatever a man sows, this he will also reap. For the one who sows to his own flesh shall from the flesh reap corruption, but the one who sows to the Spirit shall from the Spirit reap eternal life" (NASB).

- Revelation 22:12—"Behold, I am coming soon! My reward is with Me, and I will give to everyone according to what he has done" (NIV).

Gauge Your Spiritual Growth

Ask yourself the following questions. If one or more areas pose problems for you, ask God how you can deal with them through the power of the Holy Spirit.

- How do you feel about the fact that the "books" will be open in heaven to reveal your life?

- What examples of sowing and reaping—for good or bad—can you see in your past?

- If you were to ask a friend, what do you think he or she would say was an area in your life in which you practice self-deception?

- How do you honestly feel about "victimless crimes" such as prostitution, drug use, homosexuality, or abortion? Do you know what God's Word says about them?

- What prevalent sin are you practicing that mocks God's Laws?

- Thinking of a specific upcoming situation, how can the principle of sowing and reaping work in your life for good if you obey God's Laws?

- How do you feel about seeing Jesus as King at the judgment?

- How do these feelings reflect your deeds in this life?

Walk in the Power of the Holy Spirit

Make a list of the deeds you have sowed in the last week. Looking over the list, what will you be reaping? Now think of what you plan to do in the upcoming week. How can you change your attitude to seek God with your whole heart through what you are doing? How will this change of attitude affect your list? Commit yourself to doing everything on your schedule—minor or major duties—to serve Christ in the power of the Holy Spirit by using the Ten Commandments as your map to obeying God's will.

SEVENTEEN

CHOOSE LIFE!

H ave you heard the phrase "written in stone"? It usually refers to some statement that cannot be changed. But I like to think of the one set of statements that were truly written in stone —the Ten Commandments. When Moses climbed up Mount Sinai, it "was covered with smoke because the LORD had descended on it in the form of fire. The smoke billowed into the sky like smoke from a furnace, and the whole mountain shook with a violent earthquake" (Exodus 19:18). This scene introduced the moment when God gave the Ten Commandments. Imagine! Within this awe-inspiring tumult, Moses stayed on the mountain for forty days and forty nights listening to God's words.

You would think that the Israelites, who waited at the base of the mountain for Moses' return, would have been so awestruck at the sight of the presence of God on the mountain that they would have carefully kept their promise to obey God's Law. Instead, they built a golden calf to worship in God's place. While Moses was receiving the Ten Commandments, the people were already breaking the first two. As God's finger traced the holy words on tablets of stone, His people turned stony hearts against Him.

Aware of the people's disobedience, God told Moses to go back down the mountain. As Moses strode downward clutching the stone tablets, he heard curious noises like the sounds of celebration. As he approached, he saw God's people worshiping a golden calf. The people who had promised to obey all of God's Law had not obeyed for even two months after they left Egypt! In anguish over the sight, Moses hurled the tablets to the ground, shattering them.

Then God said to Moses, "Prepare two stone tablets like the first ones. I will write on them the same words that were on the tablets you smashed" (Exodus 34:1). Once again, Moses climbed that cloud-covered mountain clutching tablets; once more God etched the Ten Commandments into stone with His finger.

Do you see the picture in this account? God wrote the Commandments in stone. No one can erase or alter them; they are absolute truth. Moses, in his anger, shattered the stone tablets. As humans we can break God's commandments, but we cannot change them. The broken laws are not any less true. God just wrote them on stone once more. Nothing we can do will ever change God's absolute truth.

Let me contrast those tragic days of Israel's disobedience with another incident barely forty years later. Joshua led the people into the Land of Canaan where the people were careful to do all that God commanded them. When they obeyed, God miraculously crumbled the walls of Jericho and gave the Hebrews a mighty victory over the city of Ai. Then Joshua built an altar to worship God, and all the people, from the smallest to the oldest, from the greatest to the most humble, worshiped God. Joshua 8 says, "There, in the presence of the Israelites, Joshua copied on stones the law of Moses... There was not a word of all that Moses had commanded that Joshua did not read to the whole assembly of Israel, including the women and children, and the aliens who lived among them" (vv. 32,35, NIV).

There are two truths I have seen validated repeatedly during my five decades of ministry. First, if we break the Ten Commandments, our lives will be broken. Second, if we keep the Ten Commandments in the power of the Holy Spirit, our lives will be established in truth and we will be blessed.

Serving with a Heart of Love

I encourage you to make your love for Christ the motivation for keeping the Ten Commandments. Love brings fulfillment and joy to obedience.

I recently heard a story that shows how love makes relationships deeper and more meaningful. One couple, who had been married for more than half a century, played their own special game with each other. The goal of the game was to write SHMILY in a surprise place for the other person to find. They took turns leaving SHMILY around the house, and as soon as the other one discovered the letters, it became that spouse's turn to hide the letters.

They dragged SHMILY with their fingers through the sugar and flour containers, awaiting the next meal. They smeared it on the dew on the windows overlooking the patio. SHMILY was written in the steam left on the mirror after a hot shower, where it would appear bath after bath. At one point, the elderly woman even unrolled and re-rolled an entire roll of toilet paper to leave SHMILY on the very last sheet.

There was no end to places where SHMILY would pop up. Little notes were hurriedly scribbled and taped on dashboards, car seats, and steering wheels. Notes were stuffed inside shoes and left under pillows. SHMILY was written in the dust on the mantel and traced on the ashes in the fireplace.

SHMILY became a way of life. It highlighted a relationship that had love down pat. Grandma and Grandpa would hold hands every chance they could. They stole kisses as they bumped into each other in the kitchen. They finished each other's sentences and shared the daily crossword puzzle and word jumble. Grandma often whispered to her grandchildren how handsome Grandpa was and how she really knew "how to pick 'em."

One day, Grandma was diagnosed with breast cancer. The disease had first appeared ten years earlier and now had returned. As always, Grandpa went with her every step of the way. He comforted her in her yellow room, painted that color so she would always be surrounded by sunshine. With the help of a cane and her husband's steady hand, she went to church every Sunday morning. Then finally, she didn't have the strength to go anymore so Grandpa went alone.

Then one day, it happened. Grandma was gone.

SHMILY was scrawled in yellow on the pink ribbons of the funeral bouquet. As the crowd thinned, the aunts, uncles, cousins, and other family members gathered around Grandma one last time. Grandpa sang a throaty lullaby to the one he had loved for all those years. And everyone knew the truth of SHMILY—See How Much I Love You.

God has etched SHMILY in red across a cross for us. He gave us the proof of His love when He gave His Son, Jesus, to die for us.

How will we etch SHMILY in gratitude for Him? By obeying the Laws He has given us, the ones that will protect us and give us joy. We truly show our love for Him when we take the Commandments written by God's hand and write them on our hearts.

Make the Choice for Life

Looking ahead to the days of battle when the Israelites would need to fight for the Promised Land, Moses knew if they didn't keep the Law before them as their guide for living, the Hebrews would surely perish at the hands of their enemies. With this in mind, Moses stood before all Israel, setting before them a life-altering choice. Either Israel could follow after the rebellious dictates of their own hearts and die, or they could walk in the path of obedience to God and His commandments and live.

As I conclude this book, I want to remind you of the liberating power of the Ten Commandments and encourage you to demonstrate your love for Christ by living in obedience to the commandments of God. Consider the words Moses declared to the nation of Israel at that momentous occasion: "All the commandments that I am commanding you today you shall be careful to do, that you may live and multiply, and go in and possess the land which the LORD swore to give to your forefathers...Therefore, you shall keep the commandments of the LORD your God, to walk in His ways and to fear Him...I call heaven and earth to witness against you today, that I have set before you life and death, the blessing and the curse. So choose life in order that you may live, you and your descendents" (Deuteronomy 8:1,6; 30:19, NASB).

We cannot keep the Ten Commandments in our strength. We can

obey them only through the power of the Holy Spirit. But in my many years of walking with the Lord, I can assure you that keeping the Ten Commandments is the most wonderful way to live and to enjoy God. They are not burdensome; they are simple, profound, liberating keys to life. They unlock God's love and forgiveness.

I encourage you to review the chapters with the commandments you find most difficult to keep. Apply the principles and the practical suggestions at the end of each chapter. Live by the Ten Commandments day by day—yes, even moment by moment.

Also, read and study Psalm 119 about the endurance and truth of God's Word. Verse 160 says, "All Your words are true; all Your just laws will stand forever." Not only are the Ten Commandments absolutely true, they will last forever! We can count on God's truth for eternity.

Choose life in its fullest! Experience a relationship of love with God in its fullness as you follow in His commands.

I pray that God will bless you as you walk the path of obedience to His Law in the security of His love, filled with the power of His Spirit.

A P P E N D I X   A

THE FOUR SPIRITUAL LAWS

Just as there are physical laws that govern the physical universe, so are there spiritual laws that govern your relationship with God.

LAW 1: *God loves you and offers a wonderful plan for your life.*

God's Love
"God so loved the world that He gave His one and only Son, that whoever believes in Him shall not perish but have eternal life" (John 3:16, NIV).

God's Plan
[Christ speaking] "I came that they might have life, and might have it abundantly" [that it might be full and meaningful] (John 10:10).

Why is it that most people are not experiencing the abundant life? Because...

LAW 2: *Man is sinful and separated from God. Therefore, he cannot know and experience God's love and plan for his life.*

Man Is Sinful
"All have sinned and fall short of the glory of God" (Romans 3:23).

Man was created to have fellowship with God; but, because of his own stubborn self-will, he chose to go his own independent way and fellowship with God was broken. This self-will, characterized by an attitude of active rebellion or passive indifference, is an evidence of what the Bible calls sin.

Man Is Separated

"The wages of sin is death" [spiritual separation from God] (Romans 6:23).

This diagram illustrates that God is holy and man is sinful. A great gulf separates the two. The arrows illustrate that man is continually trying to reach God and the abundant life through his own efforts, such as a good life, philosophy, or religion—but he inevitably fails.

The third law explains the only way to bridge this gulf…

LAW 3: *Jesus Christ is God's* **only** *provision for man's sin. Through Him you can know and experience God's love and plan for your life.*

He Died In Our Place

"God demonstrates His own love toward us, in that while we were yet sinners, Christ died for us" (Romans 5:8).

He Is the Only Way to God

"Jesus said to him, 'I am the way, and the truth, and the life; no one comes to the Father but through Me'" (John 14:6).

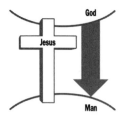

This diagram illustrates that God has bridged the gulf that separates us from Him by sending His Son, Jesus Christ, to die on the cross in our place to pay the penalty for our sins.

It is not enough just to know these three laws…

LAW 4: *We must individually* **receive** *Jesus Christ as Savior and Lord; then we can know and experience God's love and plan for our lives.*

We Must Receive Christ

"As many as received Him, to them He gave the right to become children of God, even to those who believe in His name" (John 1:12).

We Receive Christ Through Faith

"By grace you have been saved through faith; and that not of yourselves, it is the gift of God; not as a result of works that no one should boast" (Ephesians 2:8,9).

When We Receive Christ, We Experience a New Birth
(Read John 3:1–8.)

We Receive Christ Through Personal Invitation
[Christ speaking] "Behold, I stand at the door and knock; if any one hears My voice and opens the door, I will come in to him" (Revelation 3:20).

Receiving Christ involves turning to God from self (repentance) and trusting Christ to come into our lives to forgive our sins and to make us what He wants us to be. Just to agree intellectually that Jesus Christ is the Son of God and that He died on the cross for our sins is not enough. Nor is it enough to have an emotional experience. We receive Jesus Christ by faith, as an act of the will.

These two circles represent two kinds of lives:

Self-Directed Life
S – Self is on the throne
† – Christ is outside the life
● – Interests are directed by self, often resulting in discord and frustration

Christ-Directed Life
† – Christ is in the life and on the throne
S – Self is yielding to Christ
● – Interests are directed by Christ, resulting in harmony with God's plan

Which circle best represents your life?
Which circle would you like to have represent your life?

The following explains how you can receive Christ:

You Can Receive Christ Right Now by Faith Through Prayer
(Prayer is talking with God)
God knows your heart and is not so concerned with your words as He is with the attitude of your heart. The following is a suggested prayer:

> *Lord Jesus, I need You. Thank You for dying on the cross for my sins. I open the door of my life and receive You as my Savior and Lord. Thank You for forgiving my sins and giving me eternal life. Take control of the throne of my life. Make me the kind of person You want me to be.*

Does this prayer express the desire of your heart?

If it does, I invite you to pray this prayer right now, and Christ will come into your life, as He promised.

How to Know That Christ Is in Your Life
Did you receive Christ into your life? According to His promise in Reve-

lation 3:20, where is Christ right now in relation to you? Christ said that He would come into your life. Would He mislead you? On what authority do you know that God has answered your prayer? (The trustworthiness of God Himself and His Word.)

The Bible Promises Eternal Life to All Who Receive Christ

"God has given us eternal life, and this life is in His Son. He who has the Son has the life; he who does not have the Son of God does not have the life" (1 John 5:11–13).

Thank God often that Christ is in your life and that He will never leave you (Hebrews 13:5). You can know on the basis of His promise that Christ lives in you and that you have eternal life from the very moment you invite Him in. He will not deceive you.

An important reminder…

Do Not Depend on Feelings

The promise of God's Word, the Bible—not our feelings—is our authority. The Christian lives by faith (trust) in the trustworthiness of God Himself and His Word. This train diagram illustrates the relationship among *fact* (God and His Word), *faith* (our trust in God and His Word), and *feeling* (the result of our faith and obedience). (Read John 14:21.)

The train will run with or without the caboose. However, it would be useless to attempt to pull the train by the caboose. In the same way, as Christians we do not depend on feelings or emotions, but we place our faith (trust) in the trustworthiness of God and the promises of His Word.

Now That You Have Received Christ

The moment you received Christ by faith, as an act of the will, many things happened, including the following:

- Christ came into your life (Revelation 3:20; Colossians 1:27).
- Your sins were forgiven (Colossians 1:14).
- You became a child of God (John 1:12).
- You received eternal life (John 5:24).
- You began the great adventure for which God created you (John 10:10).

Can you think of anything more wonderful that could happen to you than receiving Christ? Would you like to thank God in prayer right now for what He has done for you? By thanking God, you demonstrate your faith.

To enjoy your new life to the fullest...

Suggestions for Christian Growth

Spiritual growth results from trusting Jesus Christ. A life of faith will enable you to trust God increasingly with every detail of your life, and to practice the following:

G *Go* to God in prayer daily (John 15:7).

R *Read* God's Word daily (Acts 17:11); begin with the Gospel of John.

O *Obey* God moment by moment (John 14:21).

W *Witness* for Christ by your life and words (Matthew 4:19; John 15:8).

T *Trust* God for every detail of your life (1 Peter 5:7).

H *Holy Spirit*—allow Him to control and empower your daily life and witness (Galatians 5:16,17; Acts 1:8; Ephesians 5:18).

Fellowship in a Good Church

God's Word instructs us not to forsake "the assembling of ourselves together" (Hebrews 10:25). If you do not belong to a church, do not wait to be invited. Take the initiative; call the pastor of a nearby church where Christ is honored and His Word is preached. Start this week, and make plans to attend regularly.

THE SPIRIT-FILLED LIFE

Every day can be an exciting adventure for the Christian who knows the reality of being filled with the Holy Spirit and who lives constantly, moment by moment, under His gracious direction.

The Bible tells us that there are three kinds of people:

1. **Natural Man:** One who has not received Christ.

   Self-Directed Life
   S – Self is on the throne
   ✝ – Christ is outside the life
   ● – Interests are directed by
       self, often resulting in
       discord and frustration

   "A natural man does not accept the things of the Spirit of God; for they are foolishness to him, and he cannot understand them, because they are spiritually appraised" (1 Corinthians 2:14, NASB).

2. **Spiritual Man:** One who is directed and empowered by the Holy Spirit. "He who is spiritual appraises all things" (1 Corinthians 2:15, NASB).

   Christ-Directed Life
   S – Christ is in the life and
       on the throne
   ✝ – Self is yielding to Christ
   ● – Interests are directed by
       Christ, resulting in harmony
       with God's plan

3. **Carnal Man:** One who has received Christ, but who lives in defeat because he trusts in his own efforts to live the Christian life.

Self-Directed Life

S – Self is on the throne

† – Christ is outside the life

● – Interests are directed by self, often resulting in discord and frustration

"I, brethren, could not speak to you as to spiritual people but as to carnal, as to babes in Christ. I fed you with milk and not with solid food; for until now you were not able to receive it, and even now you are still not able; for you are still carnal. For when there are envy, strife, and divisions among you, are you not carnal and behaving like mere men?" (1 Corinthians 3:1–3).

The following are four principles for living the Spirit-filled life:

1 God has provided for us an abundant and fruitful Christian life.

"Jesus said, 'I have come that they may have life, and that they may have it more abundantly'" (John 10:10, NKJ).

"The fruit of the Spirit is love, joy, peace, patience, kindness, goodness, faithfulness, gentleness, self-control; against such things there is no law" (Galatians 5:22,23).

Read John 15:5 and Acts 1:8.

The following are some personal traits of the spiritual man that result from trusting God:

- Love
- Joy
- Peace
- Patience
- Kindness
- Faithfulness
- Goodness

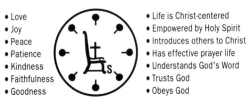

- Life is Christ-centered
- Empowered by Holy Spirit
- Introduces others to Christ
- Has effective prayer life
- Understands God's Word
- Trusts God
- Obeys God

The degree to which these traits are manifested in the life depends on the extent to which the Christian trusts the Lord with every detail of his life, and on his maturity in Christ. One who is only beginning to understand the ministry of the Holy Spirit should not be discouraged if he is not as fruitful as more mature Christians who have known and experienced this truth for a longer period.

Why is it that most Christians are not experiencing the abundant life?

2 Carnal Christians cannot experience the abundant and fruitful Christian life.

The carnal man trusts in his own efforts to live the Christian life:

- He is either uninformed about, or has forgotten, God's love, forgiveness, and power (Romans 5:8–10; Hebrews 10:1–25; 1 John 1; 2:1–3; 2 Peter 1:9).
- He has an up-and-down spiritual experience.
- He wants to do what is right, but cannot.
- He fails to draw on the power of the Holy Spirit to live the Christian life (1 Corinthians 3:1–3; Romans 7:15–24; 8:7; Galatians 5:16–18).

Some or all of the following traits may characterize the carnal man—the Christian who does not fully trust God:

- Legalistic attitude
- Impure thoughts
- Jealousy
- Guilt
- Worry
- Discouragement
- Critical spirit
- Frustration

- Aimlessness
- Fear
- Ignorance of his spiritual heritage
- Unbelief
- Disobedience
- Loss of love for God and for others
- Poor prayer life
- No desire for Bible study

(The individual who professes to be a Christian but who continues to practice sin should realize that he may not be a Christian at all, according to 1 John 2:3; 3:6–9; and Ephesians 5:5.)

The third truth gives us the only solution to this problem...

3 Jesus promised the abundant and fruitful life as the result of being filled (directed and empowered) by the Holy Spirit.

The Spirit-filled life is the Christ-directed life by which Christ lives His life in and through us in the power of the Holy Spirit (John 15).

- One becomes a Christian through the ministry of the Holy Spirit (John 3:1–8.) From the moment of spiritual birth, the Christian is indwelt by the Holy Spirit at all times (John 1:12; Colossians 2:9,10; John 14:16,17).

  All Christians are indwelt by the Holy Spirit, but not all Christians are filled (directed, controlled, and empowered) by the Holy Spirit on an ongoing basis.

- The Holy Spirit is the source of the overflowing life (John 7:37–39).

- In His last command before His ascension, Christ promised the power of the Holy Spirit to enable us to be witnesses for Him (Acts 1:1–9).

How, then, can one be filled with the Holy Spirit?

4 We are filled (directed and empowered) by the Holy Spirit by faith; then we can experience the abundant and fruitful life that Christ promised to each Christian.

You can appropriate the filling of the Holy Spirit right now if you:

- Sincerely desire to be directed and empowered by the Holy Spirit (Matthew 5:6; John 7:37–39).

- Confess your sins. By faith, thank God that He has forgiven all of your sins—past, present, and future—because Christ died for you (Colossians 2:13–15).

- Present every area of your life to God (Romans 12:1,2).

- By faith claim the fullness of the Holy Spirit, according to:

His command: Be filled with the Spirit. "Do not get drunk on wine, which leads to debauchery. Instead, be filled with the Spirit" (Ephesians 5:18).

His promise: He will always answer when we pray according to His will. "This is the confidence we have in approaching God: that if we ask anything according to his will, he hears us. And if we know that He hears us—whatever we ask—we know that we have what we asked of Him" (1 John 5:14,15).

How to Pray in Faith to be Filled With the Holy Spirit

We are filled with the Holy Spirit by faith alone. However, true prayer is one way of expressing your faith. The following is a suggested prayer:

Dear Father, I need You. I acknowledge that I have been directing my own life and that, as a result, I have sinned against You. I thank You that You have forgiven my sins through Christ's death on the cross for me. I now invite Christ to again take His place on the throne of my life. Fill me with the Holy Spirit as You commanded me to be filled, and as You promised in Your Word that You would do if I asked in faith. I pray this in the name of Jesus. As an expression of my faith, I now thank You for directing my life and for filling me with the Holy Spirit.

Does this prayer express the desire of your heart? If so, bow in prayer and trust God to fill you with the Holy Spirit right now.

END NOTES

Chapter 1: Finding True Happiness

1. Ronald Reagan, *Gales Quotations CD-ROM* (Detroit, MI: Gale Research Inc., 1995).
2. Adapted from Joel Helgerson, *Nuclear Accidents* (New York: Franklin Watts/An Impact Book, 1988), pp. 40–54; Dr. Robert Gale and Thomas Hauser, *Final Warning: The Legacy of Chernobyl* (New York: Warner Books, 1988), pp. 24,25.

Chapter 2: Why We Need the Ten Commandments

1. A. W. Pink, *The Ten Commandments* (public domain), p. 6.
2. H. Wayne House, *The Christian and American Law: Christianity's Impact on America's Founding Documents and Future Direction* (Grand Rapids, MI: Kregel Publications, 1998), p. 213.
3. D. James Kennedy, *What If the Bible Had Never Been Written?* (Nashville, TN: Thomas Nelson Publishers, 1998), p. 56.
4. Donald S. Lutz and Charles S. Hyneman, "The Relative Influence of European Writers on Law: Eighteenth Century Political Thought," *American Political Science Review*, 1984, pp. 189–197.
5. Dr. Larry Walker, "The Abiding Value of Biblical Law, *The Christian and American Law*, H. Wayne House, ed. (Grand Rapids, MI: Kregel Publications, 1998), p. 215.
6. J. Gresham Machen, *Christianity and Liberalism* (New York: The Macmillan Company, 1923).
7. House, *The Christian and American Law*, p. 42.
8. Candace Atherton, "Ted Turner's Nine Commandments," *The Investigator Report*, August 9, 2000 (http://money.crosswalk.com/articles/item/1,1237,855,00.htm).
9. *Christianity Today*, Oct. 26, 1992, p. 30.

Chapter 3: The Blessing of Obedience

1. Lyle W. Dorsett, "Ministry Maverick," Moody Magazine Online, www.moodypress.org/MOODYMAG/maverick.htm.
2. Lee Strobel, *What Jesus Would Say* (Grand Rapids, MI: Zondervan Publishing House, 1994).
3. *Good Housekeeping*, October 1990, pp. 87,88.
4. Bruce Larson, *Wind and Fire: Living Out the Book of Acts* (Waco, TX: Word Books, 1984).
5. St. Augustine, Bishop of Hippo, *Confessions and Enchiridion*, Albert C. Outler, trans. and ed. (Philadephia, PA: Westminster Press, 1955), Book 1.
6. "Out of the Mouths of Babes," *Parables Etc.* (Platteville, CO: Saratoga Press), Sept. 1986.
7. C. H. Spurgeon, sermon on Romans 10:4, "Christ the End of the Law."
8. "The Fable of the Birds," *Sunday Sermons* (Margate, NJ: Voicings Publications), vol. 17, no. 4, July/Aug. 1987, p. 3.

Chapter 4: God's Law Leads to Grace in Christ

1. Paul Lee Tan, *Encyclopedia of 7700 Illustrations* (Rockville, MD: Assurance Publishers, 1979).
2. "Changed Lives," *The Pastor's Story File* (Platteville, CO: Saratoga Press), Jan. 1992.
3. *The Navigator's Daily Walk*, July 25, 1991.
4. *Signposts Aloft* video, Moody Science Classics (Chicago, IL: Moody Institute of Science).

Chapter 5: Cheap Grace and Legalism

1. Jack Gulledge, *Ideas and Illustrations for Inspirational Talks* (Nashville: Broadman Press, 1986).
2. Dietrich Bonhoeffer, *The Cost of Discipleship* (New York: Simon & Schuster, 1995).
3. Ibid., p.45.
4. "The Choice," *Parables, Etc.* (Plattville, CO: Saratoga Press), February 1989.
5. Warren Wiersbe and Lloyd M. Perry, *Wycliffe Handbook of Preaching & Preachers* (Chicago, IL: Moody Press), p. 235.

Chapter 6: You Shall Have No Other Gods Before Me

1. Michael P. Green, ed., *Illustrations for Biblical Preaching* (Grand Rapids, MI: Baker Books, 1990), Illus. 506.
2. "Conversion," *Parables, Etc.* (Plattville, CO: Saratoga Press), March 1986.
3. *U.S. News & World Report*, June 17, 1996, p. 25.
4. "There's a Bad Feeling About Self-Esteem Trend," Cecelia Goodnow, *Seattle Post-Intelligencer* (*The Dallas Morning News*, July 2, 1996), p. 1C.
5. Al Brant, ed., *1,000 New Illusrations* (Grand Rapids, MI: Zondervan Publishers, 1957), p. 162.
6. G. Campbell Morgan, *The Ten Commandments* (Chicago: The Bible Institute Colportage Association, 1901), pp. 18,19.
7. *Our Daily Bread* (Grand Rapids, MI: RBC Ministries), Sept. 20, 1992.
8. D. J. Fant, *A. W. Tozer* (Harrisburg, PA: Christian Publications, 1964), p. 90.
9. Leighton Ford, *Good News Is For Sharing* (Elgin, IL: D.C. Cook Publishers, 1977), p. 16.
10. Maxie Dunnam, *Commentary on Galatians*, quoted in James S. Hewett, ed., *Illustrations Unlimited* (Wheaton, IL: Tyndale House Publishers, 1988), pp. 81,82.
11. J. I. Packer, *A Quest for Godliness* (Wheaton, IL: Crossway Books, 1990), p. 249.

Chapter 7: Do Not Worship Idols

1. Henri Nouwen, *The Wounded Healer: Ministry in Contemporary Society* (Garden City, NJ: Doubleday, 1972).
2. *Today in the Word* (Chicago, IL: Moody Bible Institute, August 1991), p. 23.
3. Robert P. Dugan, Jr., *Winning the New Civil War: Recapturing America's Values* (Portland, OR: Multnomah Publishers, 1991), p. 169.
4. Michael McManus, *Baptist Press* release, March 1995.
5. Gayle White, "Gays & God," *The Atlanta Journal and Constitution*, May 31, 1998, p. A01.

Chapter 8: Do Not Take God's Name in Vain

1. William J. Federer, *America's God and Country: Encyclopedia of Quotations* (Coppell, TX: Fame Publishing, Inc., 1994), p. 638.
2. Lawson Stone, "What Does It Really Mean to Take the Lord's Name in Vain?"

Decision Magazine, March 2000.

3. "How We Spend Time," *The Pastor's Story File* (Platteville, CO: Saratoga Press), January 1995.

4. "The Chastening Love of God," *The Pastor's Story File* (Platteville, CO: Saratoga Press), May 1991.

5. Charles Swindoll, *Living on the Ragged Edge: Coming to Terms with Reality* (Waco, TX: Word Publishing, 1985).

Chapter 9: Keep the Sabbath Holy

1. Letter of Barnabas, 15:6-8 [A.D. 74].

2. *Our Daily Bread* (Grand Rapids, MI: RBC Ministries), June 6, 1994.

3. *Preaching Magazine*, vol. 6, no. 4.

4. *Decision Magazine*, February 1987, p. 4.

5. "Working on Sunday," *Parables, Etc.* (Platteville, CO: Saratoga Press), May 1990.

6. "No Joy Allowed," *Parables, Etc.* (Platteville, CO: Saratoga Press), Sept. 1994.

7. George W. Noble, *The Book of 750 Bible and Gospel Studies* (Chicago, 1909).

8. Mark Harkrider, *Baptist Standard* (Dallas, TX), July 23, 1997, p. 5.

Chapter 10: Honor Your Parents

1. Joy Davidman, *Smoke on the Mountain* (Philadelphia: The Westminster Press, 1954), pp. 60,61.

2. *Houston Post*, April 3, 1995, p. D-3.

3. "Law and Order," *Parables, Etc.* (Platteville, CO: Saratoga Press), October 1994.

4. J. Oswald Sanders, *A Spiritual Clinic* (Chicago: Moody Press, 1958), p. 90.

5. Josh McDowell, *More Than a Carpenter* (Wheaton, IL: Tyndale House Publishers, 1977), p. 126.

6. Ibid., p. 127.

7. *Homemade*, January 1993, p. 1.

8. Michael P. Green, ed., *Illustrations for Biblical Preaching* (Grand Rapids, MI: Baker Books, 1990), Illus. 516.

9. *National and International Religion Report*, vol. 8, no. 11.

10. William J. Scanlon, "Financial Strain of Long-Term Heath Care," Congressional Testimony, 03-09-1998.

11. "Baby-Boomer Outlook," *Consumers' Research Magazine*, vol. 81, June 1, 1998, p. 16(4).

12. Charis Conn and Ilena Silverman, eds., *What Counts: The Complete Harper's Index*, (New York: Holt, 1991).

13. J. A. Petersen, ed., *For Families Only* (Wheaton, IL: Tyndale House Publishers, 1977), p. 253.

14. *Our Daily Bread* (Grand Rapids, MI: RBC Ministries), May 8.

Chapter 11: Do Not Murder

1. "South honors fatal culture of violence," Cynthia Tucker, *The Atlanta-Journal Constitution*, Nov. 28, 1999.

2. Dirk Johnson, "Illinois, Citing Faulty Verdicts, Bars Executions," *The New York Times*, February 1, 2000.

3. Gladys Williams, "Alvin C. York," http:volweb.utk.edu/Schools/York/biography.html.

4. Randall Watters, *War, Evil and Self Defense*.

5. Central Illinois Right To Life, www.cirtl.org/abfacts.htm.

6. *Canticle Magazine*, Winter 2000, www.roenomore.org.

7. "Roe v. McCorvey," April 24, 2001, www.roenomore.org.
8. "Plan to Provide Aid-in-Dying to Terminally Ill to End Pain, Religious Groups Oppose Move," *The New York Times*, October 6, www.pregnantpause.org/euth/nyt33.htm.
9. Ibid.
10. Campaign to End Genocide (Washington, D.C.: The World Federalist Assoc.), www.endgenocide.org/aboutgen.html.
11. National Institute of Mental Health (Bethesda, MD), www.nimh.nih.gov/research/suifact.htmg.
12. The Christian Life Commission, June 1995.
13. *Marriage Partnership*, Summer 1991, p. 87.
14. *National and International Religion Report*, vol. 7, no. 3.
15. Ibid.
16. Ibid.
17. "Interview from Death Row: Reporter Kathy Chiero's developing relationship with Karla," CBN Interview Online, January 30, 1998.
18. *Leadership Journal*, Fall 1988, p. 33.

Chapter 12: Do Not Commit Adultery

1. Gordon MacDonald, *Rebuilding Your Broken World* (Nashville, TN: Oliver Nelson, 1988), p. 53.
2. Centers for Disease Control and Prevention (Atlanta, GA: US Department of Health and Human Services), www.cdc.gov/hiv/stats/cumulati.htm.
3. "Fact Sheet," National Institute of Allergy and Infectious Diseases (Bethesda, MD: National Institutes of Health, July 1999), www.niaid.nih.gov/factsheets/stdinfo.htm.
4. John Haggai, *Lead On!: Leadership That Endures In a Changing World* (Waco, TX: Word Books, 1986), pp. 50,51.
5. Karen S. Peterson, *USA Today*, March 14, 1996.
6. Joanne Weintraub, *Milwaukee Journal Sentinel*, February 11, 1999 (internet).
7. *National and International Religion Report*, September 18, 1995.
8. Kerby Anderson, ed., *Marriage, Family & Sexuality: Probing the Headlines That Impact Your Family* (Grand Rapids, MI: Kregel Books), pp. 92,93.
9. *The Pastor's Story File* (Platteville, CO: Saratoga Press), May 1995.
10. For more information, call 800-FLTODAY (358-6329) or see www.familylife.com.

Chapter 13: Do Not Steal

1. *Moody Magazine*, July/Aug. 1996, p. 39.
2. *U.S. News & World Report*, Sept. 23, 1996.
3. Doug Sherman and William Hendricks, *Keeping Your Ethical Edge Sharp: How to Cultivate a Personal Character That Is Honest, Faithful, Just, and Morally Clean* (Colorado Springs, CO: NavPress, 1990).
4. *The Confessions of St. Augustine*, Rex Warner, trans. (New York: New American Library, 1963), p. 45.
5. *National and International Religion Report*, vol. 9, no. 8.
6. *The Baptist Standard* (Dallas: Baptist Standard Publishing Co.), Sept. 11, 1996, p. 12.
7. *National and International Religion Report*, March 4, 1996.
8. Joanna Elachi, "Washington Welfare Reform: Quick Fix or Cure?" (San Francisco, CA: Pacific Research Institute for Public Policy Action Alert), no. 24, June 21, 1999.
9. Michael Bauman, "What Went Wrong with Welfare?" Covenant Syndicate, vol. 1,

no. 17.
10. Chris Tilley, www.newpower.org (welfare).
11. Bauman, "What Went Wrong with Welfare?"
12. Dr. Phil Stringer, "Gambling and the Work Ethic," www.usiap.org/viewpoints/Society/Vice/GamblingAndtheWorkEthic.html.
13. Ibid.
14. "Cox Report," The Congressional Record, November 5, 1997.
15. The Houston Chronicle, April 24, 1992, p. 2.
16. National and International Religion Report, vol. 9, no. 10.

Chapter 14: Do Not Bear False Witness
1. "Poll: Most Americans think Clinton committed perjury" (CNN, All Politics, Dec. 10, 1998), www.cnn.com/ALLPOLITICS/stories/1998/12/10/poll/.
2. "John Harvard Statue" (Cambridge, MA: Harvard University), http://map.harvard.edu/level4/Yard/johnharvard.shmtl.
3. "The Greatest Sermon in History," Part 9, Lee Strobel, Willow Creek Community Church, Nov. 7, 1993.
4. "Lying," Parables, Etc. (Platteville, CO: Saratoga Press), May 1989.
5. Bits and Pieces, December 9, 1993, pp. 12,13.
6. Michael P. Green, ed., Illustrations for Biblical Preaching (Grand Rapids, MI: Baker Books, 1990), Illus. 606.
7. Pulpit Helps, vol. 18, no. 11, Nov. 1993, www.suite101.com/article.cfm/science_for_kids/18650.
8. "Edification," Warren Doud (Austin, TX: Grace Notes), www.realtime.net/~wdoud/topics/edification.html.
9. USA Today, January 9, 1992, p. 4D.

Chapter 15: Do Not Covet
1. Charles Swindoll, Laugh Again (Dallas: Word Publishing, 1992), pp. 50,51.
2. Our Daily Bread (Grand Rapids, MI: RBC Ministries), May 18, 1994.
3. Today in the Word, December 13, 1995, p. 20.
4. Thomas Watson, The Art of Divine Contentment: An Exposition of Philippians 4:11, 1885 Edition (Glasgow, UK: Free Presbyterian Publications), Ch. VI.
5. Ibid., Ch. V, Q2.
6. Madeline Begun Kane, Midwest Today, January 1997, www.midtod.com/9612/humor.
7. Bank Rate Monitor, various issues; American Bankers Association, Consumer Credit Delinquency Bulletin; U.S. Department of Commerce, Bureau of Economic Analysis; and Board of Governors of the Federal Reserve System.
8. "Stewardship Titles," The Pastor's Story File (Platteville, CO: Saratoga Press), Oct. 1997.
9. Matthew Henry, Commentary on the Whole Bible (1706).

Chapter 16: The Principle of Sowing and Reaping
1. Our Daily Bread (Grand Rapids: RBC Ministries), Sept. 10, 1990.
2. Today in the Word (Chicago: Moody Bible Institute, May 1990), p. 7.
3. Arthur S. Reber, Penguin Dictionary of Psychology (New York: Penguin, 1985).
4. George Munzing, "Living a Life of Integrity," Preaching Today, tape no. 32.
5. Charles Livingstone Allen, All Things Are Possible Through Prayer (Westwood, NJ: Fleming H. Revell, 1958), pp. 28,29.
6. Preaching Magazine, vol. 9, no. 6.